*"This warrior woman knows when to fight
like a lion . . . The courage of her convictions
is her shield, her soul is her spear, and
her will is her cauldron."*

Many women are searching for an image of the divine that reflects
who they want to be: strong, nurturing, and feminine. Many find
themselves drawn to Celtic spirituality, a tradition that honors all
aspects of the divine feminine.

Celtic Women's Spirituality embraces the feminine archetypes of
the Celtic tradition so any woman can draw on the sacred aspects of
the warrior, mother, crone, virgin, sovereign and shapeshifter. This
wonderful resource will show you how to develop an empowering,
deeply meaningful connection with the divine that will enrich your
spiritual life and beliefs.

With this book of rituals, meditations, magickal techniques, exercises, and festivals, you can craft a complete practice built around
honoring the goddess in every woman. You may even choose to perform the rituals to dedicate yourself as a Celtic warrior woman or
become a Celtic priestess.

Embrace the deepest mysteries of your spirit when you explore
the timeless wisdom of *Celtic Women's Spirituality*.

About the Author

Edain McCoy became a self-initiated Witch in 1981, and has been an active part of the Pagan community since her formal initiation into a large San Antonio coven in 1983. She has been researching alternative spiritualities since her teens, when she was first introduced to Kaballah (Jewish mysticism). Since then, she has studied a variety of magickal paths, including Celtic Witchcraft, Appalachian folk magick, and Curanderismo, a Mexican-American folk tradition. Today she is part of the Wittan Irish Pagan tradition, in which she is a priestess of Brighid and an elder. An alumnus of the University of Texas with a B.A. in history, she currently pursues part-time graduate and undergraduate studies at Indiana University as her schedule permits. She is also active in several professional writer's organizations, and occasionally presents workshops on magickal topics, or works individually with students who wish to study Witchcraft. This former woodwind player for the Lynchburg (VA) symphony claims both the infamous feuding McCoy family of Kentucky and Sir Roger Williams, the seventeenth-century religious dissenter, as branches on her ethnically diverse family tree.

To Write to the Author

If you wish to contact the author or would like more information about this book, please write to the author in care of Llewellyn Worldwide and we will forward your request. Both the author and publisher appreciate hearing of your enjoyment of the book and how it has helped you. Llewellyn Worldwide cannot guarantee that every letter written to the author can be answered, but all will be forwarded. Please write to:

Edain McCoy
℅ Llewellyn Worldwide
P.O. Box 64383, Dept. K672-6
St. Paul, MN 55164-0383, U.S.A.

Please enclose a self-addressed stamped envelope for reply, or $1.00 to cover costs.
If outside U.S.A., enclose international postal reply coupon.

CELTIC
WOMEN'S
SPIRITUALITY

ACCESSING
THE
CAULDRON OF LIFE

EDAIN MCCOY

1999
Llewellyn Publications
St. Paul, Minnesota U.S.A.

FIRST EDITION
Third Printing, 1999

Book design by Rebecca Zins
Cover art by Moon Deer
Cover design by Anne Marie Garrison
Editing and typesetting by Marguerite Krause

Library of Congress Cataloging-in-Publication Data
McCoy, Edain, 1957–
   Celtic women's spirituality: accessing the cauldron of life /
Edain McCoy.—1st ed.
      p.   cm.
   Includes bibliographical references and index.
   ISBN 1-56718-672-6 (pbk.)
   1. Magic, Celtic. 2. Mythology, Celtic. 3. Goddesses, Celtic.
4. Goddess religion. 5. Women—Religious life. I. Title.
BF1622.C45M34   1998
299'.16'082—dc21   97–45110
                                                         CIP

Llewellyn Worldwide does not participate in, endorse, or have any authority or responsibility concerning private business transactions between our authors and the public.
   All mail addressed to the author is forwarded but the publisher cannot, unless specifically instructed by the author, give out an address or phone number.

Llewellyn Publications
A Division of Llewellyn Worldwide, Ltd.
P.O. Box 64383, Dept. K672-6
St. Paul, MN 66164-0383, U.S.A.

Printed in the United States of America

Other Books by Edain McCoy

This book is dedicated with much love
to the memory of my
teacher, mentor, friend,
and favorite warrior woman
MOLLIE SIOBHAN MALONE
1939–1991

CONTENTS

CONTENTS

The Celtic woman walks in peace, but unobtrusively carries her battle weapons; she sees herself as part of the web of all creation, but also as a unique individual of great worth. She loves and respects her family, friends, and community, but also finds inspiration in her solitude. She is a leader, but knows when it is time to let others show the way. She strives to learn and to teach, to share and to keep secrets, to change and yet to remain herself, to be human and be Goddess.

The planet needs more Celtic women, whose bottomless cauldron of inner strength serves as a womb from which a new and better world may be born.

The Celtic spiritual traditions are arguably some of the most popular in the modern Pagan revival. One explanation for this phenomenon is that in the United States and Canada, where a large percentage of today's Pagans reside, the ancestral gene pool is primarily Celtic. Perhaps our interest is one of ethnic pride, or perhaps it is a deeper intrigue born of genetic memory. Women have also flocked to the new spiritualities seeking divine images to which we can better relate, deities who are like ourselves—female! We call this path "women's spirituality," yet we rarely give it a single cultural focus.

The term "spirituality" is often preferred over the label "religion" by practitioners of alternative worship. Some Pagans balk at the use of the word "spirituality," feeling it casts what they believe and practice into a lesser role. This is simply not true. A religion is a broad framework in which spirituality may or may not play a part. A religion, properly defined, is a set of beliefs, a dogma with a definable and static outward form. It has little or nothing to do with inner connections to the divine. Catholicism is a religion. Judaism is a religion. Islam is a religion. Even Paganism, in its broadest sense, is a religion. How many non-practicing people do you know who nonetheless claim a religious label but who seem to feel nothing for the deeper meaning of the faith to which they so tenaciously claim allegiance?

For the majority of English-speaking people, the word "religion" has come to mean a set of unnatural rules for living. One book on Paganism defines religion as "that which is taboo or restrictive." The word religion actually comes from the Latin *religio*, meaning to "re-link." *Ligio* is the same root word from which we get the word "ligaments," those tissues that link bone and muscle and allow our bodies to move. There is nothing in it that means taboo. However, languages evolve over time, and the word spirituality now strikes most of us as the term that best sums up the idea of re-linking ourselves with the divine. It is the divine to which we aspire to reconnect through ritual, and in the rituals of women's spirituality it is almost exclusively an aspect of the Goddess to which we desire to re-link ourselves.

Spirituality is an inner quality that speaks to our feelings about our faith. Spirituality can be either coexistent with the practice of any religion (by proper definition) or celebrated outside of orthodox religious forms altogether. It implies an active role in religious life that goes beyond outer expressions, attempting to take the mysteries of the faith and fully incorporate them into all aspects of the self, uniting that self with the divine.

In most of the religions women have abandoned in order to embrace Paganism, we were not wanted as full participants. We were needed merely as warm bodies to fill pews, as followers who could be told what to do and think by others who were supposedly in closer connection with the divine, and as necessary vessels in which to breed new followers of the faith.

When we practice a spirituality, we cannot help but connect with the divine, in both its inner and outer aspects, and experience it on a deep level that creates a lasting and positive effect on our lives and, presumably, upon our afterlives as well. No mere religion can do all that because it does not encourage the experiential explorations that allow spirituality to happen. The fact that women are rediscovering this fact scares the mainstream religious leaders to the bottoms of their clerical collars. The Pope himself cautioned women against earth-centered (read Pagan) spiritual teachings that could lead to, oh horror of horrors, the practice of Witchcraft![1]

In spite of the extreme popularity of both the Celtic Pagan and women's spirituality paths, they are rarely seen united, as if the outward label and the spiritual inner-connections are somehow incompatible. The idea that women's spirituality and Celtic Paganism must be mutually exclusive is silly. It is true that many of the best-documented Goddess-worshiping cultures were African or Mediterranean, but the Celts provide us with some of the strongest, most archetypally accessible images of strong women onto which we can focus our spiritual impulses. Warriors and queens, mothers and crones, sovereigns and shapeshifters are all to be found within the Celtic pantheon, and all have important lessons to teach us about ourselves and our universe. When we combine our interest in Celtic Paganism with that of women's spirituality, we naturally create for ourselves a personalized pathway that links two important aspects of ourselves: the feminine and the hereditary (or adopted) Celtic. This union can help make us more whole, more powerful, and awaken us to new realities previously untapped by our subconscious minds.

One path is not contradictory to the other. For several years I was part of a mixed-gender Celtic coven and very happy with it. Still, I sought some contact for the times in between the solar and lunar festivals, and became part of a fledgling women's spirituality group. Eight of us from diverse backgrounds and varying levels of experience soon discovered we shared a passion for all things Celtic. Though we never developed into a fully working coven, the experience taught me that women's spirituality can function beautifully hand-in-hand with Celtic Paganism, or within virtually any other culturally-based Pagan tradition.

Because Celtic women's spirituality is not a *tradition* with a set of long-held rules and a preprogrammed set of rituals and rites to be followed, it can be blended with or added to any other spiritual paths you may be following. Celtic women's spirituality can be your solitary path while you enjoy another one with a group or it can be used to enhance your existing practice, regardless of its cultural basis. No one is going to excommunicate you from Paganism for forging a personal tradition from the archetypes and myths that interest you and in which you find meaning.

Numerous books and groups teach about Paganism in general, and all should be explored if the Pagan path is new to you. Also, in recent years, a huge number of books have been published that look more deeply at the Celtic aspects of Paganism. As with any culturally-based path, certain elements characterize it and make it stand apart from the others. In general, the defining characteristics of Celtic Pagan spirituality are:

- An acceptance that the spiritual traditions of the ancient Celts still have something to teach humankind
- An acceptance that the divine is manifest in all living things
- A belief in the Otherworld as a mirror of the physical world
- An acceptance that part of the self is manifest in the Otherworld

- A belief that the Otherworld, and the spirits and deities who dwell there, can be accessed by human beings
- A belief in reincarnation or in the natural cycles of regeneration following physical death
- The acceptance of dual divinity, Goddess and God, of which the feminine archetype in her three forms (virgin, mother, crone) is the stronger element
- Belief in an eternal Goddess and an eternally reborn God
- Belief that a rightful king (as God incarnate) weds the land (the Goddess incarnate), and that what befalls the king befalls the land
- Acceptance of the number three as sacred
- Acceptance of the warrior-self as an important aspect of spiritual development
- Looking to nature for spiritual guidance and for determining the date of festivals and sacred days
- Belief in the faery world and an acceptance that its denizens can interact with and aid or hinder humanity
- Lack of a definable creation myth but a belief that the Goddess, in union with the God, manifested all things
- Belief in magick as a natural operation of the universe
- Acceptance of omnipresent time as opposed to linear time

Women's spirituality has been even less likely than other sects of Paganism to identify itself by a particular label, though a few all-women traditions have sprung up over the last few decades, including the Wise Woman, Woman-Spirit, and Dianic. Because of this fierce independence, their common ground is not as readily evident but, in general, the defining characteristics of women's spirituality are:

- Emphasis on the supremacy of the divine feminine or Goddess
- Acceptance of all women as Goddesses incarnate
- Acceptance that all women have inner strengths that were gifts of the Goddess and that can be accessed through ritual
- Belief that all women are worthy of being priestesses of the divine feminine
- Belief that all women are natural psychics
- Belief that following the Goddess path will restore balance to the self and to the world

Blending Two Paths Into One

Women's spirituality can be as easily crafted from Celtic Paganism as from any other cultural path. However, resistance often comes from the persistent warrior images that are unavoidable in Celtic history. Women following general women's spirituality paths like to emphasize in their spiritual life the ideals of peace and reciprocity usually found only in cultures nearer the equator, where an abundance of natural resources made warfare less necessary.

These women are missing the point of the warrior archetype and losing out on a valuable tool for self-expression. As they crusade for women's rights and other causes dear to them, they fail to recognize that they are already calling upon their warrior selves. Celtic women's spirituality, with its emphasis on the warrior self, can provide a framework for consciously recognizing and drawing upon this important aspect of the inner-self.

This focus on the feminine side of Celtic Paganism is not intended as a slam on men. Too often both women's and men's spirituality groups routinely bash and trash the opposite sex as part of their ritual experience. We have all given in to the impulse occasionally. This is simply the way the battle of the sexes has shaped up over the centuries and, at times, it is an understandable and acceptable emotional outlet. What is not acceptable is making it a routine part of our spiritual practice. Admittedly, it is difficult for women looking back on five thousand years of oppressive history, during which a great deal of trashing was done to our Goddesses, to remember that the patriarchy that shaped our modern world also hurt a great many men in its zeal to purvey one worldview upon us. Men who wanted to live in peace, not chase wealth as the highest goal, and who had no wish to worship only one preselected male God were silenced just as quickly as their female counterparts. This not-so-subtle conversion campaign continues today, and it remains one of society's most effective control measures. Trust that when the Witch-hunters come knocking on your door, they won't spare the males under your roof out of respect for a common Y chromosome. As women fight for their own spiritual rights, we fight also for those of the men who are our allies.

Women and men have pursued divergent spiritual paths since the first religious impulse was recognized in the human soul. Though the end goal may be the same—that of union with the divine—the necessary archetypes, symbols, and mysteries that make sense to us and open up the door of initiation clearly contain some gender divisions. Early-twentieth-century psychologist and student of the occult mysteries Carl G. Jung believed that without courting these divisions, men and women became like "devils" to each other, impeding the progression of spiritual fulfillment.[2]

Many modern women feel a need to follow a separate spiritual path that emphasizes the Goddess and challenges them to seek out the divine feminine within themselves. This is best done in a non-judgmental atmosphere, either alone or with a small group of committed women. Women have had a much harder time than men in accepting themselves as valuable people, and old wounds often require treatment in an all-female setting in order to be fully healed. The overweight or underweight woman, the too-tall or too-short woman, the small-busted or large-busted woman, the woman with the large nose or limp hair, and all our other sisters who somehow feel they do not measure up physically can feel very intimidated in mixed-gender circles. The problem of personal insecurity can be compounded if the woman becomes involved in a coven that practices ritual nudity, known as going skyclad. Unused to viewing themselves as Goddess because—willingly or not—they have bought into the feminine stereotypes of our modern world, they lack the confidence to stand in a mixed-gender circle and demand their right to be treated with dignity as an incarnation of the divine. Even when we know intellectually that any lesser self-image is both wrong and detrimental to our mental and emotional well-being, it can be very hard to overcome, especially when men are present. Even Pagan men, who from my observations have largely overcome the need to denigrate or elevate women based on their physical appearance, can be viewed as a threat to self-esteem simply because women have not learned to love and trust themselves. When we overcome this conditioning by exploring the powerful archetypes on the Celtic women's spiritual path, we learn to recognize ourselves as powerful and beautiful and we can command the respect that will allow us to rise above any further attempts to manipulate our sense of self-worth.

It is only when we learn about and accept our own wholeness of being, via archetypes that at first seem more masculine than feminine, that we can begin to work in tandem with men in dual gender-oriented spiritual rites and fulfill our full spiritual potential as Goddesses incarnate. The same is true for men. They must connect with the divine masculine within themselves before they can hope to connect with their feminine aspects and come to us as Gods incarnate in a true spiritual partnership.

Many Pagan men are discovering the spiritual value of single-sex rituals and are delving more and more into men's sacred rites, as evidenced by the books on the male mysteries that have appeared over the last few years. I see these two separate gender paths as being a positive experience for the entire Pagan community. These gender-based explorations can only serve to make us more powerful as a whole when we work together; each group in perfect balance, each member confident in his or her personal power, his or her self as the divine incarnate, and both proudly representing two halves of the whole, able to unite and to spark raw ideas into full manifestation.

The great challenge in putting together a system of Celtic women's spirituality lies in the unalterable historical fact that the patriarchy, the era of rule by men, was already in place when Celtic history was being made in Europe. While the fables of the golden age of universal matriarchy are largely untrue, there were small tribes living in Europe that had a matricentric[3] focus and lived in relative peace, using reciprocity as an economic base. One of the explanations for why the patriarchy came about has to do with a change in land use and economic base when these peaceful hunter–gatherer societies came into conflict with herding societies.

The Celts were primarily herders. Coming out of the Caucasus into Europe as early as 2000 B.C.E.,[4] they sought to conquer and "possess" great tracts of land for grazing. To most hunter–gatherer societies, the concept that one could actually own the land and all its bounty was foreign, and even when another tribe clearly dominated a territory, the idea that its resources could not be shared was inconsistent with their economic system of reciprocity. To the Celts wealth meant cattle, and this would remain so for nearly another 3000 years.[5]

Celtic clan leaders were often men, the strongest warriors of the tribe, though many women achieved this rank and, as a whole, lived enviable lives for their time period in terms of personal freedom and communal status. Celtic Goddesses continued to hold an exalted place in the spiritual system of the Celts until the new religion[6] was forced to adopt some of these unvanquishable deities into their pantheon of saints. Most Celtic myths were not committed to paper until well into the Christian period, yet they retain strong female imagery that speaks volumes about how substantial their imagery must have been, since it is generally believed that Christian clerics watered down aspects of a strong divine feminine in any myths they transcribed.[7] To have endured centuries of subtle alteration in oral custom as the patriarchy advanced and then to be transcribed, either in the same or very similar form, is a testament to the power of the feminine Celtic archetypes.

Crafting New Ways From the Old

Whenever we work within the Celtic Pagan traditions, there always arises the inevitable debate over the classification of information. Everyone wants to know what material comes from a source known to be a rock-solid fact, what comes from a source we think we know to be fact, and what comes from a source we only suppose we know, based on conjecture. Unfortunately, almost every bit of historical information we possess can be classified and re-classified—all with sound arguments to back up each decision—depending upon which scholar is doing the classifying. History, especially prehistory, is just not that amenable to our modern need to categorize. It is not a hard science, as many suppose, but a discipline whose conclusions are based upon argument and counter-argument, always fluid and ever-changing . . . just like spirituality itself.

If we were able to hop into a time machine, push all the right buttons, and travel back 2500 years to witness ancient Celtic rites, any attempt at bringing them unaltered into the present would render them useless in a spiritual sense. They would be a religion; an outer form incapable of speaking to us on deeper levels. Certainly we could connect with the Celtic reverence for nature, the high placement of a feminine divinity, and the cycle of seasons, but so few of the actual rites of the past would have any meaning for us today. We would also find that the Celts were not the cohesive people many modern Pagans would like to believe. Though the common culture gave them many similarities in spiritual belief and practice, the precise way in which those beliefs were put into action would vary from country to country, clan to clan, and century to century.[8]

Religions must evolve along with people. They must become spiritualities. If a religion does not change to meet the deepest spiritual needs of its followers, the religion loses out, and people flock to systems that do work for them, that speak to their souls. A simple look at the statistics showing the rapid decline in attendance and membership in churches and synagogues that have increasingly purveyed religion over spirituality for purposes of control tells the tale very well.

If we tried to accurately recapture the Celtic past, we would be disappointed by more than just the lack of spiritual connection. Celtic women had communal status far higher than women of other cultures during the same time period, but it was not a perfect society. A patriarchy was already in place, and by the second century CE, women's status had fallen considerably and was destined to sink even further in the years to come.

We can certainly learn from the past. Women can take the old Goddesses, the observance of the yearly cycles, the myths, and combine them with our current needs to synthesize a new style of Celtic Paganism—one that celebrates the Goddess in each of us in a way that we, as modern women, can understand, work with, and use to help us grow spiritually.

Celtic Paganism has often been touted as a path of the individual. Certainly it is true that in any spiritual system we derive the deepest insights from solitary introspection, but it is also true that the Celts highly valued their clans and community. Some rituals simply cannot be satisfactorily worked in solitude, and it for this reason that I have included one group ritual, and many suggestions for adapting solitary ones to group settings, in this text. The vast majority, however, remain for the female solitary.

Dipping Into the Bottomless Cauldron

The subtitle of this book, *Accessing the Cauldron of Life*, comes from the primal symbol of Celtic Paganism—the magickal cauldron. Though it becomes a portable grail or chalice in later legends, the cauldron is used widely in old Celtic myths and within modern Celtic Paganism. At its most basic, it represents the womb of the Goddess from which all life flows and to which all life must return to await rebirth. In some myths, the cauldron even functions as a portal between the physical world and the Otherworld from which the dead are brought back to life. Most of the famous Celtic cauldrons were bottomless, providing endless sustenance (Bran's), endless knowledge (Cerridwen's), and endless life (Badb's). Even the word for the cauldron's smaller cousin, the chalice or grail, comes from an old French word *graal*, meaning "a bottomless bowl."

The cauldron's fertile powers extend to the physical when it becomes a pot in which food is prepared. In a number of myths we see the cauldron as a vessel of never-ending abundance from which all may eat and drink their fill, the contents ever-renewing themselves. It is also a source of status, inspiration, wisdom, and transformation. Though no Celtic creation myth has survived, the link between the liquids within the cauldron and the womb blood of the original mother Goddess is clear.

The five fictions of the Celtic mythic cauldron can be summoned up in five broad categories, each relating to a specific element:

Creation = Water

Sustenance = Earth

Inspiration = Air

Transformation = Fire

Regeneration = Spirit

Using Celtic archetypes, such as the cauldron, women can successfully combine their need to connect with the divine feminine with their interest in Celtic Pagan spirituality. Through this path we can awaken the warrior queen within and establish new avenues of spiritual awareness, explore and probe women's mysteries through a Celtic framework, and connect with the power of the very potent and evocative Goddesses who dominate the Celtic pantheon. *Celtic Women's Spirituality: Accessing the Cauldron of Life*, draws on the limitless power of the Goddess and presents Celtic women's spirituality in what, I hope, is an understandable and workable format, one that women can use and build upon to create powerful and meaningful traditions for themselves, their daughters, their sisters, and their friends.

Notes

1 I cannot recall now the time, date, or place where this statement was made, though I am sure it was in the early 1990s. Sadly, I cannot recall the precise wording either. The Pagan and feminist presses had a proverbial field day with this statement before it became old news.

2 Jung, Carl G. *Memories, Dreams, Reflections* (New York: Vintage Books, 1965), 381.

3 The term "matriarchy" implies rule by women, or of a woman or group of women having hegemony over men and younger women. Few, if any, early societies can be proven to have lived under such a system. On the other hand, "matricentric" refers to societies in which the central focus of the clan or tribe was a mother figure. These societies usually had a Goddess as a supreme being and counted their clan as those linked though blood ties to a female ancestor.

4 B.C.E. means "Before the Common Era" and refers to what is generally called B.C. (Before Christ) by some writers. Likewise C.E., "Common Era," makes a similar reference for AD. I prefer these more scholarly and ecumenical designations, and they will be used throughout this book when dating events.

5 Hubert, Henri. *The Rise of the Celts* (New York: Bilbo and Tannen, 1966).

6 The "new religion" is a Pagan term referring to Christianity in Europe as replacing the "old religion" of Paganism.

7 See Chapter 1 for a full discussion on theories about Celtic myths and their relationship to the lives of Celtic women.

8 This is why there is no practice we can refer to today as being representative of "the" Celtic tradition. Many variations on the Celtic theme abound, and all can make a case for themselves—a dichotomy that would likely be understood and appreciated by our Celtic ancestors.

WOMEN IN CELTIC SOCIETY

The first Celtic tribes burst out of the Caucasus and moved into far southeastern Europe sometime around 2000 B.C.E. When it came to protecting the lands their clans had conquered through warfare, they were reputed to work as one awesome force. However, although connected by common language roots and cultural similarities, the Celts were never the cohesive people that modern Pagans would like to believe. They were just as likely to raid each other's livestock and go to war against one another as they were to fight with outsiders. It isn't even known for sure how much similarity one group of Celts recognized between themselves and other Celtic tribes. The very name we know them by—Celts— was derived from the word *Keltoi*, a label applied to them by the Greeks.[1]

Unlike other Pagan people of ancient Europe, the Celts did not have a set hierarchy of deities that remained in place wherever their clans settled. While there were some deities with similar names and legends, each separate area where the Celts eventually settled had its own varying versions of these deities, as well as a host of local divinities related to the trees, streams, and stones that populated their environment.

By 1200 B.C.E., when the tentative leading edge of the Celtic "invasion" had reached as far west as Ireland,[2] the Celts had been known from the Black Sea in the east to the western coast of Spain, and from Turkey and Italy in the south to the Shetland Islands in the north.[3] By the time the Celts were recognized as a distinct group by other European cultures, the patriarchy (the time of rule by men) had already been in place in Europe and the Middle East for nearly 3000 years.

As Celtic civilization flourished and changed during their slow westward migration, the role of Celtic women changed as well. Some of the changes came in response to the persuasions of patriarchy; later, much more was due to the conversion of Europe to Christianity and its attendant belief in the inferior moral and spiritual status of women. All these factors make pinning down precise statements on women's roles in Celtic society difficult at best, since the subject covers a wide range of time, space, and conditions. Women in 800 B.C.E. Gaul lived and were treated differently than those in 200 C.E. Ireland.

The Mythic Woman

Myths are our maps to the mysteries, codes that unlock their secrets. These living, ever-evolving tales have striking similarities worldwide. They follow patterns that our subconscious minds can understand. We can translate myths into tools of personal growth by relating the ideas they present to other aspects of ourselves. Once these mysteries are understood they cease to be mysteries and we absorb them into facets of our total being. A mythic mystery is not a "fiction" as we think of the word. Nor is it an old wives' tale or a superstition, but the revelation of profound and life-altering truths.

It is often to the Celtic myths that we look when seeking answers about our spirituality and about our place as women within that framework.

It has been argued that the high status of women in Celtic mythology, particularly those myths from Ireland that were the least tampered with over time, give evidence to the high status of women in that culture. The connection here seems weak, since there is a notable lack of women in celebrated leadership roles in Celtic societies. We have the legends of Boudicca of Iceni, Cartimandua, Nessa, Connacht's Queen Maeve, and several others who may or may not have been based on historical woman, but no known women ever ruled as High Queen of any Celtic country.[4]

That the old Celtic oral traditions had been tampered with before being committed to paper is a given, though it is doubtful whether this was done deliberately. Oral traditions change drastically over time and, through thousands of years of patriarchy, the myths would have slowly altered themselves to reflect the new aims and concerns of societies. The strong female figures of Celtic mythology tend to have made it onto paper with a tinge of pettiness and viciousness attached to them, as if the only acceptable strong woman was one who had great personal flaws or who was able to act like a man. Flamboyant Queen Maeve, with her driving need to go to war to increase her own prosperity, is one apt example.

When Christianity's grip on the Celtic world tightened, many of the old legends involving women/Goddesses were deliberately altered in ways that reduced powerful women to the level of animals or hags, the latter eventually leading to the ugly legends of the modern Halloween witch cackling over the cauldron in which she would cook a Christian child. One example of the codification of this demotion from Goddess to animal/crone is seen in the myth of an Irish Goddess from Meath, Carravogue. Her original divine function is not known today, but by the time she meets up with St. Patrick (circa 400 C.E.) she is a crone who has been turned into a giant serpent for eating berries he had forbidden to her.[5] It may have been that these were blackberries, a fruit once sacred to the widely worshiped Goddess Brighid. St. Patrick was forced to kill Carravogue by dousing her with holy water, which melted her like the Wicked Witch of the West in the *The Wizard of Oz*. But the mythic memory of the Celts seemed to be able to rise above the distorted legend, and it was said that Carravogue turned into a lake from which she would someday be reborn.

In the classical mythology of Greece we see a similar trend, in which older, once-powerful Goddesses are turned into harridans and come under the yoke of their Gods, fathers, or brothers. Even in their demoted state, these Goddesses wield a good deal of power, certainly much more than women were ever granted under Greek law. Greek history is long and well-recorded, certainly much more so than that of the Celts, and if anyone looked for a correlation between Greek mythic women's role in society they would be hard pressed to find one, outside of a few mystery cults that were long gone by the time the current versions of the classical myths were recorded.

The slow change in Welsh women's status over time may also be recorded in myth, encoded in the stories surrounding the Welsh Goddess Arianrhod, whose name means "silver wheel." She was a powerful deity of fertility and regeneration, the personification of the ever-turning Wheel of the Year. Arianrhod lived in a stellar realm with her female attendants—some sources say nine in all—and there she decided the fate of the dead. She was a very sexual deity, and mated freely with any man she chose at any time. This freedom was not questioned until a magician named Math publicly accused her of conceiving two children whom she had not borne. He forced her to jump over his magickal staff, after which she gave birth to twin sons. The staff in this case is a phallic symbol, a metaphor for her rape by Math. Because Math took away her sexual freedom and her right to choose if and when she gave birth, some feminist scholars feel that Arianrhod's myth represents the shift from the time of Celtic women's full freedom to that of male-centered clans and male domination of women.

Women Under the Law

The best resources we have for uncovering how Celtic women actually lived is through the remains of their old laws. The Celts cherished law and held their judges and their pronouncements in high regard. Some of the laws varied from place to place since the extended clan, or *tuath*, remained the principal unit of government well into the common era. But certain basic tenets did survive, many pertaining to women's rights.

Like the Celtic myths, the famous Brehon Laws of Ireland changed over time to reflect changes in Celtic society. Some version of the Brehon Laws likely governed the Irish Celts as early as 500 B.C.E., and it is speculated that these laws had roots in pre-Celtic times, though the extant version we possess probably dates from around 500 C.E.[6] A lot can happen in a millennium.

The Irish name for the Brehon Laws was *Senchus Mor*, meaning "the great wisdom," and indeed the Laws wisely saw the Celts through some difficult conflicts with each other. Several myths tell of how disputes were settled by a Brehon, or judge, inarguably interpreting the Law for the warring factions. The Laws were remarkably equitable for their time, and adequately covered the needs and rights of both King and peasant.

Celtic society was highly stratified, with the warrior elite and the Druids being the highest caste, cattle barons in the middle, and small farmers and traders at the bottom. The Celts continued to court these sharp divisions, which arguably aided their eventual downfall. Because of this, the most marked difference between Celtic individuals was not based on gender but on societal ranking. Many of the provisions granted to, or restrictions placed upon, women under the law were also placed upon men of the same rank.

In comparison with her contemporaries in Greece and Rome, a woman in Celtic Ireland held an enviable position. A freeborn Irish woman was not chattel but a partner to the husband whom she was free to choose. The only pressure placed on her was to select a spouse of comparable rank.[7] All young people, regardless of gender, were urged to marry, for neither man nor woman achieved full adult status in the eyes of the community until wed. This is still largely true in modern Ireland, and is probably a carryover from the ancient beliefs in man and woman being the God and Goddess incarnate—two halves of one whole.

Anyone who was unsure of the suitability of a potential marriage partner was permitted to contract one of the now famous annual, or trial marriages. These prototypes of the handfasting rituals[8] of modern Celtic Paganism were undertaken for a period of a year and a day, a term of magickal importance in Celtic mythology. They could be made between any two consenting parties, regardless of rank, and if not mutually renewed at the period's end, they were automatically void. Though this idea sounds intriguingly fair and open-minded to modern people, the purpose was not so much to discern personal compatibility as it was to determine the fecundity of a potential partner. In most cases, trial marriages that did not produce children were usually allowed to expire and the partners were free to seek other mates.

Irish women were permitted to own property, to seek divorce, and to retain their own property and expect the return of their dowry afterwards. They could demand an honor price (*eric* in Old Irish) for damages to or the murder of one of their kinspeople (the price being based on one's rank in society), and they could take grievances before the judges. The child of an unmarried woman was not declared illegitimate; no such stigma existed among the Celts. All freeborn people had a rank that automatically entitled them to certain rights under the law.

Women could seek divorce if their husbands did not provide the food they wished to eat, or satisfy them sexually, and they could claim abandonment, even in times of war. The ahead-of-its time concept of no-fault divorce was also a part of early Irish Law, and it could be obtained by either partner. Though called "no-fault," there were still provisions for these failures, but no one was held personally responsible for them. These provisions included mental incapacity, infertility, illness, lack of physical support, the withholding of sex, and use of magick against the other partner.[9]

Celtic women not only enjoyed higher status than other woman of their time but they also shared in the responsibilities and burdens of being free. Female property owners were required to fight for their land just as the men were, and if a woman transgressed the laws of her country or clan, she was punished with equal severity. Community was important to the Celts, not just for survival, but for a sense of personal identity. One of the worst things that could befall a Celt of either gender was banishment from the protection of the law. In Old Irish, this person was declared a *deorad*. Although a deorad might continue to live along the fringes of the community, like a charity case, he or she was no longer considered one of the tribe and was not allowed to contribute to the greater good. This encoded importance of community and clan may be one of the reasons many Celtic Pagans today feel they are best served in a group or coven situation, rather than as a solitary.

Young Irish women could be given out as fosterlings just like young men, but they commanded a higher price from their foster family due to a belief that the girls took more time to teach. Fostering was an old Celtic custom by which children were sent to another household or clan until they turned seventeen to learn skills they would need as adults. This helped to keep down a certain amount of both inner- and inter-tribal warfare because the loyalties of the young people were divided between two sets of parents they loved. Likewise, when a fosterling was being considered, the woman of the household had as much right to accept or deny the child as the man. She was equally as obligated to the child's education as her husband, and equally entitled to the fostering fee.

In many foster situations, a young man was given into the care of his mother's brother; for example, the Ulster warrior Cuchulain, son of Dechtere, was given into the foster care of his uncle King Cormac. This practice is an ancient one, seen in many Pagan cultures. It speaks again of the power of the bonds of "mother blood," the unity of a clan resting on the strength of a common female relative. In some Native American tribes and some east Asian principalities, the natural line of succession went from a man to his sister's son rather than to his own son.

Even in the highly stratified society of the Celts, rank and property were not always a given. They could be forfeited by transgressing certain Brehon Laws, and in this women and men were treated differently, at least in the extant version of the Laws. Among the breaches of society's rules that could cause a woman to lose property or become an outcast were theft, satirizing others, lying, wounding the partner to draw blood, or being inhospitable. By 500 C.E., the Laws further stated that a woman owed her sexual loyalty to her husband, whereas in earlier legends it is made clear that broad sexual freedom was given to and expected from married individuals. Amazingly, the Laws still recognized a woman's right to petition for divorce, even if she was the one who had been sexually unfaithful.[10] Even today in tribal societies where women have sexual freedom, it can be noted that women's communal status is also quite high. It may have been this earlier freedom that allowed women to keep their relatively higher status even after patriarchal pressures came to bear on the Celts.[11]

Though the Brehon Laws were not as hard on the infidelitous male, one very intriguing passage gives the wronged wife the freedom to take whatever retaliatory actions she wished against both her husband and his paramour for three days, with full exemption from legal retribution.[12]

Children were of great importance to the Celts, and to purposely take any action that could cause the miscarriage of a child was viewed as a crime against the entire community. Both men and women could be charged with *deliberately* causing a miscarriage to occur,[13] a radical departure from most modern laws, which place this burden on the woman alone. A man could also be charged with an *eric* by his wife's clan if he did anything to put the mother or child at risk during birth. He was required by law to see to her comfort and safety, and to call upon the services of a qualified midwife just as soon as they were needed. All children were provided for by the clan as well as by the parents and foster parents, and so no one feared the inability to support a child.

There is also evidence that women held positions as warriors (see Chapter 4), queens, judges, and Druids (see Chapter 2), though these avenues had largely closed by 100 C.E. Particulars about women in these functions are virtually nonexistent due to the fact that written historical documents were not kept by the early Celts. The keeping of history was the duty of the clan bard, or Druid, and much Celtic history was not committed to paper until the early Christian period (around 600 C.E.).

There is also evidence of female clan leaders. Though the recognizable Celtic surnames of today reflect clans that have been traced through a masculine ancestor (the Mac, Ap, and O' prefixes meaning "son of"), vestiges of an older, matrilineal descent can be seen in the oral traditions,[14] in which women take the names of their mothers and then pass their own names along to sons, with or without the patronymic prefix. Nessa, mother of High King Cormac MacNessa, is one example that appears in written myths as well as oral legends.

Though generally there were no female High Queens, there were regional queens such as the much-lauded Queen Maeve of Connacht, a warrior and thinker of great repute. There were also strong Celtic women who took the High King's throne and held it in trust for their sons. One is the aforementioned Irish warrior-scholar Nessa, mother of High King Cormac MacNessa; and another is Cornwall's Vennolandua, who killed her husband in battle, drowned his mistress, and claimed the High Queenship of Cornwall for herself until her son came of age.

Women archetypally represent the sovereignty of land in many cultures, though in the Celtic this link runs particularly deep and strong (see Chapter

12), and it is from these ancient beliefs that the image of the woman as sacred caretaker of the land may have arisen. In a very old Irish legend, probably one with pre-Celtic roots, we hear of two sisters, "princesses" called Ain and Iaine, who marry their brothers so that no other family but theirs would be able to rule the land. The sisters are also credited with inventing warfare, so that they would have a way to claim the rest of the island for themselves. Some legends go so far as to say that these sisters and their actions are the reason that the Brehon Laws acknowledged women's rights to property in a time and place where this was not the norm.

By the time Christianity held sway in the old Celtic lands—on paper if not in fact—women's roles had been largely reduced to those we are often told are "acceptable" today: housekeeper, servant, and caregiver. Even the great healing skills women possessed and once passed along to their daughters were branded evil, and any woman brave enough to use her knowledge openly risked execution for practicing Witchcraft (see Chapter 13). The later invasions of Celtic lands, most notably by the Norse and Normans, lead to other social and spiritual changes that left permanent marks on Celtic society and its women, bringing them more firmly into the patriarchal world by removing or eroding the equitable rule of old Celtic laws.

Questions For Celtic Pagan Women

The following questions are the first of many that will be posed to you as you work through this text. There are no right or wrong answers. They are designed only as guideposts to help you decide upon your next spiritual step, to be markers of your learning and understanding, forcing you to think critically about all that you learn. Always question what you read; the material in this book included. Take what feels right and what makes sense in terms of your current studies, and let the rest go. However, keep an open mind. What you discard today may have new meaning tomorrow.

How do I define Paganism and/or Witchcraft (or Wicca)?

Why am I interested in the Celtic aspects of Paganism in particular?

How much do I know about the culture of the Celts? Their religion? Their cosmology?

What sets apart Celtic Pagan expressions from other culturally based Pagan traditions?

What works on Celtic Paganism have I already studied? Which
did I like or not like, and why?

With which points do I strongly agree? Why?

With which points do I strongly disagree? Why?

How does agreeing or disagreeing with a writer make me feel?

Do certain words trigger strong reactions in me? Wicca? Celt? Craft?
Faery? Women's spirituality?

About how many specific Celtic traditions do I have some knowledge?
Do I want to learn more about any of them?

Am I more of a Celtic eclectic than a traditionalist? If I did follow a single
Celtic tradition, which would I prefer? Irish? Scottish? Welsh? Gaulish?
Another?

What are my spiritual goals in terms of my chosen path? How does
being a solitary or part of a group help meet them?

How do I feel about the societal stratification of the Celts?

How do I reconcile the more negative aspects of the Celtic world
to my own Celtic spiritual practice?

What do I see as the role of women in old Celtic societies?

What do I see as the role of women in modern Celtic Paganism?

What attracts me to the women's spiritual aspects of Celtic Paganism? How
do I reconcile these with my other Celtic Pagan interests and practices?

What do I hope to get out of the study of Celtic women's spirituality?

What can this study allow me to give back to my Pagan and/or secular
community?

Notes

1 Herm, Gerhard. *The Celts: The People Who Came Out of the Darkness* (New York: St. Martin's Press, 1975), 3.

2 Though the taking of Ireland by the Celts is referred to in myth (such as those surrounding the Sons of Mil) as an invasion, in truth the Celts arrived in small waves, not as a unified force.

3 Green, Miranda. *Celtic Goddesses: Warriors, Virgins and Mothers* (London: British Museum Press, 1995), 10.

4 Ibid, 15.

5 Monaghan, Patricia. *The Book of Goddesses and Heroines* (St. Paul, Minn.: Llewellyn, 1990), 69.

6 Power, Patrick C. *Sex and Marriage in Ancient Ireland* (Dublin: Mercier Press, 1976), 10 and 48.

7 Ibid, 25.

8 Handfasting is the term given to Pagan/Wiccan marriage rites by those following traditions that originated in western Europe, particularly Britain and Ireland.

9 Power, 49-50.

10 Ibid, 31.

11 Markale, Jean. *Women of the Celts* (Rochester, Vt.: Inner Traditions International, Ltd., 1972), 39.

12 Power, 44.

13 Ibid, 33.

14 Markale, 38.

THE FEMININE
MYSTERY CULTS

It has only been during the Celtic Pagan revival of the late twentieth century that women have been able to reclaim their roles as Goddess incarnate, priestess, and spiritual warrior on a widespread basis. We have taken what precious little we still know about the old feminine mystery cults and rebirthed them into a new incarnation to fulfill our current-day needs.

Women's role in old Celtic religious life is a decidedly hazier sky to peer into than that of women's role in Celtic society. Virtually nothing of substance comes to us in native writing, and our only choice is to study the past through symbols left to us by the Celts, by the writings of those who observed Celtic culture, and by comparing what we know of women's mystery schools in other parts of Europe—and even from other eras—with the archaeological remnants discovered in Celtic lands.

In most early cultures, women and men carried on separate spiritual traditions. In some areas these overlapped, and perhaps even met, but in most respects they remained separate, with each sex cultivating its own mysteries and rituals that were likely kept secret from both the opposite sex and from the uninitiated. Even in later centuries, under patriarchy, the flourishing of women's spiritual traditions has been known, particularly among the freedom-loving Celts. This is reflected in a law known today as the Golden Statute. It was enacted in early Ireland, the first known declaration of the legality of universal freedom of religion. Knowing what we do about the divisions of Celtic society being based on rank and not gender, there is no doubt that this law applied to women as well as to men.

These gender-based divisions of spiritual pursuits are known in other European cultures as well. The most famous of these is easily the Eleusian mysteries of Greece. For centuries, the city of Eleusia was a center for Goddess worship, and many pilgrimages were made to its temples and priestesses by women seeking the Goddess mysteries. Over time, the Goddess was eroded as a figure of power, replaced by the supreme male being of the new religion.

For several hundred years into Ireland's Christian period, women's spirituality most certainly functioned as a separate spiritual practice and likely was hidden from the male-oriented new religion, just as it had been kept from the male priests of the old. The persistent folklore surrounding "faery women," possibly meaning Pagan in this case, who married human males has led some scholars to believe these are stories about the gender-segregated spiritual spheres that existed until around 500 C.E., and perhaps longer. At least one ancient worship site remains today as evidence of this separation. Off the coast of County Sligo, on the small island of Innishmurray, stands an abandoned monastery dating to the sixth century C.E. The old ruins boast both a separate women's chapel and a women's cemetery that are clearly not part of the standard convent arrangements of the modern Catholic Church.[1] Nearby are the famous Five Speckled Stones, standing stones of neolithic origin, inscribed with an abundance of Pagan symbolism. Another women's cemetery in County Tyrone boasts, "No women here alive; No men here dead."

Later in Celtic history the feminine deities and their cults were diabolized, and Witch hunts to track down and destroy their followers—including some men—became standard practice not only in the old Celtic lands but throughout all of Europe.

Women as Druids

There has been much debate, both among scholars and Pagans, as to the place of women among the ranks of the Druids. The Druids were defined as both priests and philosophers, bards and historians, magicians and advisors, singers and storytellers; indeed, different Druids probably fulfilled all those roles at various times. Unlike Celtic clans, Druids appeared not to be bound by tribal territories[2] but could travel and study where they chose, their learning and judgment honored and respected by nearly all Celtic tribes. That they came to represent a very powerful force in Celtic life is a given, as is their eventual domination by males.

Some Celtic scholars have adamantly stated that there is no evidence of female Druids at all,[3] but that the role of women was likely that of prophets, healers, magicians, and keepers of sacred flames, all without the high status given to the initiated Druids. Much of this belief is derived from the writings of Julius Caesar, in which he described his campaign against the Gauls in the first century C.E. He refers several times to the power the Druids had to stop battles and advise kings, and refers to them all with masculine pronouns. Other scholars, however, cite early writings in which there are direct references to what they believe are female Druids, including those of the Roman warrior Tacitus. Tacitus described meeting a robed contingent that included women at Anglesey, a well-known Druidic stronghold until 61 C.E.[4] Like the male Druids they accompanied, these women appeared to Tacitus to be leveling curses and making other magick against the invaders.

It was in the role of prophets, or seers, that women clearly flourished, and this talent appears to have been greatly respected.[5] That this was one of the chief roles the Druids performed for their kings and clan chiefs is a given. One modern Druid writer claims that there was an entire class of women seers called *ueledas* in Old Irish, or *banfhili* ("woman-seers").[6] The latter word is clearly related to the term *fili*, the name of a specific function and class of Druids.

Celtic legends also record the names of women who are cited as Druids, or who function as Druids within their stories. Among the women said to be Druids in Celtic myth and legends are Amerach, who was able to cast spells of agelessness; Argante, a healer of Anglesey; Birog, who helped a warrior take revenge on the Formorian God Balor; Chlaus Haistic, whose legends portray her as both Goddess and Druid; Dubh, the namesake of Dublin who magickally drowned her husband for his infidelity; Franconian-die-Drud, who is associated with dreams and the horse Goddess Mare; and Maer, who attempted to use love magick on the warrior hero Fionn MacCumhal. The Irish Goddess Facha, Goddess of poetry, is said by some to be a patron deity of the Druidic bards.

Another possibility for the mystery surrounding female Druids may have been that the path of the Druidic initiate was gender-segregated from the start, and that it was the men's path that eventually became dominant in the hierarchy of Celtic society, while the women's path took other forms out of the mainstream. This lessening of the women's role may have been partly deliberate. Certainly the male Druids' eventual insistence on the superiority of males as religious leaders and teachers—something that had taken place or was taking place in virtually all cultures during this time period—probably helped pave the way for the Roman church's victory over the British Isles, as did many of the other sharp divisions in Celtic society.

Modern Druid sects are still predominantly male, but most are open to women. Women have also reclaimed this part of their spiritual past on their own and now boast distinct Druidic traditions with their own names, degrees of advancement, and mysteries. They do not appear to be as widespread as the "traditional" Druid groups nor as keen on taking part in the endless debates on what constitutes genuine Druidry. Members of one very interesting all-women Druid group I ran across while living in Texas call themselves the Dryads, named for the tree faeries known as Dryads; who, the women claim, bestowed their name upon the sect many centuries before. One of their primary deities is the Breton Goddess Druantia, a Goddess of trees.

Celtic Priestesses

It is possible that, as the Druids began to exclude women or as Druidism itself was eroded by the church, women broke away to form or to strengthen their own spiritual societies which were never based on Druidic structures.[7] These cults are easier to document, and evidence of their existence extends well into the modern era.

Archaeological digs in Celtic lands have retrieved pieces of iconography that appear to be figures of priestesses, or at least of women who are clearly performing ritual functions,[8] though arguably these might also be Goddess figures. Early literature that refers to women in priestly roles serving in temples or at the court of rulers is more precise.[9] Queen Maeve of Connacht employed at least one priestess at her stronghold, Cruachain, who made it into print—a woman named Erne. Likely there were others as well—probably eight more, to be exact.

The Celts held the number three to be sacred, and the greatest manifestation of this was seen in three times three, or nine. Unlike many modern Celtic covens who strive to keep their numbers to thirteen,[10] the early Celtic priestesshoods likely took advantage of the sacred symbolism found in the number nine, and kept their membership to this. This idea is born out in a piece of ancient Welsh poetry in which we are told that nine maidens attend the cauldron of rebirth in the Otherworld, and that only their breath may heat the fire that burns beneath it, and also in the classical writings of Strabo, who records that committees of nine women would greet returning warriors.

In Greece, Rome, and other early European cultures, women as priestesses often were given the care of sacred fires. The most well-known of these are the Vestal Virgins of ancient Rome, who tended the sacred flames of the hearth and fire Goddess Vesta. In Ireland and Gaul, two similar sacred flames were kept by women labeled "virgins" (see Chapter 8 for a full discussion on Celtic virgin Goddesses and heroines). One was at the hot springs in Gaul, sacred to the fire Goddess Sulis, a deity who found her way to England as Sul; the other was in southern Ireland at Kildare, where a sacred flame honoring the Goddess Brighid burned continuously for centuries.

Brighid was one of the Celtic Goddesses whose image and archetype was venerated over much of Celtic Europe. In Ireland she was known as Brighid, in England and Wales as Brigantia, and in Gaul as Brigindo. A Goddess of fire, childbirth, inspiration, fertility, medicine, music, animal husbandry, and crafting, she was a mother, a sovereign, a warrior, and a patron of warriors and of children. Brighid was widely and vigorously worshiped.

The early churchmen in Ireland sought to eradicate her worship, and even invented some very creative legends to link her with their own Goddess substitute, the Virgin Mary. The result of this merging of legends was the spurious creation of St. Brighid,[11] whose myths today contain a curious mixture of maiden and mother images, and whose feast day now falls on February 2, the old date of Brighid's festival once called Imbolg, now known as *La Fheile Brid* (the Feast of Brighid). Sometime during the fifth century C.E., Brighid's shrine at Kildare and its eternal flame were taken over by the church, and for many centuries afterward its nuns tended the sacred fire. It is believed the flame that represented the eternal light of Brighid's divinity burned unquenched until the mid-sixteenth century.[12]

Brighid's image as a Goddess of fertility is retained in modern Ireland through the many holy wells that bear her name, albeit in her guise of saint. Water and earth, being the two "feminine" elements,[13] are symbols of fertility in their own right, and many extant Irish wells bear the name of *Tobar Brid*, or the "Well of Brighid." Pilgrimages for healing, fertility, and the protection of children are especially popular at these sites.[14]

This adoption of sacred Goddess sites was a common practice among the churchmen, whose purpose was to coerce the native Celtic population to focus their adoration on the God of the new religion and on Mary as his earthly mother.[15] In southern Munster, Aine, a native cattle, fire, and sun Goddess, was given a sacred site at Knockaine. Until the early twentieth century, torchlight processions were held on her hillside each midsummer day, the one day of the year when her symbol, the sun, was at its zenith. These torches were also passed over fields and under animals to ensure their fertility.

As time passed, and the worship of the old religion was officially suppressed by the church, the once-venerated Celtic Goddesses fell to the status of faery women, such as the death-heralding *beansidhe* (banshee in English), or of demons, such as the blue-faced Cailleach of Highland Scotland who brings death with the touch of her skull-topped walking staff. The Celtic priestesses went into hiding, preserving there the thin thread of the old Celtic religion upon which we build today.

In the earliest days of Ireland's Christian period, women participated as full members of the clergy, serving as priestesses, abbesses, deacons, and even bishops.[16] The strong presence of women in the Pagan priesthood allowed greater choices for them when the Celtic lands began being Christianized in the second to fifth centuries c.e. Many ancient monastic sites in Ireland have ruins that contain separate women's chapels and cemeteries, not a common feature of any church institution, including the modern Roman Catholic. One of the most famous of these sites is at Innishmurray, off the coast of County Sligo. Another is at the modern pilgrimage site of Glendalough in County Wicklow, where a small stone church known as the Teampall na mBan, or Women's Church, sits just outside the main monastic enclosure.[17]

Kele-De, Smirgat, and Sheila-na-Gig

Among the most well-known of the feminine mystery cults was that of Kele-De, the Goddess for whom the Catholic monks known as the Culdees took their name. Her all-female followers were known as the *Kelles*, and her priestesses were exempt from all patriarchal laws, including the Brehon Laws that, by several centuries into the common era, forbid sexual freedom. The Kelles took any and all lovers they chose, whenever they chose.[18]

Kele-De's name has been a source of contention among scholars, with some saying it means "servant" or "bride of God,"[19] and others relating it to pre-Celtic beliefs in an "all-power" or deity of creation whose myths have been lost to us. In her image as a devourer of sexual energy, a power linked by many ancient people to the life force, she is sometimes thought to be a derivation of the infamous Indian devourer Goddess Kali-Ma.[20]

One little-known woman from Irish lore who represents the guardian spirit of feminine mysteries is Smirgat. Likely she was once a priestess, and was probably involved in an Irish feminine spiritual cult, though this cannot be proven today. We make this assumption based on a myth in which she told her lover, the hero Fionn MacCumhal, that if he ever drank from a horn he would die. To the Celts, the horn was a vessel of completeness, representing the womb of the Goddess on the inside and the phallus of the God on the outside. Drinking from the horn, particularly if it had been consecrated by a priestess for use in religious rites, would be a form of initiation into the greater mysteries—a type of spiritual rebirth.

Another divine feminine image that has been a source of controversy is the Sheila-na-Gig. Nothing at all is known about this mysterious figure beyond the fact that her blatantly sexual image has been found carved on stone thresholds, usually at sacred sites or other places of worship. One of these figures graced the entrance to Brighid's shrine at Kildare.[21] The Sheila is a crudely rendered figure of a squatting woman who invitingly holds wide her vulva in a vaguely triangular pattern. On her stick-figure-like face is a faint smile, one which is serene and almost knowingly complacent. Many of these Sheila carvings were used by nuns to adorn the doors of Irish convents. When the renderings were discovered by horrified churchmen, many of them were taken away and destroyed. In the late nineteenth century, an archaeologist found a pile of them buried near the ruins of an old Irish convent.

The meaning behind the Sheila-na-Gig has been argued to be one of blessing or protection, though it is more likely that she offers an invitation into the feminine mysteries. The triangular pattern of her vulva evokes the sacred number three of the Triple Goddess of the Celts; the virgin, mother, and crone in one who represents the full cycle of birth, death, and regeneration. In this aspect, the Sheila-na-Gig symbolizes an open gateway to the Otherworld for those brave enough to accept initiation into her mysteries. It may be that worshippers reverently touched the carving of her yawning vulva when entering the temple for worship, just as women in other cultures made a similar gesture of homage when entering the palace of the feminine mysteries.[22]

The true meaning of the Sheila, and the impact she and similar divine

Sheila-na-Gig

images have had on modern women's lives, is probably even more complex. In her physical form she represents the insatiable, devouring power long attributed to the feminine sex organs, an image potent enough to have caused many men—and some women—to fear and oppress this Goddess and her sisters, and to take out that fear on woman throughout the ages. This fearful image is one of the reasons why many of the old Goddesses, Celtic and otherwise, have been diabolized and recreated into vampiric demons, ugly hags, and evil faeries. Somehow they seemed less threatening in this form than when they were worshiped as deities and creators.[23]

The devouring female who could not control her bodily urges was such an inspiration for terror that it can reasonably be cited as the primary reason why so many of today's woman literally starve themselves to gain the approval of men. Making themselves appear weak, small, and childlike, devoid of normal human appetites, makes them less threatening and less Goddess-like.[24] With the diminishing of that status, the power of creation inherent in deities also vanished, leaving in its wake a feminine figure with no procreative powers, one who serves no purpose beyond that of servant and sex object. Today's magickal women must never forget that will becomes reality; with this desire to appear less powerful came the true loss of power, and this allowed women to come more easily under the domination of men.

The Sheila-na-Gig is not hungry to devour just for the fun of it, nor to satisfy some insatiable physical appetite. In keeping with the eternal cycles of birth, death, and regeneration, the creator *must* devour in order to offer us rebirth. Rebirth in this instance is not just physical but can refer to a spiritual rebirth as well, an initiation into the greater mysteries of our gender. Therefore the Sheila is in truth offering us a gift, a positive manifestation of the never-ending cycle of existence that is such an important part of Celtic cosmology and religion.

Notes

1 Day, Catharina. *Ireland* (Chester, Conn.: The Globe Pequot Press, 1986), 310-311.

2 Herm, Gerhard. *The Celts: The People Who Came Out of the Darkness* (New York: St. Martin's Press, 1975), 148.

3 Markale, Jean. *Women of the Celts* (Rochester, Vt.: Inner Traditions International, Ltd., 1972), 38.

4 Green, Miranda. *Celtic Goddesses: Warriors, Virgins and Mothers* (London: British Museum Press, 1995), 138-139.

5 Ibid, 139.

6 MacCrossan, Tadhg. *The Sacred Cauldron* (St. Paul, Minn.: Llewellyn, 1992), 6.

7 Valiente, Doreen. *An ABC of Witchcraft: Past and Present* (Custer, Wash.: Phoenix Publishing, Inc., 1988), 97.

8 Green, 143.

9 Ibid.

10 Thirteen has been the traditional number for members in European culture-based covens for at least several centuries. The reason most often given for this is that these are the number of lunar cycles in the average solar year.

11 Condren, Mary. *The Serpent and the Goddess: Women, Religion and Power in Celtic Ireland* (San Francisco: Harper & Row, 1989), 66.

12 Ibid, 107.

13 The other elements, the masculine ones, are fire and air.

14 For an excellent discussion of the holy wells of Ireland see Patrick Logan's *The Holy Wells of Ireland* (Gerrards Cross, Buckinghamshire: Smythe, 1980).

15 Markale, 16.

16 Rodgers, Michael and Marcus Losack. *Glendalough: A Celtic Pilgrimage* (Blackrock, Co. Dublin: The Columba Press, 1996), 72.

17 Ibid, 69.

18 Walker, Barbara G. *The Crone: Woman of Age, Wisdom, and Power* (San Francisco: HarperCollins, 1985), 78.

19 Ibid.

20 Ibid, 80.

21 Condren, 65.

22 Walker, 80.

23 Keane, Patrick J. *Terrible Beauty: Yeats, Joyce, Ireland, and the Myth of the Devouring Female* (Columbia, Mo.: The University of Missouri Press, 1988).

24 Chernin, Kim. *The Hungry Self* (New York: Perennial Library, 1985).

ENTERING THE SHEILA-NA-GIG

Guided Meditation

The ultimate spiritual mysteries are those that pertain to the self that have practical applications. Sometimes the message we receive when exploring is universal in nature, sometimes it is gender-specific, but always it applies to the individual at whatever stage of spiritual development and physical-world difficulties she finds herself. The guided meditation in this chapter is designed to allow you to accept the invitation of the Sheila-na-Gig to enter her realm of mysteries.

Guided meditations are one of the most potent tools we have for aligning ourselves with the energies of deities and mythic figures. They force us to test the limits of our personal power as they stimulate our deep minds to facilitate interaction with the divine and stir our creative selves to wakefulness.

Guided meditation can be best defined as a structured mental journey into the inner or archetypal or astral plane for the purpose of making a lasting change on both the conscious and subconscious mind. The spiritual uses of this type of meditation are as old as the art of storytelling itself, a skill highly regarded by both ancient and modern Celts. Using ancient myths and legends, storytellers transported many persons into other worlds and back again without most of them realizing this inner transformation ever took place.

Most guided meditations will work for you just as they are written, but they should always be considered as maps—schemes that show the starting and ending points of a journey, but that offer you a myriad of options for traveling the roads in between. As you work with one set of guided images over and over again, the beings who populate them will become familiar to you, and will step out of their prewritten roles to offer assistance and insight far beyond the scope of the original meditation. This is as it should be. It is a sign that you are truly working in another realm of existence, and that your presence has been accepted there.

The guided meditation in this chapter may be used as is, or be broken down into smaller components as needed. It may be changed, adapted, reordered, or rewritten as your needs dictate. At various points along the path there are places where you are offered the chance to leave the meditation. If you do this, you may return later at any time to explore its other aspects. You may want to read through the meditation in advance and make some tentative plans on how you think you may want to progress. Everyone learns at a different rate. Some women may wish to take each teaching one slow step at a time, and others will want the full range of learning all at once. There is no right or wrong way. The choice is yours to make.

You will note also that it makes use of an alternate form of Celtic circle structure, one that does not work through directions and elements in a circular pattern but evokes the east, south, north, and then the west, a representation of an arm from the symbol known as Brighid's Cross (see Chapter 6). You are certainly welcome to reorder the meditation if you prefer to use a circular pattern, but it is recommended that you make the west the last point in the meditation, since this is the place of power in most Celtic traditions, the direction from which the greatest knowledge can be obtained.

Guided meditation can be a powerful tool for self-exploration and change, and entering into it should not be taken lightly. Make sure you are in a receptive and reverent frame of mind, and have only the highest of intentions. As you keep working with this technique you will eventually find that you are fully projecting your consciousness into these images, an art that is known as astral projection. These places you will visit exist as much inside as outside of yourself, and you should never assume that this inner-self aspect somehow makes them not "real." The mind is the seat of all creation, the place where all magick is born, and it is a very fluid and real place where your every thought has consequence and form.

The sections in the meditation marked off by brackets [ ] are either clarifications of terms and words used in the text, or are instructions to the one who is reading the meditation aloud. These sections are not to be read aloud to the journeyer—a name I use for the person making the inner world or astral world voyage—nor to be considered part of the body of the meditation. You may prerecord the path and play it back for yourself, or work with a partner who will read the text to you. If you are unfamiliar with the practice of guided meditation, unsure how to achieve the altered state of consciousness necessary for successful inner-world work, or unsure how to ground yourself afterward, please refer to Appendix E for a full discussion, instructions, and tips.

Sheila-na-Gig Meditation

Close your eyes and slow your thoughts; breathe rhythmically and deeply, center your spirit, relax, and let go. Focus inward and outward, drawing your consciousness away from the physical world.

Know that you are protected by your own inner powers and by the love of the Goddess. If you wish, at this time you may mentally call out to your Goddess and ask her help and assistance, or you may wish to weave some other mental magick for the protection of your physical body as you start to become unaware of it. You may also ask her for protection and guidance in your spiritual travels. [Pause to allow the journeyer time to do these things. Three to five minutes should suffice.]

Know that you are always in control and that you have the power to return to full waking consciousness at any time you choose. If you wish to return at any point in your journey, you can do so by thinking the words "I am home." Thought is action on the astral plane. This simple act of will, constructed in a cohesive thoughtform, will trigger both your subconscious and conscious minds that you wish to return immediately to your normal consciousness, and it will immediately happen. You can then open your eyes and go about your daily life unharmed.

Knowing that you are protected and in control, you can fully relax. Take one more deep breath and release yourself to the experience that the Sheila-na-Gig aspect of the Goddess has in store for you at this time.

Will yourself free of the confines of your normal consciousness and allow yourself to pass through the void that separates what we think of as "reality" from the Otherworld. [Pause for a moment to allow this visualization to take place.]

When your inner vision clears, you find that you are standing in the courtyard of a small stone temple. All around you is the silence of a dense, primeval forest. In the courtyard of the temple is a small well from which two streams flow: one blood red and the other snow white. Knowing that your destiny lies beyond the door, you step over the well. As you do you seem to hear a celestial chord playing from deep within yourself, as if you are merging in harmony with something greater than yourself.

As you walk up to the heavy wooden door, you see that the carving upon it is of a large Sheila-na-Gig. You study the image for a moment, trying to learn all you can about her. Is she smiling secretively or not? Do her lips seem pursed in silence, or ready to impart mysteries to waiting ears? And what is the secret of her gaping void? On impulse, you place your fingers against the gateway she holds open to you, and you hear again the chord that is being echoed now within yourself. As the sounds blend and merge, the Sheila grows larger, towering over you. At first you think she might swallow you whole. Then you notice that, no matter how big she grows, you remain teetering on her edge, as if the choice to go in or not is yours alone. Knowing that the Sheila is here to transform you through her teachings, you allow yourself to fall into her dark void.

You find yourself in a place of nothingness in which there is no light, no warmth, no cold, and nothing onto which you can grab. You are everywhere and nowhere. You are neither falling nor floating, flying nor swimming—you are just there, deep inside the comforting womb-like interior of the Sheila. To your surprise, you find that you could learn to like it here. In this place you find it hard to recall your physical life. All your problems, worries, and endless list of "have to do" chores that plague you every day are gone. Your only responsibility here is to yourself.

Just when you begin to get really comfortable, you notice light beginning to form around you. As the light vanquishes the shadows, shapes can be seen coming to clarity. You feel solid earth now underneath you, and you find yourself in a clearing in a rich wooded area; perhaps the same area where the temple once sat, perhaps not. You recognize that this is sacred space. Not only does it vibrate with spiritual energy but at its perimeter are small menhirs, or standing stones, forming a perfect circle.

In the center stands a stone dolmen [this is an altar-like edifice made of stone that can be of any size; this one should be visualized as the size of a normal altar] and, to your surprise, standing behind it are nine women who smile at you in welcome. Three of them are wearing robes of white, three wear robes of red, and three wear robes of black. They seem to you to be almost ageless, though the ones in white seem the youngest and the ones in black the oldest. They are not cookie-cutter images of each other; each individual is unique and beautiful in her own way. One is heavy, one is short, one is tall, and one is slender. One is stern, another jolly, and still another motherly and nurturing.

You can see that this sacred space is on a small island surrounded by a river that seems to spring from the west and flow clockwise as it travels to the north, counterclockwise as it travels to the south. At the east, where the two currents meet, they seem to submerge rather than churn. Across the river, at each cardinal point, stands a large cauldron.

One of the women in black beckons you over to the dolmen and you gladly go to stand in front of it. You can now see that the dolmen serves as an altar and contains a variety of ritual and magickal items relating to women's rites. Chalices, stones, and shields, all enhanced with Goddess symbols, predominate. In the center of the stone, surrounded by the Goddess tools, is a deep and very lifelike carving of the Sheila-na-Gig.

"Welcome, sister," one of the women in white speaks.

"You have been expected," one of the women in red speaks. "The first step in discovering the women's mysteries awaits you."

"Remember that true initiation is not an event, but a process. No one can open the door to the greater mysteries but you," one of the women in black tells you. "The greater mysteries are why you have come, and you are anxious to start learning."

"Understanding of the self is the first step," says a woman in white. "As a young person, the female is often steered away from her true path. The only paths she is allowed to take with ease are those that others deem appropriate. But now you are here like a girl again, ready to set out on your chosen way. As when you were young, the impediments to your true path are still there, and staying the course may not be easy—that is why other sisters, like us, are here to help you. But we can only point the way. The walk is long and you must make it alone. The cauldron of the east contains answers to many of your questions about beginnings as a new woman, but it will ask many questions of you in return. Are you willing to accept the challenge of the cauldron of the east, to take its teachings and weave them into your web of wisdom?"

You tell her that you are willing and she hands you an athame [or whatever tool you or your Celtic tradition uses to represent the east and the element of air], and points you in the direction of the east.

As you walk to the edge of the island at the eastern quarter, a fierce wind begins to blow against you, as if trying to hold you back from fording the river. The waters are being stirred up, and since you have no idea how deep this channel is, you hesitate to cross. Each time you try to stick a foot into the water, the wind and surf become more violent. But you really want the knowledge that the elusive cauldron on the other bank can give you, so you stop to think of a way to overcome the elements.

[Pause a moment or two for the journeyer to reflect. At this point the journeyer may find her own way out, or you may direct her to use her athame or other east and air tool to master the wind and its effect on the river. Allow her two to three minutes of quiet time to perform this action.]

When you finally arrive on the other bank you note that the wind has become a gentle spring breeze. Several small animals are in the clearing around the cauldron—rabbits, squirrels, goats, and other totems of the young Goddess.

But it is the cauldron that holds your interest. You approach it reverently, your inner senses open to any sign that you are not welcome at this time. [If the journeyer feels she is not supposed to be here at this time, she will know it, and may decide to come out of her meditative state on her own. Pause a moment for the journeyer to make this decision.] But you feel nothing but welcome, and you venture to the rim of the vessel.

Peering over its edge, you find that it is not filled with a liquid as you expected, but with a cyclonic mass of energy that, as you watch, begins to reveal a message to you about yourself.

[Pause five to ten minutes so that the journeyer can view the symbols, "movies," or other images that may be shown to her at this time. The journeyer may hear or sense questions being asked of her as answers to other questions are given.]

When the last of the images fade, you step back from the cauldron and thank the Goddesses and feminine spirits of the east for showing you these things. You have discovered new insights of self-understanding that will help you on both your spiritual and physical paths at this time. As you finish thanking air, a gust of whirling wind engulfs you and lifts you up, carrying you safely across the river and setting you gently down in front of the altar once more.

One of the women in red smiles at you like a loving mother. "Are you ready for the next challenge?" she asks.

[At this point you may wish to will yourself back to the stone temple and out of the meditation, saving the teachings of the other three cauldrons for a later time.]

You indicate that you are ready to go on.

"Some limitations, we have been taught, are our lot as women. Intellectually we know this teaching to be false and detrimental to all living things. But emotionally we are scarred. The teachings of our youth, no matter how false or destructive, can remain a powerful force over us. They must be burned away, purged with the fire of passion and overturned by confident action. Acknowledging and banishing these fears, thereby accepting our full range of abilities, is the second step in gaining wisdom," a woman in red tells you. "The cauldron of the south contains answers to many of your questions in this respect, but it will ask many questions of you in return. Are you willing to accept the challenge of the cauldron of the south, to take its teachings and weave them into your web of wisdom?"

You tell her that you are willing and she hands you a wand [or whatever tool you or your Celtic tradition uses to represent the south and the element of fire], and points you in the direction of the south.

As you walk to the edge of the island at the southern quarter, an oppressive heat rises around you and you are tempted to run back and cool yourself in the gentle breezes of the east. The waters of the river here are boiling, as if a giant bonfire blazes beneath its surface, and you know that you cannot walk through it without being scalded. But you really want the knowledge that the elusive cauldron on the other bank can give you, so you stop to think of a way to overcome the elements.

[Pause a moment or two for the journeyer to reflect. At this point the journeyer may find her own way out, or you may direct her to use her wand or other south and fire tool to master the heat and its effect on the river. Allow her two to three minutes of quiet time to perform this action.]

When you finally arrive at the other bank, you note that the heat has mellowed to that of a balmy summer afternoon. You approach the cauldron reverently, your inner senses open to any sign that you are not welcome at this time. [If the journeyer feels she is not supposed to be here at this time, she will know it, and may decide to come out of her meditative state on her own. Pause a moment for the journeyer to make this decision.] But you feel nothing but welcome, and you venture to the rim of the vessel.

Peering over its edge, you find that its bottom is covered with a layer of richly woven fire. Reds, golds, yellows, oranges, and blues dance in its depths.

As you watch, images of sun Goddesses flare in the flames that now begin to reveal a message to you about your innermost fears, your insecurities, and your personal power and abilities.

[Pause five to ten minutes so that the journeyer can view the symbols, "movies," or other images that may be shown to her at this time. The journeyer may hear or sense questions being asked of her as answers to other questions are given.]

When the last of the images fade, you step back from the cauldron and thank the Goddesses and feminine spirits of the south for showing you these things. You have discovered new insights about those things that are now preventing you from being all that you can be in your spiritual and physical life and as a woman of power. As you finish thanking fire, a maverick blaze rises up from the ground and lifts you up with the care of a loving mother, carries you safely across the river, and sets you gently down in front of the altar once more.

One of the women in black smiles at you knowingly. "Are you ready for the next challenge?" she asks.

[At this point you may wish to will yourself back to the stone temple and out of the meditation, saving the teachings of the other two cauldrons for a later time.]

You indicate that you are ready to continue.

"Women are conditioned not to trust in their knowledge. When our experience and insights are belittled they stagnate, and in this way our enemies prevent them from becoming part of our wisdom. For wisdom makes us strong, and this is a threat to all they have tried to build for four millennia. Learning to take your beliefs and experiences and accepting them as knowledge, then weaving them into a strong cloak of wisdom, is the third step on your quest. You cannot function as a warrior, teacher, or priestess without understanding this aspect of yourself. Also remember that it is from the north that the powers of sovereignty come, from the stone of the mother earth that cries aloud when a rightful and just ruler steps upon her back [see Chapter 9]. We have more power than we usually realize," the woman in black tells you. "If we did not, no one would have battled so hard for so long to make us forget it. The cauldron of the north contains answers to many of your questions in this regard, but it will ask many questions of you in return. Are you willing to accept the challenge of the cauldron of the north, to take its teachings and weave them into your web of wisdom?"

"The north?" you ask. "Why not the west?"

"The north is the place of cold and darkness, where the greatest stumbling blocks to our progress lie. While there is much good in darkness, and much to learn, we have to shed light into it to be able to use it. Darkness cannot be seen without light, and light blinds without darkness to balance its glare."

The woman hands you a stone [or whatever tool you or your Celtic tradition uses to represent the north and the element of earth], and points you in the direction of the north.

As you walk to the edge of the island at the northern quarter, a deep rumble from below nearly knocks you off your feet. An earthquake! You are sure it is trying to hold you back from fording the river. The waters are being slapped in a dozen different directions and the riverbed vibrates and changes course. This is a tough challenge, to be sure, but you really want the knowledge that the elusive cauldron on the other bank can give you, so you stop to think of a way to overcome the elements.

[Pause a moment or two for the journeyer to reflect. At this point the journeyer may find her own way out, or you may direct her to use her stone or other north and earth tool to master the earthquake and its effect on the river. Allow her two to three minutes of quiet time to perform this action.]

When you finally arrive on the other bank you note that the earth is still and calm once more, and the carpet of thick green grass feels like a soft blanket beneath your feet.

But it is the cauldron that holds your interest. You approach it reverently, your inner senses open to any sign that you are not welcome at this time. [If the journeyer feels she is not supposed to be here at this time, she will know it, and may decide to come out of her meditative state on her own. Pause a moment for the journeyer to make this decision.] But you feel nothing but welcome, and you venture to the rim of the vessel.

Peering over its edge you find that it is filled with a rich variety of vibrant crystals which, as you watch, begin to reveal a message to you about yourself.

[Pause five to ten minutes so that the journeyer can view the symbols, "movies," or other images that may be shown to her at this time. The journeyer may hear or sense questions being asked to her as answers to other questions are given.]

When the last of the images fade, you step back from the cauldron and thank the Goddesses and feminine spirits of the north for showing you these things. You have discovered new insights, gaining wisdom that will help you on both your spiritual and physical paths at this time. As you finish thanking earth, a giant rift in the ground tosses you upward and sets you safely down across the river in front of the altar once more.

You stand impatiently now, waiting for someone to offer you access to the cauldron of the west. Yet as long as you wait, none of the nine women offers you the west.

[The journeyer may now go to the end of the meditation and leave if she chooses, or she can stay and work with the energies of the west.]

Finally you speak up and announce that you wish to visit the western cauldron. All nine women seem pleased with your choice, yet they also seem hesitant to let you go. The oldest of the women in black steps forward and speaks to you. "The west is the place of greatest power in our Celtic traditions," she reminds you. "It is the home of our ancestors, our deities, and our beloved and eternal mother from whom we are all born and to whom we must all return one day. It is a place in which all things—all thoughts, peoples, places, time, and space—meet, coalesce, and regenerate. It is a place that can make you strong or expose your greatest weakness for all the universe to see. It can recreate you better than before, or it can destroy you altogether. It is a place you must enter by choice, not just by invitation, fully knowing its power. It is a place from which you cannot return unchanged. Our myths tell us that over and over again. Are you sure you wish to take the challenge of the western cauldron at this time?" [Again, the journeyer has the choice to leave the meditation or go on.]

When you tell her you are ready to continue she looks pleased and hands you a chalice [or whatever tool you or your Celtic tradition uses to represent the west and the element of water], and points you in the direction of the west.

As you walk to the edge of the island at the western quarter, a driving rain begins to beat down on you, as if trying to hold you back from fording the river. The chalice you hold quickly fills and overflows, and the river looks as if it will soon overflow its banks and wash you away. But you really want the knowledge that the elusive cauldron on the other bank can give you, so you stop to think of a way to overcome the elements.

[Pause a moment or two for the journeyer to reflect. At this point the journeyer may find her own way out, or you may direct her to use her chalice or other west and water tool to master the rain and its effect on the river. Allow her two to three minutes of quiet time to perform this action.]

When you finally arrive at the other bank you note that the rain is gone, and now there is only a damp mist blanketing everything in a gentle haze. Several tall trees hover over the cauldron, and in them you notice some large-eyed owls—birds of the old Goddess—watching you carefully.

But it is the cauldron that holds your interest. You approach it reverently, your inner senses open to any sign that you are not welcome at this time. [If the journeyer feels she is not supposed to be here at this time, she will know it, and may decide to come out of her meditative state on her own. Pause a moment for the journeyer to make this decision.] But you feel nothing but welcome, and you venture to the rim of the vessel.

Peering over its edge, you find that it is filled with a liquid as red as blood and dark as midnight. You have a sense that it is bottomless. Its energies seem the strongest of any cauldron you have worked with yet, and you have to fight to overcome your fear of what will be revealed to you here. As you look into the cauldron's depths, the dark waters begin to reveal a message to you pertaining to knowledge and wisdom.

[Pause five to ten minutes so that the journeyer can view the symbols, "movies," or other images that may be shown to her at this time. The journeyer may hear or sense questions being asked of her as answers to other questions are given.]

When the last of the images fade, you step back from the cauldron and thank the Goddesses, feminine spirits, and ancestor mothers of the west for showing you these things. You have been given hints on how to rebirth yourself into the woman you need and want to be. As you finish thanking water, a huge waterspout engulfs and lifts you, carrying you safely across the river and setting you gently down in front of the altar once more.

When you return you find that the women all cheer for you, honoring you as an emerging spiritual warrior and priestess-in-training. Each of them kisses you on the forehead and murmurs a woman's blessings in your ear. [Pause about three minutes for this.]

The sounds of the bodhran [pronounced "bow rawn" (rhymes with cow lawn), it is the traditional Irish goatskin drum] fill the clearing, and the women have you lead them in an ecstatic circle dance. You spiral in and out from the center of the circle—which represents the eternal cycle of life, the unity of negativity and positivity, the polarities of life and death—for all these things belong to woman. It is she who births and creates, and to whom all things must go to be reborn. You dance in joyous knowledge that you are part of that cycle—part of the power.

The tempo increases and the dance becomes manic. You and the other women are twirling and spiraling in and out, allowing the power of the elements around you to come alive and join in the dance of praise and joy. At this point you notice another dancer just in front of you. This figure is now leading the rest of you in twists and turns so unexpected that they leave you breathless. It is the Sheila in all her unrestrained, voracious glory!

You follow her in the wild dance that now takes on an Otherworldly quality, and you seem to swirl through a blending of the elements, through time and space, your consciousness expanding to encompass all possibilities and realities.

As you dance you hear a woman's voice whispering in your ear. Is it the Sheila? You are not sure, yet her words ring true. "Remember that true initiation is not an event, but a process. To take the vows and ignore the process is waste, a slap in the face of the Goddess who gave you life. Take your learning and allow it to become part of your whole existence. Live it. Die it. And live it again and again. For this is the essence of feminine power, the foundation of all our wisdom."

As the last vibration of the voice fades away, the Sheila in front of you grows to mammoth proportions and you are once again engulfed in her. You find yourself in that place of nothingness and silence once more.

With a sensation that is almost jarring, you realize you are again standing in front of the stone temple, facing the carving of the huge Sheila that took you into her mysteries in the first place. In awe you watch as she shrinks in size again, and recedes into the relief on the door. You reverently touch her once more as you silently offer her your thanks.

Feeling as if you have truly been born anew and have received your first initiation into the Celtic women's tradition, you turn away from her and step back across the blood red and snow white streams. With this act you feel your consciousness start to separate from this place. You are walking toward the edge of the forest when you feel this world of mystery beginning to fade away. As you feel yourself fading from the temple site, closing off your world from this one, say to yourself the words, "I am home."

Gently your consciousness transfers itself back to your physical body. Feel now the awareness of your physical self returning to your legs, arms, back, stomach, and neck. Flex them and relish in the joy of being a living human being.

You are once again part of the waking physical world, and you open your eyes and feel exhilarated, energized, and glad to be home with your new wisdom attained from the Sheila-na-Gig. Do not forget to ground yourself [see Appendix C if you are unfamiliar with this concept]. Touch the earth, eat, scream, or do anything else that firmly roots you in the present. Then be sure to record this experience in your Book of Shadows, or other magickal journal, for later reference.

THE WARRIOR AND HER GODDESSES

Much iconographic evidence exists to support the predominance of unnamed war "Goddesses." Some icons contain no identifying inscriptions, so these could be merely statues and reliefs depicting Celtic women ready for battle.[1] It has been easy to name these ancient renderings "Goddesses" simply because of our modern prejudice against human women as capable fighters. What these icons do show clearly is that Celtic feminine figures were deeply associated with their society's primary preoccupation: war.

It is almost impossible to overestimate the importance of warrior culture to the Celts. Warriors represented the highest caste attainable in their society, ranking only below kings and queens and possibly the most skilled of Druids. Though we usually think of war as being something started, conducted, and concluded by men, a surviving pre-Celtic legend from Ireland tells us that war was invented by women, two sisters named Ain and Iaine who married their own brothers to entail their property in perpetuity so that no other family would be able to rule the island. The institution of war was their way of seeing to it that the land they ruled stayed within their family if their right to it was ever challenged. Celtic women served as warriors until at least the seventh century, although after about 50 CE they were likely few in number.

Debate rages today among feminists and Celtic scholars as to the issue of women's impressment, with several feminist revisionist historians putting forth the theory that women were forced to serve as warriors. There are two holes in this theory, one pertaining to the old Celtic laws and another that relates to the high ranking of the warrior cast.

Under old Irish Celtic law, all landowners were required to serve their clans as warriors. Since women had the privilege of owning land, they also had the obligation to defend it in this culture where war was always a constant threat.[2] Early Irish law was one of the least sexist legal codes ever conceived and executed, and it made no distinction between women and men when it came to property rights. Non-propertied women were free to fight or not when the opportunity presented itself, though formal admission into the warrior class was harder to come by for them.

In living memory, many of our young people have chosen to flee their homelands rather than serve as warriors/soldiers, but we live in a world where the value of war has been eroded—despite all evidence to the contrary—which makes it difficult for us to fully comprehend the status of the warrior elite of the Celts. Young men and women aspired to membership in the warrior class in the same way that western young people today dream of being doctors, lawyers, or high-powered executives. To achieve this status was to rise like cream to the top of the human milk pail. Those not born to the warrior class, or who did not own land had only one avenue to warriorhood open to them: fosterage. If the parents of the young woman could afford the foster price, they could have their daughter (or son, though the foster price was higher for girls than for boys) fostered by a warrior whom she would serve and by whom she would be taught many of her first battle skills. If the foster price was not within the means of the family, a few young people managed to rise in rank due to their prowess in defending their clans and lands, but these instances were rare, especially if the young warrior was not awarded land for her successes.

To suggest that large numbers of Celtic woman were forced to become warriors is as ludicrous as suggesting that large numbers of modern women have been forced to become successful, respected, and wealthy against their will. True, there may have been the occasional Celtic woman unhappy in her role as warrior, but in a society that valued war and warriors above all else there would have been too many eager to take her place for her to be "impressed" for long into battle service. If she did not want the honor, someone else would gladly take it.

Women were not restricted from battle service until 697 C.E., when an Irish and Scottish law known as the *Cain Adamnain* was drafted by a bishop named Arculf, who later became St. Adamnain. Church legend tells us that the saint's mother was dismayed at seeing women fighting with one another, and persuaded her son to put an end to the practice. His law declared that women, children, and clerics must be exempt from the terrors of war and protected from all its acts.[3] This, in effect, had the result of denying women the right to serve as warriors. The very fact that this law was created attests to the fact that there were still women with warrior status well into the seventh century, though it is a given that many of their privileges as warriors had been eroded.

At the time that Celtic society flourished, women had not been routinely starved, corsetted, and given debilitating drugs to curb unfeminine ambition.[4] These were not the emaciated models of our own time who make a living out of destroying their natural bodies for the sake of attaining a culturally-approved appearance, nor were they fragile Victorian flowers who had to be carefully tended by their menfolk lest they wither, but women who were confident that they were the equal of anyone just as they were. Diodorus Siculus, a Sicilian historian and geographer living in the first century B.C.E., wrote of Celtic women as possessing unprecedented strength; as being as large and tall as the men, just as quarrelsome, and always ready to fight. He goes on to describe their intense battle fury and their enviable and frightening warrior abilities.[5] The warrior emperor Julius Caesar wrote in his chronicle of his battle in Gaul that an entire Roman battalion would barely stand a chance against the Celts should their women be called into the fray.[6]

The idea that a woman would even want to be thought of as too delicate to engage in physical actively was completely beyond the scope of the Celtic mindset until well into the common era. Women were appreciated for their physical prowess as much as for any other attribute they possessed. Irish myths give us numerous examples of athletic heroines. Luaths Lurgann, known as "the speedy footed one," was not only the aunt of famous fianna warrior Fionn MacCumhal, but was also noted as Ireland's fastest runner. When she met her death in a running mishap, her thigh bone became the center point around which grew the lake known as Lough Lurgann. In the legend of "Deirdre of the Sorrows," the attributes of her servant, Lavercam, are often downplayed to those of the traditional nursemaid. But Lavercam was a poet, bard, and athlete reputed to be able to run the entire length of Ireland in a single day and report back to the Ulster king all she had seen and heard. Taillte is largely viewed today as a harvest Goddess, but myths tell us that she made her home at Tara and was also revered as a patron deity of competition. She ordered the once-wooded Plain of Oenach Taillten cleared to create a playing field. Annual games festivals were held at this site (now called Teltown) until 1169. These formal, organized games were considered to be an Irish version of the Olympics. Taillte's games were revived in the late nineteenth century when the Celtic Renaissance began.

Women warriors not only enjoyed the high status of the warrior elite, but its obligations as well. One of these was the teaching of new warriors, usually young men.[7] It is an old Anglo-Celtic magickal belief that teachings flow best from female to male and from male to female. This polarity mirrored their beliefs in the unified nature of their world; God and Goddess, upperworld and underworld, male and female—all merely two halves of one whole that had to be connected to function properly. Legends portraying women battle teachers have been preserved in the myths. In Irish mythology, the famous fraternal warriors of Ulster known as the Red Branch, one of whom was the highly-honored Cuchulain, were taught by the warrior Goddess Scathach.

The etymology of Scathach's name is open for debate; it may mean "victorious" or "shadowed" or "one who strikes fear." Her mysterious and hard-to-reach Isle of Shadow in the Hebrides was the home of her famous school, where she taught those men who could prove themselves worthy of her invincible battle teachings. The most famous of these were her leaps and her battle yells, the latter of which were reputed to paralyze enemies with fear. More Goddess than woman, Scathach was Amazonian in size and was said to have lived for many centuries. She is one of the many examples of a myth so clouded by divine overtones that it is hard to know where the historical woman ends and the mythic one begins. This dichotomy is a feature of myths worldwide and is one of the reasons why religions are founded on mythology rather than firm history; mythology presents a much more intriguing picture for serving as a cultural rallying point.

All Celtic warriors, male and female, were bound by certain codes of honor that arguably may have mutated into the chivalric code of the Middle Ages. Among the most strictly enforced of these were the laws of hospitality. So important were these that any warrior who broke them was risking divine retribution, as can be seen in many of the myths, including the "Attack of the Hostel of Da Derga" that resulted in the death of a king.[8]

The rules of hospitality were simple but unbreachable, and primarily designed to prevent warriors from being tempted to wage war in undefended communities. The concept of a fair fight was important to the Celts, and there was no honor in a battle not won by evenly matched forces.[9] If one accepted the "protection of bread and salt" offered by the host, the guest was honor bound to respect the host's household as her own. This included not raiding the host's stock or making war on her clan. In return, the host was not permitted to ask the guest's intentions, nor could she ask her to leave until she was ready. This could go on for up to a year and a day. So ingrained was this code of hospitality that vestiges of it persisted in rural Scotland and Ireland until the early twentieth century.

The Initiation of the Warrior

The official dedication or initiation of the young male warriors consisted of three parts: arming, naming, and sexual initiation.[10]

Women warriors had the distinction of being not only the battle teachers of young men but the sexual initiators as well. As mentioned in Chapter 1, the unprecedented sexual freedom of Celtic women was one of the reasons they held a higher status in Celtic society than did their contemporaries in other parts of Europe. This initiation had nothing to do with whether or not the young man had already become sexually active. In Celtic society, it was almost a given that he would be long before his warrior's initiation. This initiation was a sacred act, similar to the sacred sexual acts that are still an integral part of modern Pagan practice (see Chapter 9). In this respect the women functioned similarly to the sacred prostitutes well documented in Roman culture as priestesses of the Goddess Vesta. In Celtic society, they also functioned as personifications of mythic imagery of the Goddess as mother and lover, and were the ones who hallowed the sacred kings and granted them their power and right to rule (see Chapter 12). Goddesses who serve as deities of both battle and love (or "earthly pleasure") are well documented in Europe. This linkage of divine imagery and function may have been a way of ritually impressing on both teacher and student the oneness of life and death as they prepared for battle.[11]

The aforementioned battle teacher Scathach had a sister named Aife who also had an encampment on the Isle of Shadow where she trained warriors, though her reputation was less renowned. The difference is that Aife's myths show her as the sexual initiator of the new warriors, while Scathach gives them their armaments. Aife commanded a legion of fierce horsewomen, horses being a symbol of sexual prowess for the Celts, while Scathach taught them how to fight. The myths of the war hero Cuchulain, who was trained on the Isle of Shadow, shows all three elements of the warrior's initiation. First, he was given a special naming due to his keeping of an honor debt (called a *geis* in Irish); second, he was armed by Scathach as a reward for his skills; and third, he was given a sexual initiation by Aife, who bore him a son. Only after all three of these elements were in place did Cuchulain return to Ireland as a virtually invincible warrior.

Probably the most famous instance of woman arming man is found in the Arthurian legends, in which the Lady of the Lake bestows upon young King Arthur the sword known as Excalibur. Not only is this an instance of arming, but one of hallowing him as the sacred king to represent the physical aspects of the land, an important Celtic practice that will be discussed at length in Chapter 9.

The importance of names to the Celts is well known, and warriors often earned special ones due to their prowess. A Celt may have possessed many names: a spiritual name, an earned name, a clan name, a warrior's name, a rank name, a childhood name, a coming of age name, and so on. Some were held secret, either by the Celt alone or by a few trusted others. One's name reflected the true self, and to know it was to have power over that person. The naming aspect of a warrior's initiation, in conjunction with his/her arming, is reflected in extant myths.

The major myth of the Welsh Goddess Arianrhod, whose archetype represents reincarnation, fertility, and feminine authority, involves naming and arming. More importantly, it may be that her myth marks the shift from woman-centered clans to patriarchal authority, when her power to name and arm her child were taken from her by trickery. Arianrhod's body was her own to do with as she chose. She mated freely with whomever she wished, as was her right under the law. This right was not questioned until a male magician named Math claimed she had conceived two children to whom she had not given birth. When he forced the issue upon her, she gave birth to two sons. One swam away immediately to the sea, the other remained with his father and wished to become a warrior. But Arianrhod refused to bestow a name or arms on her unwanted son, as was her right under Welsh law. Math tricked her into providing both by disguising the son and allowing his warrior's skills to provoke her interest.

It is also significant that arms had to be bestowed by the mother. In this myth we see Arianrhod cast as a sovereign Goddess, one who gives the warrior or king his power and legitimizes his rank. The sovereign Goddess represented the land itself, and only she could choose who would rule and defend her. Logically she would choose the most powerful and fertile warrior to be magickally linked to her; therefore, this honor of naming and arming went to women—to a mother, a Goddess, or a priestess. We see this theme repeated many times in Celtic myth; by the Lady of the Lake bestowing the sword Excalibur on the young Arthur, the warrior teacher Scathach giving Cuchulain the invincible sword called the Gae Bolg, and a variety of other warriors and rulers attaining their power through cauldron or chalice images that are symbols of the Goddess.

No known Celtic precedent exists to show us that a woman's warriorhood or rulership must be given to her through another source. Nonetheless, one popular argument is that because women taught male warriors their art and men taught females, it should be surmised that men initiated the women. This argument falls apart because the art of teaching (a social act) and the art of initiation (a spiritual act) shared no common authority in Celtic society. A more sound argument is that, because the arming and naming of young people was a woman's right, and because warriors fought to defend the land that was personified by the sovereign Goddess (a female), women were the initiators of all warriors, both male and female.

This argument has some basis in Celtic mythology as well. Not only do we have the aforementioned Arianrhod as an example, but we also have the myth of the Goddess Cerridwen who is often depicted as a sow, an animal archetypally linked to the land and its abundance like the Goddesses of sovereignty. Cerridwen is famous for her cauldron of knowledge, known as *Amen*, in which she brewed a potion of wisdom known as *greal*, a word whose etymology many people have tried to link to the word "grail." This brew was required to simmer for a year and a day, a common period of magickal time passage in Celtic myths. Cerridwen's servant and student, a young man named Gwion, was entrusted with caring for the brew. When some of the bubbling mixture spilled out onto his finger he instinctively put them in his mouth and instantly gained all wisdom of past, present, and future. Knowing the brew was meant for Cerridwen's son, he decided he had to flee.

Cerridwen pursued Gwion relentlessly as they each shapeshifted through many forms. In each, Cerridwen was able to become the predator that could conceivably catch and kill the prey that Gwion had become. Cerridwen was able to apprehend Gwion when he became a speck of grain and she the hen who consumed him. The grain took root inside her womb, and she gave him rebirth as the great bard Taliesin. Some Pagans believe this magickal chase relates to various levels of initiation rites within the Celtic priesthood, and the ultimate shapeshifting into rebirth to represent the new self that emerges after initiation.

Unfortunately, this story is often interpreted as one of anger, of Cerridwen pursuing Gwion to punish him simply because he stole something that belonged to her. In any myth where issues of spiritual wisdom are at stake, it is important to look at the deeper meanings. In this case, we must look at how the story represents an initiation, in which Cerridwen functions as the teacher and Gwion as the student. While it may be hard for a teacher to watch a student exceed her, the chase does not appear to be fueled by anger or jealousy. It is the job of a teacher to challenge the student when she feels she is ready. Without challenges, the student cannot grow or hope to realize her full potential. Once Gwion the student had acquired wisdom, Cerridwen the teacher forced him to use it.

Cerridwen's rebirthing of Gwion as Taliesin has been seen by some as just another story about a devouring Goddess who consumes men's life forces indiscriminately (see Chapter 2). Even those who understand the mythic importance of a devouring Goddess, in terms of reincarnation beliefs, often miss the point that the devouring was also part of the initiation, the tangible evidence of Gwion's achievement. After he was able to meet Cerridwen's challenge, she bestowed upon him a new identity. In other words, she initiated him into the deeper mysteries and he emerged changed for the better. This is what spiritual rebirth is all about.

The Warrior Queens

Celtic clan chieftains and rulers were not always chosen on the basis of heredity, but were traditionally selected on the basis of their battle skills, with the top-ranking warrior becoming the leader. This practice left the competition open to women, and several managed to attain this high status.

Easily the most famous of the warrior queens was Ireland's Queen Maeve of Connacht,[12] whose myths tell of a strong, uncompromising woman who could command troops with the confidence of a lioness. Like many figures from ancient mythology, Celtic and otherwise, Maeve is an interesting blend of heroine, historical figure, and Goddess. Since most of her myths were not committed to paper until the eleventh century C.E.,[13] it is virtually impossible to find her precise roots or to disentangle these threads from one another. One of her origins may have been in a patron Goddess of Tara, the longtime stronghold of Irish High Kings. As the reigning Queen of Connacht in the Red Branch cycle of myths, she personifies the epitome of feminine power: warrior, seductress, and sovereign. Known for her fiery temperament and iron will, Maeve boasted she could easily sexually exhaust thirty men in any night. Her personal power is best bespoken of by the fact that battles would be put on hold while she menstruated, ancient peoples believing this "moon time" to mark the peak of a woman's personal power.

Another semi-historical figure was Nessa, mother of King Conor MacNessa, a ruler often placed on the throne around the third century C.E. Originally named Assa, meaning "gentle," she was a great scholar whose tutors were murdered by a jealous Druid, after which she became a skilled warrior and took the name Nessa, meaning "ungentle." She combined her formidable mental and physical skills to secure the throne for her son.

Among the continental Celts, a tribe known as the Bructeri was ruled by a superb horsewoman and warrior queen named Veleda. During her reign, her people were at war with Rome. Her military prowess and skillful leadership inspired her army to steal a Roman ship and tow it up the River Lippe to her stronghold, winning the battle for the Celts.

There are also a number of warrior queens whose lives we know to be firmly in the historical period. Several written references have survived about their lives and accomplishments. The most famous of these is Boudicca, a ruler of the Celtic tribe known as the Iceni during the first century C.E. She led a revolt against the Roman government in southern England, and credited her patron deity, the war Goddess Andraste, with much of her success. Boudicca routinely offered sacrifices to Andraste, usually in the form of captured enemies.

Boudicca was buried secretly after she chose to take poison rather than be captured. Legends say she was buried in the sacred oak grove where her royal ancestors were lain to rest. She was buried standing up, her sword raised in her arm, her face turned south toward the enemy Rome. This makes her a powerful feminine image in a culture that has largely portrayed their spectral warriors as male. The head of the Welsh warrior God Bran was similarly employed, and most students of Celtic myth are familiar with the warrior kings, such as Arthur and Owen, who lie sleeping, waiting for the call of their country to awaken them to fight again.

Another woman whose exploits are part of historical record is Cartimandua, a warrior queen of the Brigantes tribe who also fought against the Roman invaders. Her legends have sometimes merged with both those of the sovereign Goddess Brigantia and with the horse Goddess Epona.

Following in this noble tradition are many Celtic women who took up the sword to become warriors and outlaws when given no other choice by the society in which they lived. It is readily apparent that these "modern" warrior women knew the importance of their femininity in relation to their warrior power. Though the use of the matronymic *ni*, meaning "daughter of," was falling from favor by the medieval period in favor of the nearly universal adoption of the patronymic *mac*, meaning "son of," women used all three of these and were known by this surname label. Yet these fighting women proudly kept their matronymics even though to do so was to brand themselves as illegitimate, as having no father who would claim them. No such social distinction existed among the old Celts, but by the early Middle Ages it was common to place this burden upon those one wished to strip of status and economic power.

In Ireland the names Ebha Ruagh ni Murchu and Marie ni Ciaragain belong to the warrior ranks of the early medieval period. In the Elizabethan period (1558–1603), Ireland's Grainne ni Malley was a famous pirate who preyed on English ships. Grainne's legends have assumed epic proportions, and it is hard to know today what is true, what is merely told to make a good story, and what is overlap between the two. So successful were her attacks on English vessels that Queen Elizabeth invited Grainne to her court and offered valuable bribes in exchange for her promise to cease preying on English ships. Grainne turned down the offerings and returned to Ireland, where she held an English noblewoman hostage until the British admiralty acknowledged her sovereignty over the Irish seas.

Celtic Religion in the Waging of War

Celtic warfare had religious aspects that are difficult for modern people to understand. In today's societies, partisans may go to war, each claiming that "God" is on their side, each offering prayers for victory and for the safety of the soldiers. Then the young men (and now some young women as well) are sent off to fight, and the only time the young soldier is likely to encounter religious influences again is if she lands in a hospital and gets a visit from a government-approved chaplain.

Because the religion of each Celtic tribe was an integral part of the entire tribe's life and not factionalized like the religious life of modern societies, it was possible to bring into war—and into all its preparations, spoils, and outcomes—spiritual focus that modern people can barely imagine.

The blessings of the Druids and priestesses were essential to beginning a well-planned war campaign, and divination rites to determine the best possible course of action and its probable outcome were necessary to ensure that blessing. A variety of divination tactics might be employed, depending upon the skills of the Druid or priestess. They might cloud-gaze, crystal-gaze, do an inner-world journey, read entrails, or use any one of several other methods.

In Cornwall and Wales, a Goddess of fate named Aerfen presided over the outcome of battle. Clans would offer sacrifices every three years at her shrine, in the present-day town of Glyndyfrdwy, to ensure her benevolence in future wars.

Boudicca of the Iceni offered her sacrifices to Andraste, and used a hare—her totem animal—both as a means of divination and to signal her armies to attack. Boudicca had worked out a system of learning the outcome of battle depending upon the pattern and direction in which the hare ran.

One of the more chilling portents of battle gone wrong was the appearance of the *Luideag*, or the Washer at the Ford. Related to the better-known Celtic faery known as the banshee (*beansidhe* in Gaelic), the Washer appeared as a spectral old woman washing burial shrouds in a stream that ran red with blood. Any warrior who saw this apparition knew she was destined to perish in the upcoming conflict. Like the banshee who wails her lament the night before a death in a specific family, the Washer might also be heard keening (*caoine* in Irish). Keening is a uniquely Celtic form of a mourning wail still used today by the women of Ireland. Mythology tells us that the Goddess Brighid was the first woman to keen when she discovered her son Ruadan, her child by her husband Bres, dead on a battlefield.

Also on the night before a battle a *cath* would be told in one of the clan's communal areas. The word "cath" refers to a type of epic story concerning war that was told as an act of sympathetic magick on the eve of battle. In keeping with the high placement of the art of storytelling in Celtic society, such sessions were referred to until well into the early twentieth century as "the blessing of the story," and they constituted what modern Pagans would call a "story spell," a spell encanted in the form of a cohesive story.

All these blessings—stories, Druidic, and other—are often thought of today as being offered solely by the high-ranking males of the tribe. Perhaps in later times this was true, but the Irish word for blessing is an ancient one that still contains a telling aspect of its connection with feminine power. The Irish word for blessing is *beannacht*, which contains the root word for woman, *bean*.

Warriors often consulted priestesses, searching for the magickal spells and charms that would render them impervious to harm in battle or that could enchant their weapons to score a perfect kill every time. Celtic myths reinforce this belief with tales such as that of the famous Gae Bolg sword given to Cuchulain by Scathach. Once such magick was possessed, the rule of "keep silent" was best followed. In modern Pagan magick, keeping silent is one of the often-taught basic requirements for keeping the magick strong. Many Celtic tales tell us how the act of making a misguided confidence destroyed a warrior. An example of such a story is that of Niamh, daughter of Celtchair, chief Druid at the court of King Conchobar. Niamh married a warrior who possessed the magickal secret of not being killed in battle, then persuaded him to reveal it to her. After he confessed to her, she took the information to her father, who was able to have him slain. As a reward she was wed to the man of her choice, a son of the King.

Other battle preparations included body adornment, a war ritual of tribal peoples the world over. The Celts favored either a yellow dye made from saffron or a blue dye made from the woad plant. The blue was by far the more popular of the dyes, and was recently brought to public consciousness through the Oscar-winning film *Braveheart*. The body painting had both spiritual and physical significance. In spiritual terms, it was designed to help connect the warrior with the other fighters, to help them move as one unit, and to align them with the powers of the divine. On the physical level, it marked one clansperson as different from another so that partisans could be identified through the dust of the battle.

That certain Celtic warriors went into battle nude, sporting only weapons and ritual paint and adornments, is also documented by Greek and Roman writers. The warriors known as the *Gaesetae*, whose name means "spearmen," were famous for going into battle unclothed.[14] Presumably this helped their essences or auras merge, allowing them to move as one during the fighting.

Another aspect of Celtic warfare that has caused controversy is the taking of the heads of the enemy. The head was of supreme importance in Celtic mythology and religion. It was the seat of knowledge, the home of the eternal spirit—where something of the life-essence might remain even after death. One of the most famous "head stories" in Celtic myth concerns Bran, leader of a battalion of Welsh warriors. When he was killed his head was severed, feasted over for eighty years, and then mounted at the present site of the Tower of London so that it would ward and warn of impending invasions.

When battle ended, the victorious warriors would gather their slain enemies' heads, sometimes referred to as "the Morrigan's acorn crop." These would be mounted on the gateposts of the tribal encampment as protective amulets. The custom of taking heads in battle continued in Celtic lands until at least the fourteenth century, though both the idea of the head as a symbol of power and that of honoring the fighting spirit of the slain warrior had been forgotten.

The greatest honor a warrior could gain was to be honored by the bards with songs of praise (called being bard-sung), to sit at the right hand of the clan chief or regional monarch, and receive the "warrior's portion," the largest and finest cut of meat from that night's victory feast.

Women warriors participated in all these battle events, though their numbers waned considerably from 800 to 100 B.C.E., and if any women were seated at the right of the king and offered the warrior's portion for their battle feats, these records were either not made or did not survive. What has survived is the writing of Greco-Roman war leaders of the first century C.E., who spoke of women's role in battle as one of a supporting force.[15] They brought fresh horses, removed wounded warriors, and pronounced curses in the manner of priestesses casting spells against the enemy.

War Goddesses and Battle Furies

Though men are the warriors most often celebrated in Celtic myth—the entire Fianna cycle and most of the Ulster center on male figures—it remains a fact that Celtic war, battle, and battlefield deities (or "furies") are predominantly feminine, and contain mother or crone qualities as well. This might seem odd at first, especially the mother aspect (which we think of as a nurturing, life-affirming archetype), until we think in terms of the cauldron archetype.[16] Among other things, the cauldron represents a source of status, inspiration, wisdom, and transformation (recall the story of Cerridwen). Though no Celtic creation myth has survived, the link between the liquids within the cauldron and the blood of the mother Goddess is made clear. In instances where no cauldron exists, rivers, lakes, and wells often fulfill this archetype of regeneration powers.[17] Because the Celts envisioned their Land of the Dead as existing across or under the water, water archetypally represented one of the powerful places "in between" that the Celts felt held great power. In this case it was the point at which the physical world and the Otherworld met and melded.[18]

The cauldron's fertile powers extend to the physical world when it serves as a pot in which life-sustaining food is prepared. One of the many Goddesses to whom the Celts looked for guidance and inspiration in battle was the Irish Goddess Sin who, in later folklore, was reduced to being a minor faery queen who feeds greedily on the blood of warriors. Older legends, probably from an oral tradition, portray her as a Goddess who could make wine from water and swine from leaves in order to feed her warrior legion. Many cauldrons in Celtic myth were thought to provide unlimited sustenance for warriors, including those of some Gods, such as Bran and Dagda. Interestingly, in both cases the deities who possess this power are male, but the ultimate facilitator of regeneration is the cauldron, the primal Goddess symbol.

Without a doubt, the most pervasive image of the Celtic battle furies, the Goddesses of war and destruction, is the Triple Goddess known as the Morrigan, whose name means "great queen."[19] Sometimes she is portrayed as three crones, other times as the more traditional Triple Goddess: one virgin, one mother, and one crone, though all three are in truth aspects of one deity (see Chapter 6). The three Goddesses of the Morrigan are Badb, Macha, and Nemain.

The Celts believed that when they engaged in battle, the Morrigan flew shrieking overhead in the form of a raven or carrion crow. Sometimes she came disguised as a wolf, and would move unharmed through the furor of the battle. When a battle ended, the soldiers would leave the field until dawn so the Morrigan could claim her souls. At this point the battlefield was sacred ground. The Scots even had a Goddess of the war ground known as Bellona, whose name may be a form of Badb.

They also believed the Morrigan could reanimate a regiment of slain soldiers to a macabre spectral dance in which their lifeless bodies could continue to engage in the fight. This ability of the Morrigan to call upon legions of slain bodies is connected to many myths surrounding the Goddess's ability to take and give life. The image of a cauldron is involved in many of these myths. One such myth surrounds a Welsh war Goddess called Cymidei Cymeinfoll, whose name means "big belly of battle." The big belly may be another reference to the powers of regeneration in terms of pregnancy, since she was also reputed to give birth to a warrior every six weeks. Cymidei and her husband, Llasar Llaesyfnewid, possessed a magickal cauldron into which they could immerse warriors felled on the battlefield. They would emerge from the cauldron fully alive and able to continue the battle, but would be minus their powers of speech. This loss is viewed archetypally as being both a sacrifice on behalf of one's clan, and as a symbol of change as the result of being "reborn."

A host of minor and lesser-known war Goddesses fill the pages of Celtic myths and folklore. In Wales and Celtic England, the Goddess Agrona was often equated with the Morrigan. Though her name contains the same root word as is found in the modern English word "agronomy," meaning the study of land cultivation, no evidence of her as a harvest Goddess can be found. Possibly she was a blending of the sacred mother of the land and the crone who takes life.

The Celtic war Goddesses are usually portrayed as pleasing to look upon, though sometimes fierce of countenance. One who was characterized by her hideousness was Lot, an Irish Goddess of the pre-Dannan race known as the Formorians. This myth may simply be another byproduct of the inevitable fact that it is the victors who write the official chronicles of history. The Formorians were defeated and exiled by the Tuatha De Dannan, the former becoming ugly sea monsters and the latter becoming the beautiful Gods and Goddesses of the Celts.

These war Goddesses have been memorialized not only in myth, but in bronze and stone figurines and coinage dating from Europe's early Iron Age (1500–1200 B.C.E.). As previously mentioned, while it may be argued that these representations are of Celtic women and not deities, a few of the figures bear inscriptions that name them as Goddesses known to be associated with war. Others bear the images of geese, an aggressive bird who symbolizes guardianship and defensiveness.[20] Other icons hearken back to the horse images that seem to surround the warrior queens and depict Celtic women/Goddesses charging into battle on horseback.

The horse images seen in many of the myths of warrior queens and war Goddesses provide links to the Otherworld or divine realm.[21] Horses in Celtic myth were symbols of sexual prowess and personal power, and they provided a link between the Otherworld and the physical world. Many a Goddess in her horse form provided transportation between the worlds, as is seen in the myths of Rhiannon. It is possible that some of the ancient hill cuttings and chalk marking figures in England that depict many-breasted horses, such as those found at Uffington and Cambridge, may be related to these warrior queen/Goddess figures and were originally intended to confer both her protection and her blessing of fertility upon the land.

Battle Scars and Rites of Passage

Throughout history, war has been considered an activity that belongs to men. In spite of the successes of the warrior queens, among the Celts men still dominated the war arena. The excitement with which many young men greet the prospect of war, even in recent times, often frightens and disturbs women. Since ancient times, battles have been rites of passage for young men that helped mark them as adults within their communities. Scars were once displayed among the Celts with the same pride that a modern soldier shows off his medals. It is unlikely that battle scars served to mark women as adults.

Women have always had the advantage of having a physical point at which they are known to "come of age," to be women and not girls. Our rite of passage comes to us at menarche, the onset of menstruation. We don't have to seek it out. Nearly all ancient cultures saw the menstrual period as the time of woman's greatest personal power. Often women were required to be separate from the rest of their clan or tribe during these days. It was considered a sacred act to spend this time in communion with the Goddess, or to work on spells and rituals that would be boosted greatly.

Women can arm themselves and name themselves as warriors, and they can learn to reach deep inside themselves and pull out this warrior-self whenever it is needed. The ritual in the next chapter will show you how.

Questions For the Potential Celtic Warrior Woman

The following questions are designed to help you assess your desire and ability to be a warrior woman. Their purpose is to help you evaluate yourself; there are no right or wrong answers.

How do I define "warrior?"

What do I understand to be the role of the warrior in Celtic society? How about women warriors?

What is my perception of a warrior woman?

How does the warrior aspect of myself fit in with other expressions of my Celtic Paganism?

Do I feel it is necessary to be a warrior to be involved in Celtic women's spirituality? Why or why not?

Have I ever felt like a warrior in my life? When?

Have I ever felt that using my warrior self was not the feminine thing to do? When and why?

Do I allow others to control me too often? Or do I seek too often to control others? How would my warrior self affect these aspects, both positively and negatively?

Do I use common sense in my daily life, or do I rely too often on only magickal protections?

Are there others who depend on my protection and good judgment?

Do I feel that being a warrior could interfere with my other Celtic spiritual tasks, such as being a priestess, participating in a coven, or making personal journeys into the Otherworld? Or do I feel these would be enhanced by my warrior status? Why or why not?

Do I want to be a dedicated warrior at this time? Why or why not?

Notes

1 Green, Miranda J. *Celtic Goddesses: Warriors, Virgins and Mothers* (London: British Museum Press, 1995), 28.

2 Joyce, P. W. *A Social History of Ancient Ireland* (London: Longmans, Green and Co., 1903).

3 O'Hogain, Dr. Daithi. *Myth, Legend and Romance: An Encyclopedia of the Irish Folk Tradition* (New York: Prentice Hall Press, 1991), 18.

4 I refer here to the patent medicines popular in the late nineteenth and early twentieth centuries, many of which were created to curb women's "unfeminine" traits, such as intelligence and ambition.

5 Markale, Jean. *Women of the Celts* (Rochester, Vt.: Inner Traditions International, Ltd., 1972), 38.

6 Caesar, Julius. *The Battle For Gaul* (Boston, Mass.: David R. Godine, 1980), 63.

7 Matthews, Caitlin. *The Elements of the Celtic Tradition* (Shaftsbury, Dorset: Element Books, 1989), 76.

8 The complete text of this myth can found in *Ancient Irish Tales* (New York: Barnes and Noble, 1996). Originally published in 1936, this new version with commentary is edited by Tom P. Cross and Clark Harris Slover.

9 Exceptions to this were the "unofficial" battles such as the infamous cattle raids, always surprise events in which fairness and even matching of forces were not considered important.

10 Matthews, 75.

11 An entire chapter on this connection, called "Goddesses of Love and Battle," is found in D. J. Conway's *Falcon Feather and Valkryie Sword: Feminine Shamanism, Witchcraft and Magick* (St. Paul, Minn.: Llewellyn, 1995).

12 For an in-depth look at the lives and myths surrounding the famous warrior queens, see Rosalind Clark's *The Great Queens: Irish Goddesses from the Morrigan to Cathleen ni Houlihan* (Gerrards Cross, Buckinghamshire: Smythe, 1991).

13 Power, Patrick C. *Sex and Marriage in Ancient Ireland* (Dublin: Mercier Press, 1976), 10.

14 Ellis, Peter Berresford. *Dictionary of Celtic Mythology* (Santa Barbara, Calif.: ABC-CLIO, Inc., 1992), 166.

15 Green (1995), 29.

16 Green, Miranda J. *Symbol and Image in Celtic Religious Art* (London: Routledge & Kegan Paul, 1992), 37.

17 Matthews, John and Caitlin. *The Encyclopaedia of Celtic Wisdom* (Shaftsbury, Dorset: Element Books, 1994), 218-219.

18 Green (1995), 41.

19 *The Book of Invasions (Lebor Gabala Erenn)*, compiled in the twelfth century, chronicles many stories of the war Goddesses.

20 Green, *Celtic Goddesses*, 34.

21 Green, 32.

THE DEDICATION OF THE WARRIOR

Solitary Ritual

Today's warrior woman may not be called upon to battle enemy tribes—although she might, if she is part of our modern armed forces—but she is likely to be called to fight for her principles and beliefs, to protect herself from rape and burglary, to shield her children and loved ones from danger, or simply to safeguard her self-esteem.

Sadly, modern women have not been taught how to fight for themselves. "Baby Boomer" women, raised with the passive role models of early television, were taught that the best way to gain power was to be sneaky and always let a man think he had really solved the problems to which women had found the answers. The young women of Generation X have grown up in a violent world that has tried to teach them to equate personal power with the ability to hurt others before they get hurt. This is just as much a poor warrior model as the overly passive Donna Reeds and June Cleavers of the Baby Boomer generation. Women who grew up in the pre-World War II era, raised by the last offspring of the repressed Victorians, have even fewer positive role models than the two generations that followed them. All in all, it's amazing that any woman is sane and ego-healthy.

Modern warrior women are aware that the greatest differences between people are based more upon gender than any other arbitrary designation that separates human from human. Though we are led to believe that issues of race, religion, and politics are the greatest barriers between people, just stop and think about all the women in your life, what they have endured, how they have managed to survive and, in many cases, how they have triumphed. There is no defining category to which they belong other than their womanhood. Think of the women beaten by fathers, brothers, or husbands. Think of those who have endured sexual harassment in the workplace. Think of those who have been raped. Think of those who have had to choose between raising the children they love or working two menial wage jobs to just retain custody of them. Think of the laws, enacted by legislatures made up mostly of upper-class men from the dominant ethnic background, who have legally boxed women into situations in which people made of lesser stuff would crack. These are worldwide problems that transcend all classifications but gender.

The media goes out of its way to emphasize racial differences when a white man attacks a black woman or a black man attacks a white woman, but it really comes down to only one thing—a man attacking a woman. The implication the press gives is that somehow an attack is more acceptable if it comes from someone who shares his victim's ethnic, religious, and economic background. Convincing women that someone of another ethnic, religious, or socio-economic background is their enemy helps keep women focused on the characteristics they share with the men in their lives. It keeps us separated from other women, from seeing a natural feminine unity based on similar goals, experiences, and problems. Keeping women at war with each other keeps us isolated and it keeps us weak.

Having been blessed with friends representing a great diversity of ethnicity, national origin, religion, and culture, I have seen this principle in action for myself. I have talked at length with women from all over the world, and the one topic on which we have no trouble understanding each other is on issues of women's concerns. If you have not had such an experience, you really should seek out the opportunity. Hearing for yourself the oneness of women's experiences and perceptions is empowering. It is also very threatening to the powers-that-be. There is strength in unity, and the patriarchy knows this.

Women have also had to endure verbal attacks that serve to keep us in a lesser position. We have been called the usual round of demeaning names such as bitch, cunt, hag, harridan, tease, and so on and so forth, ad nauseum. Our very ability to function in the world has been called into question as well. In many cases we have been deemed too hysterical and emotionally unstable to hold positions of responsibility. Yet studies show that it is men who are right-brain oriented—and the right half of the brain is the hemisphere that rules the emotional side of human behavior. Women tend to be ruled by the left brain, the hemisphere of logic and reason. Women also have more connectors between the two halves, a substance known as the *corpus callosum*, which allows a greater exchange of information between the two spheres. Think about it. When was the last time you heard a report on the evening news about women whose bar fight got out of hand to the point that they resorted to shooting at each other? When is the last time you heard about a woman so upset over the break-up of her marriage that she killed her husband, her kids, and then herself? When is the last time you heard about a woman serial killer, or pedophile, or rapist?

Our natural cycles, the very cycles that enable human life to continue, have often been blamed for our supposed irrationality. Premenstrual syndrome (PMS) takes a lot of bashing in the media. It is true that many women become more aggressive during this period, though they are rarely out of control. What they are is under the influence of the male hormone testosterone which, although it remains only in small quantities, increases during the premenstrual phase. Modern medicine has documented the male phenomenon known as the "testosterone rage," a violently irrational outburst caused by sharp escalations in this hormone's production, usually due to the ingestion of bulk-building steroid drugs. Testosterone increases aggressiveness. Testosterone is the definitive male hormone, as estrogen is the defining female one. Therefore, any PMS symptoms that are perceived as unstable are due to the fact that women act more like men during this phase than at any other time in their cycles. Aggressive behavior in men is applauded—in women it is feared.

Women must integrate a warrior aspect into their lives, just as they do other magickal aspects, not only to function as a whole being, but because survival in our modern world requires it. When we become warriors we become capable of arming ourselves with the facts needed to defend ourselves and our sisters when such verbal attacks come. Words have power. If you don't accept that, you have no place in a magickal religion in which words are known to be powerful enough to shape realities. Left unchecked by us, the negative energy of these words will grow to form a repressive reality we do not want.

Being a warrior has its obligations, and its need for temperance as well. Warrior women must learn, to borrow a B-western movie term, not to "shoot from the hip" when it comes to our defenses. Becoming overly aggressive is not a solution to our collective problem. If that worked, then the world today would already be a mighty perfect place to live. Above all, we should not give in to "man-bashing." We must have the wisdom to distinguish the chest-beating baboons steeped in the involuted thinking of the patriarchy from our brothers who find this behavior and mindset just as disturbing as do we. In the heat of battle the skilled warrior knows at whom she is swinging her axe!

Evoking the powers of the warrior is not a way of gaining power over others, but of taking back power over ourselves and our lives. It reaffirms our right to make our own decisions, to choose what we do with our bodies, with whom to mate, what to study, how to live and, most importantly, how to connect with the many aspects of our Goddess. Once we learn how to call upon that warrior self, we can respond quickly and efficiently if ever we or someone/something we love is threatened. Never confuse the warrior self with one who must always resort to violence to solve her problems. Some of the most powerful warrior work you may be called upon to perform is peaceful in nature, creating change through wisdom and will. This is power indeed.

The Nature of Ritual

A ritual is a set pattern of actions and words undertaken to achieve a lasting and definable end result. Rituals can be formal or informal, planned or spontaneous, but all retain some elements of unchanging, prescribed rites whose purpose is to imprint a lasting change on the life and psyche of the participant. The language of ritual is symbolism. Symbols trigger our minds to move in desired directions, and to connect with other aspects of our inner selves and our deities. The need to forge a symbolic connection with the deep mind, or subconscious, is why ritual form necessitates a certain amount of repetition.

Often it is said that ritual leaves a lasting change on the psyche of the one who participates in the ritual. This is a good definition but unless the concept of the psyche makes sense to you it is useless. *Psyche* was the old Greek word for the soul, as well as being the name of a Greek allegorical heroine who represented the human soul and married the God of love, Eros. It refers to the totality of a person as she exists not only in this incarnation but in all forms. It refers to the physical body, the soul, the mental body, and the astral body. Properly conceived and executed, ritual is a very powerful and far-reaching tool for change. Long after the physical aspect of a ritual has ended, its energies continue to work on your behalf.

An old metaphysical adage teaches that when you change, everything around you changes. Through ritual, we attempt to control the nature of our inner changes. By doing this, we cause the world around around to change in conformation with our desires. This is why ritual is often equated with magick, since the end result is some type of change, however subtle.

Ritual most often takes place within the confines of the sacred circle. Use of the circle for religious rites and magick is an ancient practice. The circular shape is a symbol of completion, eternity, and containment, and it represents our acceptance that all things are cyclic in nature; each of us is born, dies, and then is regenerated over and over again. (For those of you unfamiliar with the casting, use, and grounding of sacred circles, Appendix C provides detailed discussion and complete instructions.)

Preparing for the Warrior Dedication Ritual

This ritual consists of eleven parts:

> Cleansing
>
> Shielding
>
> Arming
>
> The Naming of the Arms
>
> The Declaration of Intent
>
> Sacred Vows
>
> The Naming of the Warrior Self
>
> The Girdling or The Bestowing of the Torque
>
> Assuming the Warrior Stance
>
> Drinking the Warrior's Brew
>
> Consuming the Hero's Portion

For this ritual you will need the following materials:

- An incense or herb with purifying powers such as frankincense, basil, sage, or cinnamon
- Your shield (discussed in full in this chapter)
- A chosen piece of weaponry; this can be a ritual tool or a special wand, knife, or axe you want to use for your warrior rituals
- A sash or cord that will be used to make a girdle to represent your new status; or a torque, a metal neckpiece used by Celtic warriors and people of rank that is sold through many occult suppliers (see Appendix F)

- A tea made of herbs related to strength and prophetic visions such as mugwort, cinnamon, catnip, white oak bark, angelica, valerian, or spearmint
- Plans for a large, lavish, post-ritual meal

Prior to any ritual it is customary to do a cleansing of both the body and the mind. This was very much a Celtic custom, and many early observers of the Celts write in detail about the obsessive cleanliness these people practiced. The body can be cleansed either through "bathing" it in the smoke of a purifying incense or bathing in a tub, preferably with an herb known for its purifying powers. The mind can be cleansed through simple meditation: taking time to slow your thoughts, center your energies, and focus on the upcoming ritual. Whichever method(s) you choose, make sure to turn your thoughts from mundane concerns and focus them on the task at hand.

You will also need to prepare ahead of time:

- A shield, and then select a name for it
- Another weapon, and choose its name as well
- A warrior name for yourself

Your shield can be as simple or as elaborate as you like. This is to be a form of psychic protection and strength, not an actual tool of battle. It can either be drawn on a piece of paper, glued together with colored pieces of felt, embroidered in cloth, or burned or carved into a piece of wood. Shield-shaped blocks of soft basswood are easy to find in craft shops, and these carve and burn well. If your shield is small enough, it can be carried around with you as a personal talisman. If not, it can be saved for personal or group warrior rituals in which you divine outcomes for uncertain or frightening situations, or whenever you just need a boost of personal strength and stamina.

When you have the time and the privacy, begin to design your shield. Take a pencil or colored pencils and sketch out ideas as they come to you (see the sketch of my shield on page 57). The images you choose should reflect your Celtic focus as well as contain images of defense and protection. Mine include a large pentagram, which is a symbol of protection and of many Wiccan traditions; a horse, representative of the Goddess and symbolic of the ability to travel between the worlds; a boar, an animal that symbolizes the best of a Celtic warrior's attributes—strength, tenacity, and stamina[1]—and is also a sign of abundance and wisdom; a triskele to represent the Triple Goddess (see Chapter 6); a Brighid's Cross to honor my connection to this Goddess as one of her priestesses; and my chosen warrior name.

The Author's Warrior Shield

You should also choose a secret symbol to be projected mentally onto your shield during the ritual, one that you can readily call to mind to activate the shield's protective powers. This is also like having a security code for your magick. No one else should ever know what this symbol is. This will prevent anyone else from using your shield or breaking through its defenses.

The precedents for the arming and naming of warriors were discussed in the previous chapter. Names were of great importance to the Celts, who felt that a name contained the essential power of a person or thing. To name something was a serious endeavor. Naming helped shape that thing's or person's personality and helped direct its inner power. To know the true name of someone or something was to have a measure of control over it. This again is why you will want to keep your shield's unseen symbol and your weapon's name closely held secrets.

Naturally your warrior self will not be worn on the surface at every moment. Giving yourself a warrior name will allow you to call up that aspect of yourself at a moment's notice, whenever it is needed. Do not worry about it clashing with any other names you have chosen for yourself. A Pagan can have many names. Choosing a warrior name will not lessen the power of your chosen Craft name[2] or of any other names you use in magick and ritual. I have four names: my general Craft name, my priestess name, my warrior name, and the secret name my tradition has us select for ourselves upon our initiation. Because I have a secret name, as do many Pagans, I do not feel the need to closely guard my other names.

Finding the right name for yourself is not difficult, though it may take some time. When selecting special names for yourself or your tools, start by drawing from the Celtic myths. The names of warrior Goddesses or heroines are always nice to adopt. You can also go through an Irish or Welsh lexicon searching for an appropriate name. For example, my warrior name is Lorica. The Irish word *lorica* refers to a warrior's breastplate, the last line of defense in face to face battle. It also means a blessing or prayer of protection in modern Irish.

One way to select a name for your shield or weapon is to let it tell you what its true name is. To do this spend time with it; hold it, sleep with it (if it is safe to do so—sleeping with sharp knives is out!), meditate with it held against you. Open yourself to its energies and ask what it is called. It may take some persistence, but eventually a name should come to you. If it is a name or word with which you are unfamiliar, you may want to check it out before committing to it in case it is unacceptable to you. Negative names like "Spirit Killer" or "Harm Giver" should indicate that your mental programming of the weapon went wrong somewhere and you should start over, projecting more positive, defensive images into it.

To call up the power of your shield, your tool, or your warrior self, you need only to take a deep breath, center your energy, and say (or think clearly) the name three times. Allow each one to be spoken in clear, slow, deliberate tones, feeling each one empowering and awakening these inner aspects. You should also mentally conjure up the image of the secret symbol that you will project onto the shield during your dedication ritual. The combination of the name and the mental image will stir your shield and weapons to life, whether they are physically with you at the time or not. They will also bring your inner warrior to the surface. Use the energy of your shield when you need to have a defense, and the weapon when you must go on the offense.

This process is so simple to use once its components are in place that too many women dismiss it as having little use. This is another of those mysteries you should learn: the simplest magicks often have the strongest results, because they are the easiest to harness and build a working relationship with over time. Each time you use a magick, its power in relation to you is strengthened threefold. Those who you are protecting yourself from may never actually see the shield and weapon manifest around you, but trust that they will sense the power and tread cautiously around you.

I saw this warrior magick in action for myself. When I was living in Texas my best friend, also a Celtic Pagan, and I used to race-walk or jog late at night simply because it was convenient for us; it was also wise considering the south Texas heat. We always stayed together and remained in our own neighborhoods, quiet residential areas with good security. We felt that, as women, we were being as safe as we could be without forfeiting our right to move freely in the world. One night we became aware that we were being watched by a man hiding between two houses that faced the road that exited the housing development in which I lived. About a half mile beyond this was a major thoroughfare known as Bandera Road, though it was not well-traveled so far out so late at night. It was a mystery to us how this man had happened upon us, but we could both sense he was not standing there wishing us well. Immediately we both mentally called upon our shields and weapons, and visualized them in action against this interloper. We did not do this with the intent to harm, only to warn him of the dangers in messing with two warrior women. Within a few minutes he disappeared back toward Bandera Road.

Because you have worked this ritual in both the seen and unseen worlds, your warrior power will function in both. When you are astral projecting, doing a guided meditation, or practicing dream control, knowing how to call upon your warrior aspect will put you in charge. While it is always best to simply retreat from Otherworld dangers or awaken from a disturbing dream, there will be times when this is not possible. Calling upon the warrior in you, and on the power of your shield and tool, can strengthen your defenses and help you fight off a psychic attack if it comes.

The torque and the girdle are symbols of Celtic authority and personal power. The torque is more often associated with male warriors, but since torques were symbols of rank and not gender, women probably wore them as well. The ritual girdle is not anything like the hip-crunching corset popular a few decades ago, but an emblem that represents personal authority.[3] It shows that its wearer is whole and complete unto herself; she needs no other individual to make her feel complete, requires no outside approval for her choices, and asks no favors from anyone as she seeks her warrior self. The girdle was also a symbol of magickal protection for the Celts,[4] and might have been used to offer protection to warriors as they went into battle.

The Warrior Dedication Ritual

Gather all your materials and go to a private place to cast your ritual circle. Be prepared to spend at least an hour undisturbed in this place. When all the preliminaries are out of the way (see Appendix C if you are unsure how to do this), announce your purpose aloud to the universe. You might want to do this while facing south, the direction of passion ruled by fire, the element that also rules protection and battle.

Next, take out your shield and mentally impress upon it the secret symbol that you have chosen to use to empower and protect it. See it clearly in your mind, and then mentally sear it onto the face of the shield. Spend a few moments feeling your energy blending with that of the shield. You should also mentally project into it what you require it to do for you. Then make a statement in which you name it. You can state this out loud if you are alone, but you may choose to do it silently if you are with a group and do not choose to reveal the name of your shield to anyone. The naming might sound something like this:

> Shield which is my defense and protection, in the presence of
> the Goddess who knows the true name of all her creations, by
> earth, water, fire, and air, I call you (insert shield's name). As I
> call upon you, so shall you respond to my need.

Now repeat the shield's name three times. After each recitation breathe onto the shield. The breath of life was another Celtic concept used by the warriors. When a warrior lay mortally wounded on a battlefield, another warrior would come along and bestow the "kiss of life." Their lips would touch as life ebbed from the dying warrior so that some part of the life force would live on in the surviving warrior. The Celts also believed that this helped a warrior to be reborn into the clan again.

Starting with the south quarter, walk clockwise around your circle, presenting your shield to each of the elements and introducing it by name. Tell each quarter that this shield is now a part of you so that each element can recognize it as such. This type of introduction is a customary practice at the end of many Wiccan initiation rituals. The purpose is to announce to the totality of the universe the new name by which they shall know you, or in this case, your defense mechanism—your shield.

Next, take up your chosen weapon. As you did with the shield, spend time sensing the connection between you. This will be even stronger if you have crafted the tool with your own hands. Remember that it does not need to be elaborate. It does not even have to be a weapon in the traditional sense, since its function is a psychic and symbolic one. Then name the weapon:

> (Insert name of type of tool, like knife, wand, et cetera) which
> is my ally in battle, in the presence of the Goddess who knows
> the true name of all her creations, by earth, water, fire, and air, I
> call you (insert weapon's name). As I call upon you, so shall you
> respond to my need.

Repeat the weapon's name three times, and after each recitation breathe onto the shield. Then, starting with the south quarter, walk clockwise around the circle, introducing your weapon by name to each quarter.

Next, take these two newly charged armaments of defense and offense and move with them to the center of your circle. Hold your defensive shield in your left or receptive hand (usually the non-dominant one—the one you do not write with) and your offensive weapon in your right or projective hand (the dominant one—the one you write with). Now you will take the sacred vows of the warrior woman. These should be written by you and should contain the following four elements:

- Dedication of intent to protect and defend yourself
- Acknowledgement of your strength and power as a warrior
- Dedication to the way of the Goddess
- Willingness to help protect others who are not as strong as you, or who are afraid or unable to defend themselves

Still holding the tools, declare your warrior name three times by saying:

> I am the warrior called (insert name).

You may do this silently if there are other women present and you wish to keep your name a secret. If you do not, there are several empowering ways they can help you celebrate the dedication of your warrior name. They can chant your new name in rhythm while you stand basking in the glory of your strength, or they can each salute you in turn, honoring you as a warrior among women. It sounds so simple, but take it from someone who has been there: it is a very moving experience to be celebrated in such a manner.

The next step is to bestow upon yourself, or have bestowed upon you if you are in a group situation, the girdle and/or torque. As these are placed upon you, some statement should be made that they are symbols of honor, of the warrior's rank and obligation. You should also vow to see them destroyed if you should ever shame or misuse your warrior power. You may make these vows in your own words, or in the words your group has chosen. These types of oaths are common in basic Pagan initiation ceremonies, usually asking that your deities desert you and your tools turn against you should you ever use them wrongly.

After this, take a ritual drink of the warrior's brew, the tea you have prepared ahead of time. It should have been made with your ritual purpose in mind and will be used to seal your vows. In group situations, a communal cup is sometimes passed among all members. Or, if sanitation is an issue, a communal cup or cauldron can be used to fill smaller individual cups. The choice is yours. Taking the drink will also be a threefold rite; you will offer a salute to the Goddess first, drink second, and then save some to offer to Mother Earth as a libation when the ritual has ended.

Now yell, cheer, sing, and dance, assuming a warrior's fighting posture, and present yourself to each quarter with your new warrior name. Allow yourself to feel invincible. Revel in your strength.

When you are ready, you may close your circle and ground yourself (see Appendix C). Put your new talismans of warrior power in a safe place, where their energies will be protected from curious hands and unwanted random thought patterns. Encase them in a cloth made for them and place them in a closet or magickal cabinet, or you can place them under your bed, if it is clean enough under there. These are magickal tools, a part of you, and they should always be treated with respect.

After you have seen to the care of your new talismans, go out and feast on your Hero's Portion. The Hero's Portion consisted of the finest cut of meat and the best cup of wine at a celebration banquet. In Celtic mythology these feasts are mentioned frequently, as is the competition for this place of honor at the right hand of the ruler. Either go out alone to eat and treat yourself royally, enjoying your first taste of warrior self-confidence, or go out with a group of Pagan women (whether or not they were part of your dedication ritual) and celebrate your new status together.

Notes

1 King, John. *The Celtic Druids' Year: Seasonal Cycles of the Ancient Celts* (London: Blandford, 1994), 113.

2 A Craft name is a spiritual name chosen by you or for you upon your initiation into Paganism. This is similar to the confirmation names taken in some Christian sects. Some people keep these names secret, while others adopt them for everyday use. The purpose is to acknowledge a changed you; a new person who needs a new name.

3 This actually should read herself *or* himself, since men wore them, too. Ireland's King Cormac was said to have owned five girdles.

4 Matthews, Caitlin. *The Celtic Book of Days* (Rochester, Vt.: Destiny Books, 1995), 199.

THE CELTIC TRIPLE GODDESS

Though there has been plenty of argument among Pagans as to the nature of deity, we generally accept that the deities are as real as they need to be. I have always found the argument about whether the deities are real or whether they are "merely" archetypal projections from our own inner selves to be ridiculous. To assume that what is in the mind is not real invalidates all our inner-world experiences, our magick, our astral travels, and any other metaphysical endeavors on which we have labored. It is in the mind that all these things are born. We are each a universe unto ourselves, and to say any divine image that lives there is not real is the same as saying that we are not real, either.

An old magickal adage that is often repeated among people who practice any form of magick is:

> As above, so below;
> As within, so without.[1]

This statement means that we acknowledge that which is outside ourselves as a manifestation of what is inside, and what is inside is the result of what is outside. The macrocosm and the microcosm are like two huge mirrors that reflect each other, both helping to shape the image of the other. In other words, if the deities exist inside us, they must exist outside us as well, each reflecting the existence of the other.

The primary difference between the Celtic concept of deity and that of many other Pagan cultures is the fact that there was, and still is, no definable hierarchy of deities. Though some have tried to give this position to the God Dagda, there is no Celtic God of Gods such as Zeus enjoys in the Greek pantheon, and there is no Goddess who rules over the other Goddesses. There are, however, Goddesses whose mythic roles are more prominent than others or whose worship was more widespread, but they still do not become a part of any definable divine hierarchy.

The Celtic view of deity also shared some similarities with other Pagan cultures. There was a belief in the duality of the divine; a female and a male, or Goddess and God, each representing one half of the whole of the creative life force. For the Celts it was the female, or Goddess half, that reigned supreme. It was the Goddess who gave birth to all life, who nurtured us while we lived upon the earth; and it was to her that the Celtic soul returned upon death to await rebirth. In many Celtic myths the female or Goddess character plays the leading role, with the male or God character often functioning as a supporting cast member or as a consort to the Goddess.[2] The female almost always drives the direction of the story when the male appears to be the primary protagonist.

The Celts saw their Goddess(es) as the personification of the land, and this fact formed the basis for all Celtic worship.[3] This "spirit of place," or *genus locus* as it was known in Latin, is the basis of the Celtic concept of the divine. To this day the Celtic lands bear the names of ancient Goddesses. The terms Eire and Britannia, which refer to Ireland and Britain respectively, are the names of old Celtic Goddesses who were one with the earth. We also have records of Celtic Goddesses of wells, lakes, rivers, stones, and mountains, all attesting to her prominence and her inherent link with the earth.[4]

The Triple Goddess

Nearly all cultures have a cardinal number that they hold to be sacred or to possess magickal energies. For the Celts, this was the number three and all its multiples. Celtic cosmology, iconography, and mythology strongly underscore this belief. Among these significant threes are the three aspects of the Triple Goddess (and some Triple Gods), the three levels of the Otherworld, the three paths to reincarnation, the three actions that complete a spell, and the many carvings and drawings of divine trios that have survived since ancient times. This triple sacredness was embodied in a symbol known as the triskele or triskelion, a whirl of three spokes enclosed in a circle and radiating from its center point.

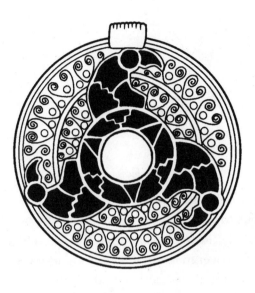

Triskele Pendant

As the natural multiple of three, nine (expressed in mathematics as "three squared") embodies the ultimate in the sacred power of three. In Celtic myths we are told stories of nine women who act as cauldron guardians, teachers, and foster mothers. In ancient Kildare these women tended the sacred flame of Brighid, in Welsh mythology they protect the Otherworldly Cauldron of Annwn, and in modern faery tales they appear to Sleeping Beauty to offer their blessings—including that of death and rebirth.

Author and researcher Miranda Green[5] writes that Celtic artifacts are unique in that they were often meant to make a statement about the nature and power of divinity. Many carvings that feature feminine trios still exist today. A good number of them contain no label or symbol to clearly identify them with a particular set of Goddesses, but they still serve to underscore the importance and sacredness of the number three and feminine triplicities to the Celts. Still other icons, particularly from the Romano-Celtic period in Gaul, are well labeled or contain symbols that connect them to known Triple Goddesses.

Animal figures and icons were also used to represent the Triple Goddess and her attributes. Several statuettes of triple-horned bulls have been unearthed on the continent. Bulls figure heavily in Celtic mythology, particularly in Ireland, and often function as a symbol of sovereignty. One of the most famous and lengthy of all Celtic myths is the *Tain Bo Cuailagny*, or the "Cattle Raid of Cooley," in which Connacht's Queen Maeve covets a famous bull belonging to an Ulsterman and leaps into an epic war to possess it.

Triple Goddesses can also be identified by their description. White, red, and black are the traditional colors of the Celtic Triple Goddess, and often a mythic feminine figure is described as having these color attributes present in body or clothing. When cherished Pagan legends came under fire from the church, the *seanachai* and the *cyfarwydd*, the storytellers who, like the old bards, preserved the oral myths of their people, wisely began to bury knowledge of the old ways within stories that were palatable to the church.

An examination of many faery tales reveals symbolism that teaches us these old ways. One such faery tale is *Snow White and the Seven Dwarves*, in which we have a young woman with white skin, red lips, and black hair (the Triple Goddess colors), who lives

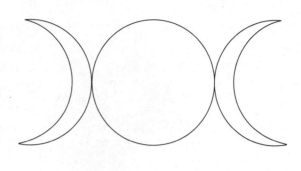

Triple Goddess Moons

in the woods and befriends wild animals and elven beings.

The Triple Goddess is not unique to Celtic mythology and religion, but it is safe to say that it is within the Celtic framework that she is seen most strongly, her image repeated over and over in myth, folklore, and legends. She is one being with three aspects: the virgin, the mother, and the crone, any or all of which may be present at any time. In the Greek tradition, where the archetype of the Triple Goddess is also strong, she came to be symbolized by the three phases of the moon: the virgin with the waxing moon, the mother with the full moon, and the crone with the waning moon.

This cycle of aging that the Triple Goddess undergoes during each twenty-nine-day lunar month coincides with the menstrual cycle of women. The word menstrual itself means "moon change."[6] This triple moon glyph is used today in many Celtic circles as a symbol of the Triple Goddess, though it has no proven roots in Celtic iconography. Certainly the relationship between the moon and the cycles of women was noted by the ancient Celts. It was just that the moon did not play as central a role in the reckoning of holidays or in the making of Goddess lore as did the sun.[7] In Celtic mythology we see very few references to what might be interpreted as moon-Goddess connections, but we see many sun/fire-Goddess links, a connection usually reserved for male deities in other Pagan traditions.

The Triple Goddess is three-in-one, yet she remains unique from the other aspects of herself. Like the three faces of the moon, she changes with the seasons; a young woman in the spring, an expectant mother in summer, and an old hag in winter. One of the most dramatic myths that illustrates this unity of the three-in-one Goddess is that of Flaithius, whose name means "royal one." One of the stories tell of a time when Niall of the Nine Hostages and eight of his other fellow warriors[8] were riding out on a routine scouting expedition and came across an old woman so ugly they could hardly bear to look upon her. She was standing before a well from which they all wished to drink. (Wells represent the birth canal of the Mother Earth, and to drink from one was a form of shamanic initiation into the Goddess mysteries, often entailing an impromptu journey into the Otherworld.[9]) The hag refused to allow the men to drink unless each man dismounted and came down to kiss her. Six refused outright, and two others deigned to give her quick pecks on the check. Only Niall gave her a lover's kiss and then proceeded to have sexual intercourse with her. Afterward, Flaithius was transformed into a beautiful young woman, a Goddess of sovereignty who made Niall High King of Ireland. (See Chapter 12 for a detailed look at the role of the sovereign.) In Triple Goddess myths this transformation represents both the unity of the three-in-one, the cycle of the seasons known today as the wheel of the year, and illustrates the powers believed to be possessed by the Goddess at various stages in her "life."

Sometimes the Celtic Triple Goddesses appear in myth in ways that make it hard to discern if they are really three aspects of one being, three beings with one aspect, three stories about the same woman, or three women who are in a similar situation in three different stories. To keep things simple and easy to follow, many storytellers and writers have lumped similarly or same-named women together as one person. For instance, many people are unaware that the Arthurian myths mention that King Arthur had three different wives, all of them named Guinevere. Queen Maeve's original myths show her as having two sisters of dissimilar temperaments, and the giantess and Goddess of the hunt, Garbh Ogh, built herself three burial cairns before she went inside them to die.

Edain, or Etain, who is considered to be a Goddess of reincarnation, appears as three different women in three different stories. Though all three bear the same name and have different adventures, there are links showing that this Edain is the same woman reborn. One of the major themes threading through each of her stories involves her search for knowledge and gifts from the spirit world.[10] In this she can be likened to the modern-day seeker of higher wisdom, who hopes that by gaining this knowledge through successive lifetimes, she can achieve perfection of the soul and move fully into the spirit world, never to incarnate again.[11]

Each aspect of the Triple Goddess has her own sphere of influence, though sometimes these overlap one another considerably in folklore; after all, she is really one being who is only showing us different faces, so this is to be expected. Below you will find a chart of basic correspondences that go with each aspect. These will all be delved into more deeply in the following chapters.

	Virgin	**Mother**	**Crone**
Age	Youth	Middle Age	Old Age
Menstrual Phase	Menarche	Pregnancy	Menopause
Life Phase	Coming of Age	Motherhood	Elderhood
Life Cycle	Birth	Nurturing	Death/Rebirth
Moon Phase	Waxing	Full	Waning
Major Festival	Imbolg	Lughnasadh	Samhain
Seasons	Spring/Summer	Summer/Autumn	Autumn/Winter
Gift to Give	Awakening	Creativity	Wisdom
Animals	Ewe/Doe	Hare/Horse	Owl/Hound
Celtic Color	White	Red	Black

The Triple Goddesses of the Celts play key parts in myths with potent imagery. The war, death, and destruction Goddesses collectively known as the Morrigan form one of these trios. Sometimes these Goddesses are described as being three crones, and other times as a virgin (Nemain), mother (Macha), and crone (Badb). They function as deities encompassing the complete cycle of Celtic life, from birth to death and back again. The Morrigan are the rulers of war and bringers of death, but they are also the keepers of the soul until it can be reborn, taking the soul full cycle and back again. Badb is the crone aspect who is said in some myths to preside over the cauldron of regeneration in the Otherworld, which makes clear the rebirthing aspect of the death-dealing Morrigan.

Another important trio were the original sovereigns of Ireland: Eire, Fodhla, and Banbha. These Goddesses were of the race of deities known as the Tuatha De Dannan, often referred to today as the "faery race" of Ireland. Each Goddess made a plea to the invading Milesians (the first Irish Celts) for why her name should be forever placed upon the land. Eire's plea was granted because it was perceived that she possessed the greater magick of the three, and hers is still the Gaelic name of Ireland today.

Sometimes the Triple Goddesses appear in the form of an animal known to be sacred to the Celtic feminine divine. One such trio appears in the form of cows, animals sacred to the Celts that represented wealth and power. These three were Bo Find ("white cow"), and her sisters Bo Dhu ("black cow") and Bo Ruadh ("red cow"), all representing a traditional color of the Celtic Triple Goddess: white, red, and black. The cow sisters belong to one of the oldest of Irish myths, and may represent some fragment of a long-lost creation myth. Together the three of them came to barren Ireland from across the western sea in the Otherworld, and each went to a different part of the island and made it fruitful. Bo Find, the principal form of the trio, was said to have given birth to twin calves near the site of present-day Tara. The male and female calves were gifts of abundance that she declared would feed the Irish people forever. Bo Find's sacred links to the land are made even more clear by the holy well named for her there called *Tabor-Bo-Find*.

In lesser-known myths we see dragons, usually representing opposing forces of light and dark God energies that battle for supremacy at the turning points of the year, as trios representing Triple Goddess aspects. In one little-known folktale we are told of a three-headed dragon who does battle with a male warrior. She loses when he severs her third head. This might be interpreted as a post-Pagan period myth, created in a time when humankind had begun to fear and hate the devourer aspect of the Goddess, which therefore had to be ruthlessly cut off from the gentler virgin and mother aspects. When the warrior severed the crone, or third head, he effectively cut himself off from the understanding and acceptance of the natural cycles of life, death, and rebirth that characterized the old Pagan faith of the Celts. In legends even less well-known, we are told that Queen Maeve had two sisters with dragon attributes, and that the scholar and warrior Nessa was once a dragon.

When dragon-like images come in feminine form, they often contain symbols or story images that link them to the element of water rather than to fire, as many of the more well-known dragon legends do. It may be that these are links to sovereign aspects, similar to the Lady of the Lake who bestowed the sword of rulership on King Arthur (see Chapter 12). The fact that the women/dragons return to water to perish in these legends may link them to lost creation myths or Otherworld legends that have been lost or fragmented over time.[12]

About the Triple Goddess Rituals in This Book

Many creative rituals exist—many in print—that revolve around the Triple Goddess or one of her aspects. The most common of these are rite of passage rituals for women in which each face of the Triple Goddess corresponds to a specific life cycle phase.[13]

Virgin Life-Cycle Ritual Events:

Wiccaning/Paganing
Presenting a newborn to the deities

Coming of Age
Celebrating menarche, or the beginning of the menstrual cycle, as a time of entering spiritual adulthood

Mother Life-Cycle Ritual Events:

Conception/Pregnancy
The act of conceiving and carrying a child in the womb,
or of adopting a child

Childbirth
The ritual of giving birth to a child or of formally adopting one

Crone Life-Cycle Ritual Events:

Croning
Celebrating menopause, the cessation of the menstrual cycle

Passing Over
Funeral rites and memorial rituals for Pagans

The Triple Goddess ritual found in Chapter 7, and the ritual suggestions at the ends of Chapters 8, 9, and 10, differ from those found in many books on women's spirituality that solely address life-cycle events. To divide up the Triple Goddess like she was a choice piece of meat at a Thanksgiving feast keeps her and her deeper mysteries away from women who are not currently at one of these junctures in their lives. Some women may never even get to celebrate these rites, either because they came to Paganism too late in life (for a coming of age celebration, for example), or because they cannot or choose not to take some of the "traditional" life cycle steps, like having children. The ritual suggestions in this book embody the symbols and archetypes of each aspect so that any woman can use them at any stage of her physical existence, tailoring them to her own needs or to those of a Celtic women's spirituality group.

This is because the Triple Goddess is not as static as some would like to make her. No matter which is her current dominant face, she always contains elements of her other two aspects. This ebb and flow of aspects is tied in with the Celtic concept of time, one now verified by science, that time is one omnipresent now and not a linear progression. Like many ancient people, the Celts understood this, and it makes their concept of deity a mutable one. A crone can have new beginnings, not just the virgin. And a virgin can be wise, not just the crone. Do you recall the saying, "out of the mouths of babes"? The mother is an archetype of creation, and we all have the ability to create in a myriad of different ways at all stages of our lives. Birthing or adopting children is only one of them.

Working with all aspects of the Triple Goddess throughout our lives is essential to understanding the greater mysteries of the Goddess and to bolstering our self-esteem and creating inner harmony. All women are the Triple Goddess. Though we may at any given time be showing one particular guise to the world, the others are alive and well in us too. We hear this acknowledged every day in the words a misogynistic world uses to describe us. "Women's intuition" and "old hag" are the crone, the inner wisdom that comes with time; "Girl talk" is the awakening of the young virgin; "Mother love," "overprotective," and "virago" are terms tossed out at the nurturing mother aspect and her warrior self; "Hysterical female," "on the rag," and "bitch" have also been given an unwelcome place in our three-fold lives. Many women have stopped fighting and simply reclaimed or reconceptualized these abusive terms and used them as tools of self-empowerment. We are the Triple Goddess. When the world slaps one of our faces, we still have two more with which to come back at it.

No aspect of the Triple Goddess is a stranger to any woman. Women have a symbiotic relationship with her from birth to death, whether or not we consciously realize it, and all her aspects can be made known to us if we take the time to seek her out.

Notes

1 Attributed to Hermes Trismegistus.

2 Stewart, R. J. *Celtic Gods, Celtic Goddesses* (London: Blandford, 1990), 66.

3 Ibid, 64.

4 Condren, Mary. *The Serpent and the Goddess: Women, Religion and Power in Celtic Ireland* (San Francisco: Harper and Row, 1989), 26.

5 *Symbol and Image in Celtic Religious Art* (London: Routledge and Kegan Paul, 1992), 169.

6 Shuttle, Penelope and Peter Redgrove. *The Wise Wound: Myths, Realities, and Meanings of Menstruation* (New York: Bantam Books, 1990), 142.

7 The famous Coligny calendar of Gaul was a lunar calendar, and clearly the moon phases played a role in the Celtic reckoning of time, but the primary divisions of the year and all its high festivals were marked by the changing of the solar seasons. See Chapter 19 for more on the wheel of the year.

8 Note the image of nine here, one of the highest sacred expressions of the number three. Note also that it refers to males here. There were numerous Triple Gods in the Celtic pantheon, though rather than being seen as young man, father, and old man, they tend to represent functions such as hunter, warrior, and king or skills such as goldsmith, herdsman, and forger or one of the three orders of the Druidic priesthood, namely bards (poets and historians), ovates (elders and judges), and filid (seers and enchanters).

9 Caldecott, Moyra. *Women in Celtic Myth* (London: Arrow Books, 1988), 88.

10 Mynne, Hugh. *The Faerie Way* (St. Paul, Minn.: Llewellyn, 1996), 33.

11 This is a New Age concept that many Pagans reject as being too pat and too reflective of linear thinking, but it can be fitted into the omnipresent time theory. Many other Pagans assert that this perfection of the soul is the purpose of living. It is counter-argued that there is no native word for "soul" in any of the Gaelic or Brythonic Celtic languages.

12 Campbell, J. F. and George Henderson. *The Celtic Dragon Myth*, bilingual edition, Irish-English (Wales: Llanerch Publishers, 1995). This facsimile edition of a nineteenth-century work outlines some fascinating theories about dragons in Celtic myths and legend, especially where they concern Goddesses and heroines.

13 For good transcripts of these kinds of rituals see either Pauline and Dan Campanelli's *Rites of Passage: The Pagan Wheel of Life* (St. Paul, Minn.: Llewellyn, 1995), or Diane Stein's *Casting the Circle: A Women's Book of Ritual* (Freedom, Calif.: The Crossing Press, 1990).

THE THREEFOLD BLESSING

Group Ritual

The ritual in this chapter has no origins that can be positively pinpointed. It may be more accurate to call this blessing a Celtic-style ritual rather than a Celtic ritual. I first saw similar blessings used in the early 1980s, and the Irish coven of which I was part in the late 1980s had its own version. While this blessing cannot be said to be ancient in form, it is certainly ancient in symbolism, and it is possible that similar ones were used by Celtic women.

The Threefold Blessing incorporates two important Celtic feminine archetypes, the Triple Goddess and the cauldron. The Irish coven I belonged to when I lived in Texas made use of this blessing in a variety of ritual settings. It was always part of our initiation rituals and our coming-of-age rites, and was employed frequently during healings. I introduced it to the women's group I briefly worked with and found it took on an added sense of mystery in the all-female setting.

The Threefold Blessing requires only one tool—a cauldron of some type containing a small amount of salted water. Do not use more than a few pinches of salt since it is corrosive and can damage carpets, clothes, and grass. A chalice can be substituted for the cauldron, but I feel this detracts from the deeper meaning of the blessing. The cauldron is such an important archetype in Celtic spirituality, representing the womb of the Goddess and a portal to the Otherworld, that trying to use anything else just does not have the same impact on the mind and soul. You don't have to spend a lot of money on a cauldron or set out to find something fancy to use. The symbolic impact is the same whether you have a $10 cauldron or a $1,000 one. Even the plastic cauldrons, found cheaply in every grocery and drug store around Halloween, will suffice. This is what I use and it has always served me well.

The blessing as it is written here requires at least four women participants—one to be blessed, and three women to portray each aspect of the Triple Goddess. It can be easily reworked for use by fewer women, or even by solitaries. For instance, two women can do this with one playing all the Goddess roles and blessing the other. Then they can reverse roles, so that both can receive the blessing. A solitary can offer the blessing to herself by rewording the ritual so that she is calling the blessing of each Goddess aspect into herself, rather than having the deities address her. Of course, this blessing can also be adapted to suit larger covens or mixed-gender group workings.

The Threefold Blessing

You may plan to do this blessing at any point within any ritual. I feel it works best as a closing element, but you should place it where it feels right to you or to the other women with whom you are working.

At the appropriate time, bring the woman (or women) to be blessed into the center of the circle or ritual space, and have the three women who are going to be portraying the Triple Goddess take the cauldron and stand before her. They speak in unison as they hold the cauldron before them.

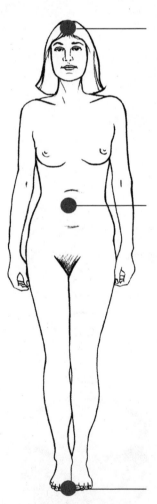

Anointing points for threefold blessing

Triple Goddess (in unison):

Behold my cauldron! Through it I give life and nourishment,
death and rest, regeneration and renewal. To look into its
depths is to peer into my womb, to see all time and space, and
to know the unity and eternalness of me. To accept my blessing
is to enter into my mysteries.

Virgin:

Blessed be the water—my blood from which all life emerges.

Mother:

Blessed be the salt—my body which nourishes and sustains.

Crone:

Blessed be the cauldron—my eternal womb which creates, and
destroys, and creates anew.

Triple Goddess (in unison):

(Each placing one hand in the water and stirring in a
clockwise motion.) Water and salt, blood and earth. Life,
death, and rebirth. All these I created, and by these I bless
her who follows me.

The person portraying the virgin aspect removes her damp hand from the
cauldron and stands in front of the woman to be blessed.

Virgin:

Do you know me?

Woman being blessed:

You are the Triple Goddess—the virgin.

The virgin kneels in front of the woman to be blessed and touches the salted
water to her feet.

Virgin:

By my blood I bless your feet that you may always walk the right
pathway as you travel this life. May your feet lead you boldly

into new ventures and bring you safely home again. May you walk in beauty and confidence, in sacredness and truth, boldly and freely as befits a warrior among women. Blessed be, sister.

The virgin aspect retreats to stand with the other aspects as the mother aspect removes her damp hand from the cauldron and stands in front of the woman being blessed.

Mother:

Do you know me?

Woman being blessed:

You are the Triple Goddess—the mother.

The mother leans over and places her damp hand low on the woman's stomach, at the level of her womb.

Mother:

By my body I bless your womb, your creative center, so that fertility and fruitfulness shall be part of every aspect of your life, both the inner and outer world. May all you touch grow, all you dream flourish, and all you hope for richly manifest. May all you achieve allow you to grow in strength, in power, and in confidence, as befits a warrior among women. Blessed be, daughter.

The mother aspect retreats to stand in line with the others while the crone aspect removes her damp hand from the cauldron and comes to stand in front of the woman being blessed.

Crone:

Do you know me?

Woman being blessed:

You are the Triple Goddess—the crone.

The crone stands as eye-to-eye with the woman as possible—she kneels to no one—and places her damp hand on the woman's forehead.

Crone:

> By my womb which gives and takes, I bless your head that you
> may find your inner wisdom. I cannot give you that which you
> do not already possess, but I can show you the way to find that
> which is within you, warrior among women. I bless you that you
> may think clearly, seek knowledge, and come to understand my
> mysteries and how they work in your life and in the universe.
> Know that you are connected to all things. You are mine, as all
> that is, was, or ever shall be, is mine. Like you they came from
> me, and like you, to me they shall return. Go forth, my warrior,
> and be wise. Blessed be, my warrior child.

If you are working with a large women's group, you may have another woman
come to the center of the circle to be blessed, and so on, until all have had
their turn. A nice finishing touch for this ritual is to have each woman in turn
tell the various aspects of the Triple Goddess how her blessings have so far
been manifesting in her life. This is also a way of offering the Triple Goddess
a blessing in return.

When you are finished with the ritual in which this blessing was used, dis-
pose of the water as befits a sacred object. Pour it onto or into an appropriate
place. If you feel you must pour it down a common drain, do so with the clear
visualization that it is somehow returning to its source—the Goddess.

THE VIRGIN

The virgin is the most nebulous aspect of the Triple Goddess, primarily due to the human need to compartmentalize—and no aspect of the feminine divine defies categorization more than the virgin.

The problem begins with the way the modern world conceptualizes the term "virgin." Because the old Latin word *virgo* meant "intact," the patriarchal world began equating the state of virginity with an intact hymen, the thin membrane that covers the opening to the vagina. The hymen is broken during first sexual intercourse, though it can be broken in any number of non-sexual ways, including participation in certain sports, the insertion of a tampon, or through a routine medical examination.

Fortunately, the hymen is a body part modern women are beginning to evolve out of, just as we do any other useless appendage. Far too much has been made of this small bit of tissue, and most of it has only served to induce fear of sexual relations among young women who are told, either by older women or through misleading novels, that losing one's hymen, or "virginity," is very painful and very bloody. I experienced no great pain or excessive bleeding with my first intercourse, nor did any of the women in my acquaintance.

The original term *virgo intacta* referred to the whole woman, not just her hymen. A virgin was one who was intact. In other words, she was complete and whole unto herself. She needed no one else, such as a male mate, to make her complete or for society to acknowledge her worth.[1] She was free to mate with any man she chose, any time she chose, something that was especially true in the culture of the early Celts. Often she might be a priestess who used sex in a sacred fashion. In this she was similar to the famous Vestal Virgins, the sacred prostitutes of the Roman temples. They were certainly not virgins in the modern sense, but they certainly were in the original meaning.

You will note that in this book I have consistently used the word "virgin" rather than "maiden," a practice in which I have been training myself. This is not easy, since the alliteration of the phrase "maiden, mother, crone" rolls off the tongue so easily. But the term maiden is too etymologically linked to the hymen, also called the "maiden head," and reeks too much of the modern conception of what a virgin is for me to be comfortable with it any longer. I feel the word *virgin* best sums up the old view of the young Goddess as sexually awakened and well aware of the power her sexuality gives her as a sovereign deity.

By the Middle Ages, the two definitions of virgin had become confused in the minds of Celtic writers. This is seen clearly in the myth of Dechtere, an Irish Goddess who conceived the hero Cuchulain by drinking a liquid into which a magfly containing the spirit of the God Lugh (said to be Cuchulain's "father") had fallen. She gave birth by vomiting up the child, thus remaining a "virgin."

There is at least one early modern precedent for the use of the word virgin for a sovereign or woman of power. England's Queen Elizabeth I was always known as the Virgin Queen, simply because she never married. Several biographers have alluded to the fact that she did this because she did not wish to share her power—her sovereignty—with anyone else, even though this meant that upon her death she would have to pass her crown to her Scottish nephew, the son of her enemy, Mary Queen of Scots. Elizabeth had numerous suitors, several of which were likely her lovers, yet she always remained "the Virgin Queen"—whole and complete unto herself.

Attributes and Correspondences of the Virgin

The virgin represents new beginnings and awakenings. To the Celts, she stood for the power of the land itself. She is the Goddess of adventure, the magickal aspect of the feminine divine.[2] By contrast, she is also the embodiment of beauty and of both joy and sorrow.[3]

Sometimes the virgin aspect of a Goddess or heroine will overlap that of the mother, and they will share attributes. When reading through Celtic myths, legends, and folklore, the virgin can best be identified using these cues:

Youthful
The virgin is almost always a younger woman.

Beautiful
She usually possesses great beauty and attracts both wanted and unwanted male attention. This attention usually results in battles or trouble of some kind, both for the woman and for the men wanting to possess her.[4] Two examples of these virgins are Ireland's Deirdre of the Sorrows, over whom the Red Branch fraternity broke up, and Wales's Gwen, who was so beautiful that no human eye could look upon her for long.

Sovereign
She grants kings the power to rule, as did Queen Guinevere in the Arthurian legends.

Presents a Weapon or Chalice to a Male Figure
Any Goddess or heroine who offers an item such as this is acting in a sovereign role, and is likely a virgin aspect.

May Have a Horse Aspect
Because the horse is linked to sovereignty, a horse Goddess is usually a virgin, though in some cases she is a mother aspect. A few human women who were historically seen as sovereigns had horse nicknames, such as the warrior Cartamandua, who was called "the silken pony."

Strong Sexual Nature
Because the young virgin's archetypal role is to mate with the king, and then with his chosen successor, she has a decidedly sexual nature. This aspect of her has been perverted over time and the women viewed as wantons or as whores. An example of this is seen in the Breton myth about a virgin Goddess named Dahud-Ahes, who left Brittany when the Christians came and was dubbed a Goddess of debauchery.

A "Faery" or Otherworld Woman Married to a Mortal
This is another type of sovereign Goddess who grants a mortal man full access to the Otherworld or to shamanic knowledge, or who makes the man divine in his own right. An example is Caer, a Goddess of sleep and dreams, who wed Aenghus MacOg, a God of love.[5] Another is Niamh of the Golden Hair,

who takes Ossian into the Otherworld to live, although he dies when he disobeys her warnings about what he may and may not do when he revisits earth.

Linked to a Land or Water Site
While this can also be a mother attribute, it is more often a virgin who is embodied in these natural features, such as Boann, the Goddess and eponym of Ireland's River Boyne; the Lady of the Lake in the Arthurian myths; Aine of the hills of Munster; or Sioann of the River Shannon.[6]

Endures Great Sorrow or Personal Tragedy
A virgin usually has a series of tragedies or personal disasters as the central focus of her myth, such as Deirdre of the Sorrows, Wales's Branwen, or the healing Goddess Airmid, who sees her jealous father slay her brother.

Embodies Joy and Takes Risks
Deirdre of the Sorrows,[7] Grainne, and other Goddesses mentioned in this chapter express a great joy in life, and they take risks to get or keep it, even though the end result is more often tragic than happy.

Gives Birth to a Son, Often by Magickal Means
Examples are Eri of the Golden Hair, who is impregnated by a beam of sunlight; Dechtere, who conceives by drinking a soul from a cup; and Finchoem, who swallowed a worm she found crawling on a magickal well and conceived Conall of the Victories. Goddesses who give birth to animals are usually related to agricultural cycles and are viewed as mother aspects.

Goes on Great Adventures
One example is Grainne,[8] who lures the young warrior Diarmuid away from her marriage feast to another man. Together they ran the length of Ireland with the Fianna warriors in pursuit.

Symbolizes Peace, Yet is Often a Warrior
Brigantia, the sovereign spirit of the Bretons, is one example. Ruling queens or chieftains, such as Queen Maeve, also fit into this category.

Part of a Romantic Triangle
A virgin is often pulled between two men, either two lovers, or a father and son. Examples are Isolde, who was in the middle of a contest between Cornwall's King Mark and Ireland's Tristan; and Grainne, who was wed to Fionn MacCumhal but fled with her lover Diarmuid.

Fought Over by Two or More Men
When two men are fighting for possession of a woman, either a sexual contest or a fight for some possession of hers, it is likely she is a virgin. The fight is

one of sovereignty, with the old king weakening and dying and needing to be replaced by a younger man. The winner will be the one who possesses the sexual favors of the sovereign Goddess. In Welsh mythology we see an example of this in Olwen's father Ysbadadden, who sets up obstacles to try and keep her from her desired lover Culwch.

Triple Goddess Aspect Embodying Virgin Attributes
Any Triple Goddess or thrice-appearing feminine archetype who embodies other attributes marking her as a virgin Goddess is likely a virgin aspect, such as Anu, the virgin aspect of Anu, Dana, and Badb, or Guinevere when she first marries King Arthur.

Questions About the Virgin For Celtic Women

The following questions may be asked of yourself at any time in your exploration of the virgin aspects. Whether you have been involved in Celtic Paganism for a long time, or whether you are just beginning to explore it, the virgin has something to teach you.

What ideas and images do the words "virgin" and "maiden" conjure up in my mind?

How do I feel about the virgin Goddess?

Do I feel the virgin has any relevance to my life now? Why or why not?

Do I feel a kinship with the virgin, or am I at odds with her?

Does the virgin make me feel jealousy? Anger? Happiness? Why?

Am I comfortable with the virgin archetype? Why or why not?

How do I imagine that the men in my life feel about the virgin Goddess? Does any aspect of their feelings threaten or comfort me?

What do I hope to get out of working with the virgin Goddess? What do I think or expect her to give to me?

What can I offer the virgin in return?

What do I not expect the virgin to be able to do for me?

Can I easily relate the virgin aspect of the Goddess to her other two forms?

What virgin aspects do I possess or not possess? Which of these would I like to change if I can?

Virgin Meditation and Exercise

Set aside a block of time when you can be the virgin. This can be a few hours or an entire day. During this time allow your thoughts and outward actions to be those archetypally belonging to the virgin. Allow everything you do or plan during this time to be an adventure; plan new things to do in the near future, make fresh starts, deal with both joy and sorrow, indulge your vanity, bestow favors and delegate authority, indulge your spontaneous side, play like a child, giggle, or set aside some time with other women just to enjoy yourselves.

During this period you must be able to interact with at least one other person who is unaware that you are indulging your virgin self. If you can interact with more, all the better. This allows you to gauge the reactions of others to your virgin aspect.

As soon as possible after this exercise, find some private time to meditate on the qualities of the virgin Goddess and how those are and are not manifested within you regardless of your chronological age. Be sure to write down your impressions in a Book of Shadows or magickal diary for future reference.

Rituals of Awakening: Celebrating the Virgin

We have awakenings all the time; spiritual, ethical, life-changing, personal, and more. All these new beginnings mark the end of old cycles and the beginning of new ones. These are the province of the virgin.

Times you may especially want to celebrate, honor, or petition the virgin through ritual are:

- When you are coming of age or when you are leading a ritual for a young woman who is coming of age (this is a ceremony, widely popular in Pagan circles, that marks spiritual adulthood)
- When you need to ask for help making a change in your life
- When change has come and you need help getting used to its flow
- When pleasant changes have come and you wish to offer thanks
- When you need help making a change in your life
- During rituals of hallowing the sacred king
- During mating rituals
- When doing divinations pertaining to awakenings, new ventures, changes, fresh starts, or self-possession
- When the sun is weak and new in later winter and early spring
- When the waxing crescent moon first appears in the night sky

In Celtic virgin rituals the featured color should be white, though blue is finding favor. You may want to find one of those thick pillar candles boasting three wicks that are seen more and more in candle and gift shops. If you find one in white you can use it to honor the virgin while still acknowledging her other two faces who are present but unseen. Spring-related libations are best for the virgin; milk, honey, cream dishes, and sweets.

A variation on the traditional ritual circle appropriate to the virgin aspect is to cast two smaller circles inside your primary circle to represent the earth world and the Otherworld form that the virgin emerges as in spring. (See Appendix C for step by step methods for circle castings.)

Notes

1 Markale, Jean. *Women of the Celts* (Rochester, Vt.: Inner Traditions International, Ltd., 1972), 131.

2 Farrar, Janet and Stewart. *The Witches' Goddess* (Custer, Wash.: Phoenix Publishing, Inc., 1987), 35.

3 Stewart, R. J. *Celtic Gods, Celtic Goddesses* (London: Blandford, 1990), 82.

4 Keane, Patrick J. *Terrible Beauty: Yeats, Joyce, Ireland, and the Myth of the Devouring Female* (Columbia, Mo.: The University of Missouri Press, 1988).

5 Green, Miranda J. *Celtic Goddesses: Warriors, Virgins and Mothers* (London: British Museum Press, 1995), 121–122.

6 Stewart, R. J. *The Power Within the Land* (Shaftsbury, Dorset: Element Books, 1991).

7 Caldecott, Moyra. *Women in Celtic Myth* (London: Arrow Books, 1988), 151.

8 Ibid, 196.

THE MOTHER

CHAPTER NINE

It is probably the mother aspect of the Triple Goddess with whom we are generally most comfortable. We all understand the archetype of a creative, nurturing woman because we see this image almost daily. In modern cultures this nurturing mother aspect is often the only acceptable one for a woman to outwardly display—so long as she continues to look like the beautiful young virgin, of course. The media and many people in our lives relentlessly pound us with this daily message.

The mother Goddesses of the pre-patriarchal world hardly looked like the emaciated women of modern preference. Extant iconography shows us a radically different picture, one of women with pendulous breasts, bulging stomach, and ample lap, who proudly displays her physical self and never hides in shame. Because patriarchy was a fact of European life by the time the Celts came to power, Celtic iconography shows us more slender Goddesses, though many still cradle grains, children, or fruits in their roomy laps.[1] Thankfully, many statues and carvings from Romano-Celtic Gaul are labeled with the names of Goddesses, eliminating the guesswork as to the precise nature of the figures.

The mother Goddess often has two faces, that of a bright or light mother and that of the dark mother. These two figures represent the waxing and waning periods of the solar year, the waxing and waning of the moon, the change from motherhood to cronage, and the physical world and the Otherworld. The light mother symbolizes a period of growth, fertility, and action, the active powers of the warrior and queen; the other represents stagnation, barrenness, and inaction, the powers of the Witch and priestess. They can also represent the change from mother aspect to crone.[2] A Celtic mother Goddess may also have three faces, being shown as a triple mother in whom one face represents the harvest, another birth, and still other menstruation.[3]

In most cultures a mother Goddess is featured in its creation myth, but the Celts are perhaps the only major culture in the world that does not have a known creation story. It is assumed that they had one once, either one of their own or one adapted from another culture with whom they made contact, but none remains today.[4] There are several Celtic myths that contain images that might link them to the creation process; Goddesses who weave or spin, who emerge from water, who bring animals or fertility to the land, who birth great Gods and heroes, or who are clearly ancestral deities. Still, no single figure emerges as anything remotely resembling a primal creation Goddess.

One of the most definable Celtic mother Goddesses is Modron, whose name literally means "great mother." She was the mother of Mabon, whose name roughly translates as "bright son." He was stolen from her when he was only three days old but, in medieval legends, was restored to her by King Arthur who, in this instance, functions as her lover/consort and provides her with a child who is really a younger aspect of himself. In the Celtic tradition the lover/consort of the Goddess is almost always his own father. Throughout the cycle of the year he is born from the Goddess, mates with her, and then dies so that he can be reborn from her.

Another mother is Ireland's Dana or Danu, whose eponym is found today throughout Europe in places the Celts inhabited, such as the Danube River Valley. Some Celtic scholars speculate that she is the most ancient of the Celtic deities of whom we have extant knowledge. The root *dan* in Old Irish means "knowledge," offering us an important insight into her character. The name of the race known as the Tuatha De Dannan, who make up the majority of deities and faery rulers of the Irish Celts, means "people of the Goddess Dana," marking her as their ancestral deity or "great mother." The Welsh mother Goddess Don, and the Irish Otherworld God Donn, are both thought to be but other versions of Dana.[5]

Over time, Dana's image merged with that of Brighid, one of the most widely worshiped Goddesses of the Celts. Brighid is viewed as both a virgin and mother. Even when this Goddess was transformed into St. Brighid of the Catholic Church, her images as virgin and mother blend and contradict each other. Because she is a protective Goddess, and this is a trait of the mother, and because she is linked to fire and the sun, other mother symbols, I feel this aspect of her is the strongest.

Brighid is also a deity of creative inspiration, another mother correspondence.[6] She is credited with inventing the Irish art of keening (*caoine*), the distinctive mourning wail she was moved to produce when she cried for her slain son Ruadan. She is probably the origin of the faery ghost known as the banshee (*beansidhe*, or "woman faery"), whose keening can be heard throughout the countryside on the night before a death. The banshee is also considered to be a protective spirit of a clan, perhaps an ancestral deity—both clearly mother Goddess attributes. She has also been worshiped as a warrior, healer, guardian of children, patron of midwives, and sovereign.

One of the most interesting mother images is Macha of the Morrigan. The myth of "The Curse of Macha" is part of the Ulster cycle of Irish myths, and directly leads to events in the famous epic known as *The Tain*. In this myth, Maeve goes to war over an Ulster-owned bull, and these events in turn lead to the death of the hero Cuchulain. This is where Macha's mother image merges with those of the crone Goddess. As a Goddess of death and destruction (crone attributes), she once guarded the *mesred machae*, the pillared gate on which the heads of conquered warriors were displayed at the Ulster fortress of the Red Branch warriors, *Emain Macha*. As a mother she was a horse Goddess whose husband, an Ulster king, declared that she could outrun any horseman who challenged her. He was dared to make good his boast, and the king asked Macha to complete a grueling race course. She protested that, since she was in the end stages of her pregnancy, she could not do this. The king was afraid of looking foolish or being killed for his boasting, so he ordered her to run the race. Macha turned to plead with the assembled warriors and asked, "Won't you help me? After all, a mother bore each of you."

Macha was given no reprieve. She completed the course victorious, but died at the end while giving birth to twins. As her life ended, she cursed all the bearded men of Ulster (meaning all adult male warriors) to have great labor pains whenever danger threatened so that they would be unable to fight. Only the famous warrior Cuchulain, who was famous for his baby face, was immune to the curse, but the rest of the warriors fell under the spell and were subsequently defeated by Connacht.[7]

Celtic Holy Wells and the Healing, Fertile Mother

Throughout the Celtic lands are a plethora of sacred or holy wells. Some of these are wells in the traditional sense, in that they provide a necessary water source for those living near them. Others are no more than small depressions in ancient stones that stand now, as in the past, at the center of sacred space. In Ireland, hundreds of these old wells have been adopted by the new religion and are today the focus of pilgrimages and special rites on Pattern Days, the feast days of specific saints for whom many of the wells are named.[8] They are used for baptismal events, personal purification rites, and especially for healing, just as they were thousands of years ago. Women often approach the wells to cure themselves of infertility, again linking the well to the power of the mother Goddess.

Healing is an attribute of the mother. Some crones and virgins were also healers, but again this type of overlap is not unusual in a culture that views the feminine divine as a three-faces-in-one deity. Still, it is the mother who retains most of the healing power, and evidence exists at many of the wells today that links them to the mother aspect. St. Kevin's Well at Glendalough, Ireland, sits cradled in a horseshoe-shaped mound of earth and is flanked by birch trees, both Goddess symbols.[9] The wells that are not named for saints often bear the name of mother Goddesses, such as the often-visited *Tobar Brid* (Brighid's Well) in County Donegal. Many wells are named for Brighid, who became St. Brighid in the new religion. Both the Christian and the Pagan Brighid were very much linked with healing powers, and both had strong mother aspects. Many Celtic Pagans and Christian pilgrims still seek her out when they need healing.

The image of the well itself is archetypally one of birth. The long, narrow opening in the earth that leads from the surface to the life-giving water source below is a symbol of the birth canal, or vagina, of the Great Mother who is the earth. Coins and other offerings are still placed in holy wells, just as they were thousands of years ago, as a way to gain the favor of the mother and of the feminine water spirits who dwell therein. Wells have also been viewed as portals between the world of form and spirit, representative of rebirth and of the shamanic journey into the Otherworld and back again.

Irish mythology and folklore tells of many Goddesses and heroines who are linked to wells, and to the healing and fertile magick of wells. For example, Aibheaog is a fire Goddess from County Donegal—fire being an element of the mother Goddess in the Celtic myths—who is linked to a sacred well there named for Brighid, indicating that Aibheaog may be but another face of

Brighid. The waters of this well are said to be very effective against toothaches, but the petitioner is required to leave a small white stone at the well to represent the decayed tooth. This is a form of magick known as magickal substitution, in which something unwanted is discarded or sacrificed for something similar in exchange. It is a popular feature of Celtic folk magick that is used liberally in places where Celtic ways still flourish.[10]

Other healing properties common to these wells are cures for headaches, backaches, mental illnesses, infertility, eye diseases, arthritis, and the healing of children's ailments.[11]

Caolainn is a local deity in County Roscommon, and is the guardian spirit of a magickal well there. She is best known for helping pilgrims get their wishes, usually teaching in the process that the wisher did not really want what she sought in the first place. The teaching of tough lessons is sometimes a mother attribute, though this is more often the province of the crone. Again, we have the overlapping spheres of influence common to the Celtic Triple Goddesses.

Near the village of Brideswell (also meaning "Brighid's well") in County Roscommon is a well that was said to grant fertility to barren women.[12] In many cases, just sprinkling one's self with the waters was sufficient to gain their powers. At other times, a more elaborate ritual was needed. In County Sligo there is a well known as Our Lady's Bed. Women who feared dying in childbirth would lie in this shallow well and turn over three times while petitioning the Goddess in the form of Christianity's Mary that they would not die in childbirth.[13] This may have been a form of "magickal substitution" in which one action or offering is made as a symbolic sacrifice in order to gain something else. In this case it may have been a form of mimicking death to lie in a shallow depression on the ground, a symbolic sacrifice of life so that the woman could hope to live through childbirth.

Stones or other objects found on or near the wells are often kept as fertility talismans by female pilgrims. This belief has precedents in Celtic mythology. Nessa, the warrior and scholar previously mentioned, refused to bear the child of the man who captured her, so she decided to impregnate herself by consuming two worms she found crawling over a holy well. When her son, the future High King Conor MacNessa, was born, he held two worms clenched in his tiny fists.

That these wells contained power forbidden to certain seekers is a recurrent theme in Celtic well mythology. Liban, a Goddess who is associated with water, reincarnation, and knowledge, was the guardian deity of Irish holy wells. One day, when she let down her vigilance, one of the wells gushed forth a flood that formed Lough Neath in Northern Ireland. Liban lost her Goddess status in Irish folklore and became a spirit doomed to reside in wells and rivers.

In folklore it is the Goddess of inspiration, Cebhfhionn, who can be found sitting atop the Well of Knowledge, from which she fills a bottomless vessel. Her intent is to keep this magickal water from humans for their own good. Like an overly protective mother, she feels we can neither handle nor appreciate true wisdom.

Another popular myth tells of Sionnan, for whom the River Shannon is named, and her haphazard approach to a well which turned out to be the Otherworld's famous Well of Knowledge (or Well of Sagais), to perform some unspecified ritual. Her irreverent action so outraged the well that its waters rose up and sucked her down. For this action she was forever denied entrance to the peace of the Otherworld, and now resides in the waters of Ireland as the queen of its rivers.

This well of knowledge is sometimes identified as a well of wisdom, and here the lines between mother and crone blur. Bean Naomha is a County Cork Goddess who swims as a trout in the Well of the Sun (*Tobar Ki-na-Greina*). In her fish form she is a Goddess of wisdom, an oracle from whom answers are not easily obtained. To use her well for divination, local legend says you must crawl as you approach it, then crawl clockwise around its rim three times. With each pass you must take a drink and then place upon the well a stone the size of a dove's eye. After you have done this, form a question in your mind and glance into Bean Naomha's well for the answer.

Attributes and Correspondences of the Mother

The mother archetype sometimes overlaps with the virgin, though more often, when overlap occurs, it is with the crone. This makes sense in terms of our perceptions of linear time, in which the Goddess ages from virgin to crone. When reading through Celtic myths, legends, and folklore, the mother can best be identified by these clues:

Gives Birth to Animals, Land Features, or Plants
Examples are Bo Find and her sisters, who give livestock to Ireland by coming from the Otherworld to birth them there.

Possesses Fertility
The mother is often presented as pregnant, as giving birth, or as granting the power of fertility to others. She can also grant fertility to the land or to its

animals. Sometimes she is capable of impregnating herself by unusual means, such as when Nessa used the worms found on the rim of a sacred well, or when Queen Etar swallowed a magfly and gave birth to Edain.

Represents Creativity and Inspiration

The mother not only has these powers herself, but can grant them to others. Brighid and the Irish faery/Goddess/vampire/mother known as the Leanansidhe both represent this aspect, and are often petitioned for aid by those in the arts. Another such Goddess is Saba, a woman who was turned into a deer before she bore her son, the poet and warrior Ossian, whose poetic talents were evident at birth.

Canola is thought to be one of the oldest of the Irish deities and is credited as the inventor of Ireland's long-cherished symbol, the harp. Folklore tells us that she fell asleep outdoors while listening to the most beautiful music she'd ever heard. When she awakened she saw that the music was coming from the sinews of a gutted whale through which a strong breeze was passing. She fashioned the harp to recreate this sound and is said to be able to bestow her musical talents to others.

Is Given Leadership of Her Clan or Country

Queens like Maeve of Connacht were not uncommon among the Celts. Female succession into positions of power, queens and chieftains who were mother-figures just as kings were father-figures, were once popular.[14] Any women with this position is likely to be an aspect of the mother Goddess.

Myths Containing Menstrual, Birth Canal, or Well Images

Nearly all the well Goddesses qualify as mothers, though some have crone attributes. Others have images linking them to the menstrual cycle, such as Wales' Gwyar. Gwyar's full Welsh name means "shedding blood" or "gore."

Linked to Agricultural Cycles or the Harvest

The earth is the mother. In her womb is planted seeds, where they grow as crops, and from her body they are born to us at harvest time.

Unlike the Goddess in most other cultures, there are not as many Celtic Goddesses who clearly function as agriculture or harvest deities, though a few do exist. These are mostly from Celtic Gaul, where contact with the Romans led to the creation of many statues and icons of Goddesses bearing harvest symbols.[15] One such Gaulish Goddess is Deae Matres, a triple deity whose name means "mother Goddesses." Though none of her legends survive, many inscriptions and sculptures attest to her worship. In one icon she is seen as a robed trio bearing baskets of flowers (spring), grain (summer), and fruit (autumn), symbols that represent the three non-winter seasons in which agricultural events take place. Other icons of Celtic mother Goddesses hold cornucopias or harvest tools to link them to these events.

Has Solar or Fire Image or Links

In many other European cultures, the mother Goddess is linked to the full moon. The Celtic mothers are linked instead to the sun (see Chapter 18 for more on this phenomenon). The sun is an active force, whereas the moon is viewed as passive. The mother is also an active force, becoming pregnant, giving birth, and nourishing her offspring.

This active principle includes the Goddesses of hot springs, too, since these were believed to have been heated by a sun deep within the earth. Celtic sun, fire, and hot springs Goddesses with mother attributes include Adsullata, Aimend, Aine, Brighid, Lassair, Rosmerta, and Sul.

Is An Ancestral Deity

The great mother is the one to whom an entire race or tribe can trace its origins. The *Tuatha De Dannan* certainly had this in Dana. Another is Cornwall's Elen, from whom all Cornish kings claimed descent. Elen's children and grandchildren were blended into some of the Arthurian legends, with Elen occasionally being romantically linked to the magician Merlin.

Has Strong Protective Instincts and Powers

The mother seeks to protect those whom she loves, especially children. Often a mother Goddess will be depicted sporting a shield or wielding a weapon. At other times, only her myths and legends tell us of her protective nature, such as those of Caireen, an Irish champion and defender of youth, probably once a patron Goddess of children.

Has A Nurturing Aspect

Women who care for others are also good candidates for mother Goddesses. Those cared for do not have to be children but anyone for whom the mother feels responsible. The Goddess Airmid, who collected healing herbs that she grew on the grave of her beloved brother, has mother attributes.

May Have a Horse Aspect

Because the horse is linked to sovereignty, a horse Goddess is usually a virgin, though sometimes, as in the case of Macha, she is a mother. When white in color, the horse is a symbol of travel between this world and the Otherworld, the dream realms, sexuality, fertility, and personal power—the latter two being exceptionally strong mother attributes. So ingrained in Celtic thought was this link that Irish folk custom taught that white horses were not welcome at funerals.

Symbolized by Caves or by Earth-Dwelling Animals

In many cultures the Goddesses who are seen as living in subterranean places are mother Goddesses, often reborn in spring as virgins. There is less of this imagery in the Celtic pantheon than in others of old Europe, but the image of the faery woman who lives beneath the ground and comes out to steal children for herself is certainly a popular one in Celtic lands. Other mother Goddesses take on the form of earth-dwelling animals, like the Irish snake Goddess Corchen, who archetypally represents rebirth.

Symbolized by or Lives in Hillsides

Hills or burghs have been thought to be the homes of Celtic faeries for centuries, faeries who were once the powerful deities of the land. Two such Goddesses are Scotland's Momu, a deity of wells and hillsides, and England's Magog, a four-breasted horse Goddess for whom two mountains are named. Magog became England's St. Margaret.

Possible Links to Lost Creation Myth

Any Goddess whose imagery could possibly link her to lost Celtic creation myths is also likely to be a mother aspect. Two examples of these are Ireland's Irnan, who could spin webs to entrap marauding enemies, and Wales' Arianrhod, who is sometimes depicted as a weaver. In other cultures, Goddesses who are weavers, spinners, or otherwise make cloth are often tied to that culture's creation myths.

Linked to the Turning of the Wheel of the Year

The ever-spinning wheel of the year (explored fully in Chapter 17) is sometimes seen as being turned by the mother. The symbol of Brighid, the Brighid's or St. Brighid's Cross, represents this turning. It has four points, one for each of the major solar festivals of the year. It also represents the unity of the Goddess as a principle of the creative life force. One is male and the other female, and their union creates all things. The Cross is also a glyph for the earth that she rules and loves as its mother.

A Brighid's Cross

Questions About the Mother For Celtic Women

The following questions may be asked of yourself at any time in your exploration of the mother aspects. Whether you have been involved in Celtic Paganism for a long time, or whether you are just beginning to explore it, the mother has something to teach you.

What images or ideas does the word "mother" conjure up in my mind?

Do the words "nurturer" or "healer" conjure up any special images?

How do I feel about the mother Goddess?

Do I feel the mother has any relevance to my life now? Why or why not?

Do I feel a kinship with the mother or am I at odds with her?

Does the mother make me feel jealousy? Anger? Happiness? Why?

Am I comfortable with the mother archetype? Why or why not?

How do I imagine that the men in my life feel about the mother Goddess? Does any aspect of their feelings threaten or comfort me?

What do I hope to get out of working with the mother Goddess? What do I think or expect her to give to me?

What can I offer the mother in return?

What do I not expect the mother to be able to do for me?

Can I easily relate the mother aspect of the Goddess to her other two forms?

What mother aspects do I possess or not possess? Which of these would I like to change if I can?

Mother Meditation and Exercise

Set aside a block of time when you can be the mother. This can be a few hours or an entire day. During this time, allow your thoughts and outward actions to be those archetypally belonging to the mother. Allow everything you do or plan to do during this time to have nurturing or protective qualities; work in your garden, walk in the woods, give some extra care to family or other loved ones, allow your creative self to flourish, or finish ("give birth to") a project on which you have working.

During this period you must be able to interact with at least one other person who is unaware that you are indulging your mother side. If you can interact with more, all the better. This contact will allow you to gauge the reactions of others to your mother self.

As soon as possible after this exercise, find some private time to meditate on the qualities of the mother Goddess and how those are and are not manifest within you, regardless of your chronological age. Be sure to write down your impressions in a Book of Shadows or magickal diary for future reference.

Rituals of Creation: Celebrating the Mother

Women are natural creators, not just because we possess a womb but because we have had to nurture our creativity to survive with sanity intact for centuries in a world that has sought to repress or vilify women's natural talents. Creativity has allowed us to express ourselves in ways that have been meaningful to us while not threatening the patriarchy. It is no accident that tapestry and needlework from the past is so exquisitely lovely; it was one of the few creative outlets allowed to women and, in the name of the church or of teaching their children, they made the most of the opportunity.

Times you may especially want to celebrate, honor, or petition the mother through ritual are:

- When you are trying to become pregnant
- When you have given or are about to give birth
- When leading a Wiccaning/Paganing ceremony for a newborn (this is a ritual dedication in which the parents present their child to the deities and ask their blessing upon the infant)
- When you wish to give thanks for your "children" (children in this case refers to any of your babies: projects seen through to completion, favorite activities that are successful, pets, organizations, and so on, as well as your own offspring)
- When you wish to offer thanks for your own talents and achievements
- When you are doing a land or garden blessing
- When you are healing or being healed
- When you need a creative boost
- During fertility rituals
- When doing divinations pertaining to creativity, fertility, childbirth, children, or matters of the home and heart
- When the sun is strong in summer
- When the fields are rich with growing crops
- During the full moon

In Celtic mother rituals the featured color should be red. You may want to find one of those thick pillar candles that boast three wicks for use in your ritual. A red one can be used to honor the mother, while still acknowledging her other two faces who are present but unseen. Summer-related libations are best for the mother: grains, eggs, and fresh meats.

A variation on the ritual circle appropriate to a mother ritual is to divide the primary circle into the three smaller sections, similar to a triskele pattern. Name one for each aspect of the Triple Goddess, for the three levels of the Otherworld, or for any other triple Celtic aspect you choose. Work the main part of your mother ritual within the circle most closely related to her attributes. (See Appendix C for step by step methods for circle castings.)

Notes

1 For photos and discussion of some of the icons, please see Miranda J. Green's *Symbol and Image in Celtic Religious Art* (London: Routledge and Kegan Paul, 1992), 34, 191.

2 Janet and Stewart Farrar's *The Witches' Goddess* (Custer, Wash.: Phoenix Publishing, Inc., 1987) devotes a brief chapter to this dichotomy (Chapter III, 18-23).

3 Green, 191.

4 Matthews, Caitlin. *The Elements of the Celtic Tradition* (Shaftsbury, Dorset: Element Books, 1989), 8.

5 Stewart, R. J. *Celtic Gods, Celtic Goddesses* (London: Blandford, 1990), 64.

6 Matthews, 50.

7 Other interpretations of the meaning of this myth can be found in Mary Condren's *The Serpent and the Goddess: Women, Religion and Power in Celtic Ireland* (San Francisco: Harper & Row, 1989), 33–36. Condren speculates that men may have imitated the birth pangs of women when going to battle so that the Goddess who protected women in childbirth would protect them as well. This theory seems to have holes in it since the purpose of Macha's actions was clearly to curse the men, not to help them.

8 For a full discussion of these wells and their uses in Ireland, see Patrick Logan's *The Holy Wells of Ireland* (Gerrards Cross, Buckinghamshire: Smythe, 1980).

9 Rodgers, Michael and Marcus Losack. *Glendalough: A Celtic Pilgrimage* (Blackrock, Co. Dublin: The Columba Press, 1996), 117.

10 For a detailed look at this type of Celtic magick as it remains today in southern Appalachia, please see my work *Mountain Magick: Folk Wisdom from the Heart of Appalachia* (St. Paul, Minn.: Llewellyn, 1995).

11 For more detail, see Logan, Chapter 6.

12 Logan, 83.

13 Ibid, 82.

14 Markale, Jean. *Women of the Celts* (Rochester, Vt.: Inner Traditions International, Ltd., 1972), 99.

15 Green, 31 and 34.

THE CRONE

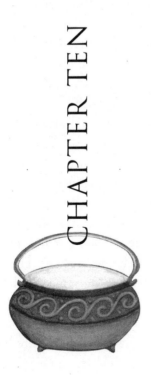

The crone both fascinates and repels, like a horror movie that we know will scare us out of a full night's sleep but still feel compelled to watch. The crone is our Halloween witch who rides her broomstick across the face of the autumn moon, she is the faery tale hag who lures children and young women to their doom with sweets,[1] and she is the woman on the street who is shunned and pushed aside simply because she is old and perceived as useless. But the crone is also our grandmother, our teacher, and our ultimate fate. We shall become her as we age, and we shall return to her when life on earth has run its course. Unfortunately, humans have always feared death; therefore, the crone becomes a constant reminder of that which we hold in dread and yet cannot avoid. This death image is further seen in the cessation of her "power times," or her menstrual cycles. Rather than shedding this blood of life, she retains it within herself, keeping the power locked inside her.

All too many books on Wiccan/Pagan practice still advise that it is best to leave this dark side of the Goddess alone, to restrict our explorations of divinity to the more comfortable virgin and mother aspects. Fortunately, this seems to be a slowly changing trend. To our own detriment, we shun the crone. To ignore her is to ignore a vital part of ourselves, and this cuts us off from some of the greatest spiritual knowledge available. As women it is especially important that we integrate the crone into our practices and recognize her within ourselves. Only by doing this can we be completely whole and open to the greater mysteries of women's spirituality. We must come face to face with her to know that important shadow self that is a part of us all.[2] When we achieve this knowledge, we can integrate all aspects of our being into one total wholeness. The resulting personal power is very strong.

The Celtic crone is a particularly strong archetype. Whereas the virgin contains most of the sovereign power and the mother most of the healing power, the crone contains the magickal or transformative power. As can be expected, there is some overlap between mother and crone imagery. This is especially seen in the crone's surprisingly sexual aspects. As a devourer of life, she is a Goddess to whom sacrifices are made. This image has caused a great deal of fear of her, especially among men.

This connection is made clearer through one of the symbols of the crone, the spinning wheel, an archetypal representation of her spinning the thread of life and clipping it at life's end. The distaff of the wheel, the spool on which the completed yarn is wound, was seen as a feminine magickal tool of great power. In the Teutonic traditions, there is even a festival honoring the distaff and its life and death imagery. One old Irish superstition says that one must never hit a male animal with a distaff or it will be rendered impotent.

Sexual sacrifice is another important part of Celtic spirituality, and is related strongly to Celtic annual fertility cycles (see Chapter 12) and to the devouring Goddess. The Sheila-na-Gig who opens her yawning vulva to us is one such image of a devourer with a sexual nature, consuming with her vagina rather than her mouth. In Latin this sexually devouring aspect was known as *vagina dentata*, meaning the "vagina with teeth."

When I was in high school, a particularly crude joke began circulating about a country boy whose mother warned him about the dangers of the "vagina with teeth" when he went off to the big city to live. Eventually the boy married, but on his wedding night refused to have sex with his bride because of what his mother had told him. The bride spread wide her legs to show her new husband that she was not hiding anything between them. The young man's eyes grew wide with fear and he said, "You can't fool me. With lips like that, there's *got* to be teeth!"

In many cultures around the world this devourer image was so greatly feared that the mouths of human women were deemed ugly and were required to be covered. Islamic and Chinese cultures provide two such examples. In

Islam, women are required to keep the lower half of their faces covered when in public, and Chinese women were once trained to lower their heads when they spoke and to cover their mouths when they laughed. There was also a prevalent belief in Europe that the reason women generally outlived men was that the old women were able to suck the life force from men to extend their own lives.[3]

Fear of having their life essence drained away by a woman, especially by an old woman, gave rise to a belief that a magickal object known as an *aiguillette*, a small noose-like piece of rope used in binding spells, was employed to take away male sexual potency. Though it is a interesting theory, no one ever has adequately explained why a woman would be motivated to do this.

This death Goddess aspect embodied by the crone is so strong that we often see her as being more pervasive in myth than she actually is. For example, the Morrigan is a much-talked-about Goddess, repeatedly explored in most texts on Celtic or women's spirituality, yet she is actually mentioned very few times in actual recorded mythology.[4] She is occasionally exaggerated to portray her in ways that emphasize her death aspects. Sometimes she is a Triple Goddess in the traditional sense of virgin, mother, and crone, but she is also portrayed as a triple crone form. This crone triplicity has little basis in mythology but still has become an important part of modern-day oral traditions.

One of the best-known aspects of the Celtic crone is the *Cailleach*, whose name means "old woman," and who has become a synonym for the "old hag" Goddess in Gaelic-speaking lands. She is sometimes portrayed as having a blue face, or as an evil faery whose magickal staff freezes to the touch, or as a veiled Goddess who hides her hideousness along with her mysteries.[5] To lift her veil is a metaphor for parting the symbolic curtain separating the Otherworld from our own. When we can do that, and successfully travel between the worlds, we have access to the mysteries of the crone. (Also see Chapter 14, "Feminine Celtic Shamanism.") The triple aspect of the Cailleach is evident from descriptions of her as having a white apron, red teeth, and black clothing.[6] The red teeth in this case are as much as indication of her devourer nature—as in the consumption of blood—as they are, in their color, part of her mother self.

In the old Breize or Brezonek language of Brittany, the crone is known as the *Groac'h*, another name that means "old woman" but that has taken on evil overtones and is now translated as "Witch." This is "Witch" in the mistaken sense, as in "a follower of the Christian anti-God Satan" and not as a follower of old European nature religions. The Groac'h appears as the antagonist in numerous Breton folktales, none of them portraying her in a flattering manner.

Attributes and Correspondences of the Crone

When reading through Celtic myths, legends, or folklore, the crone can generally be identified by these clues:

Has Shapeshifting Abilities

Other aspects of the Goddess can shapeshift; so can many Celtic faery women. However, the crone is a master shapeshifter, able to transform herself into animals at will. She is especially fond of becoming a bird. Birds in Celtic mythology represent the transition from life to death and are often used as symbols of movement between the world of the living and that of the dead. The crone can also shapeshift into her virgin form, usually in the spring. One of Ireland's great mythic books, *The Book of Lecan*,[7] emphasizes this cyclic nature of the Cailleach by telling us that she had seven youthful periods with seven different mates, after which she became a crone again. This connects her with the old cycles of regicide in which old kings had to die so that younger, stronger ones could mate with the Goddess of the land (see Chapter 12).

Depicted as a Devourer or Destroyer

The crone Goddess consumes life. Sometimes she is a war or battle Goddess like the Morrigan, who consumes in the heat of battle. At other times she is shown as physically large, her stomach full of humanity, as in the Welsh myth of Cymedei Cymeinfoll, known as the "big belly of battle." At still other times she is the Sheila-na-Gig, who offers her body as a portal to the greater mysteries, or a magician like Carman, a County Wexford Goddess, whose magick can destroy anything by thrice chanting a spell over it.

Lives in the Otherworld or Outside an Earthly Tribe

The imagery of the crone's world is clearly underworldly, concerning the dark aspects of the Otherworld. Due to modern folklore depicting the village wise woman as a crone Witch, she is sometimes seen as living on the fringes of the community, like the famous Witch Biddy Early (see Chapter 13).

Symbolized by Crows or Ravens

As carrion birds, the crow and the raven are strong Celtic symbols of the crone as a devourer. Badb, one of the Morrigan, is often seen as a crow, and in her triple form is often shown as a raven shrieking over the battlefields. Birds in Celtic mythology archetypally represent a transition from life to death,[8] and it was one of Badb's duties to help others make this transition so they could reach the Otherworld.

Takes Humans Into Otherworld Upon Death
Where sometimes a virgin Goddess or faery queen will take a human, usually a male, into the Otherworld for the purpose of mating with him, the crone takes humans into the Otherworld almost exclusively upon their death. The crow and raven imagery best shows this transition.

Presides Over War and Battles
Because war brings death, crone Goddesses like the Morrigan are present. Called an evil Witch, faery, or demon, like the Cailleach or Groac'h, the crone is often drawn in less-than-flattering terms. The words evil, old, hag, and ugly are often used to describe her.

Myths Perverted to Inspire Fear
The crone is often cast in a role where she is fearsome, as a war Goddess must be, and this image has been used to scare children into better, socially acceptable behavior. One example of this is Ireland's Moingfhion, whose name means "white-haired." Her myth concerns her attempted murder of her stepson. Archetypally, she plays the role of the crone who must kill and then mourn the dying God so that he may be reborn through her. But in modern Ireland, it is a Halloween custom to say prayers to protect one's self from her wrath, especially if one has children in the house.

Myth Makes Effort to Devalue or Diabolize Her
When it is clear that a myth or folktale has gone to extra lengths to cast one of its female figures in a lesser or demonic role, she is likely a crone being belittled out of fear. An example is the continental crone Goddess Carravogue, who was turned into a snake by a Christian saint for eating a forbidden food, a clear effort at making her a Celtic Eve responsible for the downfall of humanity.

Sometimes Shown As Having an Unpleasant Appearance
The Celtic crone cannot always be identified by her unpleasant appearance, and many Goddesses who fulfill other roles are depicted in less-than-pleasing ways. But if the image is one of hideousness coupled with old age or a devouring nature, then she is usually a crone aspect.

Possesses or Uses a Cauldron
The cauldron archetypally represents rebirth, a function over which the Celtic crone presides. Goddesses such as Cerridwen, Badb, and Cymedei Cymeinfoll are examples of cauldron bearers. In Celtic eschatology, or end of the world beliefs, it is a crone who will cause the end to come by boiling over the cauldron of life, death, and rebirth, engulfing the planet and turning it into a great wasteland.[9]

Associated with Burial Grounds or Sacred Ruins

Most of these Goddesses have become wicked faeries in modern folklore, though they were probably once crone Goddesses. Many of these now guard various burial cairns in Ireland and Scotland. Cally Berry, a north Irish version of the Cailleach, was said to have created Newgrange Cairn by dropping it into place boulder by boulder.[10]

Possesses Great Wisdom or the Gift of Prophecy

With age comes wisdom and, consequently, better divination skills, both attributes that the crone possesses in abundance. The crone Badb was said to have prophesied the downfall of the Tuatha De Dannan at the hands of the Milesians, and many believe she prophesied the Great Irish Potato Famine of 1845–1849. A Scottish Goddess of prophecy and transcendent knowledge, Corra, appears in the form of a crane. (Note the bird image!) In Wales, Drem, a prophetess in the employ of a Welsh king, had the power to know when someone was planning aggression against her country. Cerridwen and her cauldron of knowledge also readily come to mind when thinking of wise crones.

Teaches Tough Lessons

This aspect is seen more in the oral tradition and in women's traditions than in the original myths. Often the crone deals out harsh punishment or teaches hard lessons to her students or those on spiritual quests. This is a form of challenge to the seeker, who must face her deepest fears and uncertainties in order to progress, a concept found in mystery schools around the world, including the Celtic. Some guardian crone Goddesses and some of the women in Arthurian myths, such as Morgan LeFay, fit this image.

Can Control the Weather or Bring On Winter

The crone is also thought to be able to control the weather, and has been viewed as an evil faery because of this, particularly in Scotland, which has a host of weather-controlling faery lore. The Cailleach is one such example.

Because winter is the time of death and hibernation, the season in which life lies dormant awaiting rebirth, it is the season of the crone. Much Celtic folklore links the crone to this season. The already discussed Cailleach of Scotland is a prime example. In the modern folklore that has made her an evil faery, she is the queen of winter. In her gnarled blue hand she carries a staff that can turn anything it touches to ice and bring winter upon the landscape.

Questions About the Crone for Celtic Women

The following questions may be asked of yourself at any time in your exploration of the crone aspects. Whether you have been involved in Celtic Paganism for a long time, or whether you are just beginning to explore it, the crone has something to teach you.

What ideas and images does the word "crone" conjure up in my mind?

What about the words "hag," "harridan," "virago," and "Cailleach"?

How do I feel about the crone Goddess?

Do I now, or have I ever, feared the crone? What caused this fear?
How did I end the fear? Or, if it is still an issue, how do I plan
to end the fear?

Do I feel the crone has any relevance to my life now? Why or why not?

Do I feel a kinship with the crone or am I at odds with her?

Does the crone make me feel jealousy? Unease? Joy? Why?

Am I comfortable with the crone archetype? Why or why not?

How do I imagine the men in my life feel about the crone Goddess?
Does any aspect of their feelings threaten or comfort me?

What do I hope to get out of working with the crone Goddess?
What do I think or expect her to give to me?

What can I offer the crone in return?

What do I not expect the crone to be able to do for me?

Can I easily relate the crone aspect of the Goddess to her other two forms?

What crone aspects do I possess or not possess? Which of these would I
like to change if I can?

Crone Meditation and Exercise

Set aside a block of time when you can be the crone. This can be a few hours
or an entire day. During this time allow your thoughts and outward actions to
be those archetypally belonging to the crone. Allow everything you do or
plan during this time to be born of the inner wisdom of your crone self. Go
through this time fully aware of your inner power, wield it quietly and well,
and celebrate your aging processes.

During this period you must be able to interact with at least one other person who is unaware that you are indulging your crone self. If you can interact with more than one person at this time, all the better. This contact will allow you to gauge the reactions of others to your crone aspect.

As soon as possible after this exercise, find some private time to meditate on the qualities of the crone Goddess and how they are and are not manifest within you, regardless of your chronological age. Be sure to write down your impressions in a Book of Shadows or magickal diary for future reference.

Rituals of Wisdom: Celebrating the Crone

We all have flashes of wisdom, times we feel "older than our years" or when mysteries make themselves known to us and, to our delighted astonishment, we fully comprehend them. This is the province of the crone.

Times you may especially want to celebrate, honor, or petition the crone through ritual are:

- When you reach menopause, or are going to a ritual to celebrate someone else's having reached reached menopause
- Upon a death
- During rituals of passing over (these are rites that memorialize a deceased loved one)
- When doing divinations pertaining to profound change, endings, knowledge, wisdom, death, war, self-confidence, and women's mysteries
- When mourning the death of the God in autumn
- When the sun is weakening in autumn
- When the waning crescent moon first appears in the night sky

In Celtic crone rituals the featured color is almost always black, though sometimes gray, orange, or brown is seen. You may want to find one of those thick pillar candles that boasts three wicks for use in your ritual. A black one can be used to honor the crone while still acknowledging her other two faces who are present but unseen. Autumn-related libations are best for the crone: fruits (especially apples), wines, berries, pumpkins, and all late-autumn produce.

A variation on the circle appropriate to the crone is to use a half-circle. Plan your ritual space up against a wall or rocky outcropping. Physically draw it as far as you can, then mentally complete it behind the barrier. This barrier is perfect for representing the "unknown," an attribute deeply associated with the crone. (See Appendix C for step by step methods for circle castings.)

Notes

1 These images can be seen in the faery tale crones of *Snow White* and *Hansel and Gretel*.

2 Mynne, Hugh. *The Faerie Way* (St. Paul, Minn.: Llewellyn, 1996), 21.

3 Walker, Barbara G. *The Crone: Woman of Age, Wisdom, and Power* (San Francisco: HarperCollins, 1985), 18.

4 Caldecott, Moyra. *Women in Celtic Myth* (London: Arrow Books, 1988), 138.

5 Matthews, Caitlin. *The Elements of the Celtic Tradition* (Shaftsbury, Dorset: Element Books, 1989), 21.

6 Monaghan, Patricia. *The Book of Goddesses and Heroines* (St. Paul, Minn.: Llewellyn, 1990), 66.

7 Irish Educational Institute. *Yellow Book of Lecan, Vol.. 1* (Dublin: Irish Texts Society, 1940).

8 Markale, Jean. *Women of the Celts* (Rochester, Vt.: Inner Traditions International, Ltd., 1972), 113 and 116.

9 Walker devotes an entire chapter to the cauldron imagery of the crone: Chapter 5, 99–122.

10 Condren, Mary. *The Serpent and the Goddess: Women, Religion and Power in Celtic Ireland* (San Francisco: Harper & Row, 1989), 82.

THE ART OF RITUAL DRAMA
Re-Discovering Celtic Mythic Teachings

No, the spelling of re-discovery is not a typo. Many feminist writers have adopted the practice of breaking apart common words at unusual places to emphasize the deeper meanings within them. In this case, our goal is literally to discover again, or re-discover, the mythic mysteries that have been left within such easy reach, yet often go unrealized.

How To Learn from the Celtic Myths

Myths are living things, ever-evolving with the people who read and retell them. Many of them are pure fantasy, and others contain elements of historical truth blended with fantasy and spiritual teachings.

All religions are based on mythologies that tell us about the nature of our deities, the origins of the universe, our place within it, and how and when we can expect it will end. Within that framework it is easy to see how the myths have evolved over time to shove out the feminine aspects. It is the job of women's spirituality to restore those aspects to their rightful place, alongside that of the male creator deity.

So just how much change has occurred over time in the Celtic myths? That is hard to say for sure, but certain delineations are clear.

Welsh mythologist Sir John Rhys wrote at the turn of the century that any mythology is much more ancient than the oldest written verses that first codified it.[1] Certainly it is a given that in virtually all ancient societies, the original creation myth involved either a male and a female deity, or a woman alone.[2] Egocentric or not, people all insist that we are created in the image of the deities. But it is women who have the wombs. Women give birth. Therefore female deities—Goddesses—give birth to creation. This is not to take away from the masculine contribution—it takes one of each gender to create new life—but since the male God has been touted for several millennia as the sole arbiter of creation, we do no one injustice by strongly asserting the feminist viewpoint here.

The nature of Celtic deities and their relationships with one another are also telling. The Celts did not view their deities as being all-powerful or all-knowing. They had many human qualities, including common character flaws such as jealousy and anger. They were revered for the powers they represented, their mastery over certain elements, or their connection with either the Otherworld or a specific aspect of nature. Most of the time the words God and Goddess do not even appear in mythic texts. This is just as well, since the Irish words for the deities imply a lesser status for the feminine divine. The Irish word for Goddess is *Bandia*, meaning "woman God." (*Ban* = woman, *Dia* = God) Yet the word for God is simply *Dia*, not *Feardia*, which would be "man God." This implies that a God stands alone, but a Goddess must have her title qualified. In Wales the linguistic prejudice is lessened with the word *Dew* meaning God, and *Dewies* meaning Goddess. The addition of the feminine ending is much more in keeping with the English words and is less offensive to the feminist mind.

Ironically, the best guidepost we have for learning to read between the lines in myths is in the Book of Genesis in the Judeo-Christian Bible. When the old priests (the *kohanim*) began fiddling with the creation myths, they got in a rush and made a few oversights. The text concerning the creation of humanity translates into "And in his image he created them, male and female *they* created them" (emphasis mine).

Ah ha! *They* created them in *their* image—male and female. A very telling slip of the old quill pen. Like most ancient cultures, the early Hebrews also had a Goddess, a feminine half of the universal divine, known as the Shekinah. Sadly, the legends surrounding her have been so downplayed that she is little more than a caricature of a Goddess today, honored on Friday nights as the "sabbath bride" who brings peace to the sabbath day rather than as a divine presence in her own right.

When reading Celtic myths we need to be aware of places where the extant story does not fit in with the known patterns of old Pagan cultures. The monks who transcribed the Celtic myths were writing in a later period (800–1400 C.E.), at a time when the oral legends had already evolved under patriarchy. It is likely they wrote the myths very much the way they heard them at the time, though there are some clear interpolations of Christian doctrine in many of them. Read critically—good advice no matter what subject you choose to study.

The Sacred Art of Ritual Drama

One of the best ways to work with myth hands-on is through ritual drama. Ritual drama is the art of using live theater as an inherent part of spiritual rituals. This practice is as ancient as humanity, and is currently finding a great revival in modern Paganism.

The oldest roots of modern theater can be found in the religious rites of the long past. The earliest acting roles were taken by shamans, who would adorn themselves in animal skins and mimic a successful hunt on behalf of their tribes. In ancient Greece, where modern theater is said to have begun, all dramas were ritual in nature. Their main purpose was to point out how humanity was nothing more than a plaything of the deities. At the climax of every production, an actor portraying a deity would be lowered from the heavens to wisely put right all that had gone wrong during the course of the play. So widespread was this dramatic structure that even today it bears a name: *deus ex machina,* or "God from a machine."

In ancient Rome and Greece, ritual drama was employed in the temples to reenact the springtime rebirth of Kore/Persephone, who had spent the previous six months in the underworld. In Egypt, the life cycles of many deities were honored in sacred drama, most notably the resurrection of the death God Osiris. In east Asia today, many spiritual dramas are used both in and out of temples. The Passion Plays of Easter, depicting the death and resurrection of Jesus, are direct descendants of the ancient ritual drama.

Ritual drama does not appear to have had a strong Celtic following, but my Celtic coven used to create quite elaborate ritual dramas, all to good affect. Once we began working with these on a regular basis and had produced a repertoire of both semi-freeform and well-planned scripts, we added the element of invocation, and suddenly our dramas were not just for offering honor or praise to the deities, but they were learning experiences as well.

Another benefit of ritual drama is the way it allows us to incorporate desirable archetypes into our personalities as we act out their mythic themes. In the safety of an all-female environment, we can take on the persona of strong feminine figures and play "superheroes," as our brothers did while growing up. By using this role playing in a ritual setting, and by teaching it to the young girls in our care, we can see to it that tomorrow's women grow up accepting these strong feminine archetypes as integral parts of their total being. This is especially important for women who have not felt they had the freedom to express themselves in heroic roles—usually true for the majority of today's adult women. This lack is seen most vividly in adolescence, a period during which developmental psychologists say female self-esteem and self-confidence take a dramatic plunge.

Properly defined, invocation is a theurgical art, the art of drawing the essence of a deity into the physical self. The widely practiced ritual of Drawing Down the Moon, in which a priestess takes on the persona of the mother Goddess during the full moon, is a good example of a modern usage of invocation.[3] I once was of the belief that only women should invoke female deities and men invoke male deities, but I learned some years ago how limiting this is. We all possess the strengths of the other gender within us and, just like we have to acknowledge all aspects of the inner Triple Goddess to be whole, we also have to acknowledge our gender-opposite aspects.

One of the greatest eye-openers for my coven in using ritual drama was how quickly and clearly it showed us which deities shared compatible energies, which worked well together, which clashed, which were not so powerful as we had been led to believe, which are not comfortable with humans, and which were just not interested in being part of us. It was a profound learning experience, one that I still employ in solitary practice.

Yes, a solitary can work ritual drama almost as well as a group. What you lose out on is some of the interaction of energies you get when an entire group has taken the time to ritually invoke individual deities one at a time. But, in some ways, all the players are still present. Recall when you were a child, playacting alone in your room or backyard. You were literally in another world—at least as far as your mind was concerned. All around you were other characters with whom you interacted. At the time you were playing they were all very real to you. So deep into your own character were you that, if you were interrupted to come in to lunch, very often you did not hear your mundane name being called. You might even have rushed breathlessly around telling your caregiver all about your recent adventure.

The key to successful solitary ritual drama is to recapture that youthful excitement and lose yourself in the inner world that you create within your circle, just as the child you once were could do so easily. This can be done either physically or through guided meditation (see Appendix E).[4] Which method works best for you will depend on your prevailing mood and your skill level in eyes-open altered state of consciousness work. Some solitaries do better to keep their eyes closed and work solely on the inner plane rather than try and engage in physical action that, admittedly, can be jarring.

Guidelines for Creating Ritual Dramas

Treat all ritual drama as a sacred rite. Cast your circle, call your quarters, and honor your deities (see Appendix C). This is especially advised if you will be invoking divine energies rather than just "acting" them out. The divine is sacred and requires sacred space. During invocation you will be opening yourself up to allow outside energies to merge with your own, and you will want to be absolutely sure the area around you is friendly only to the highest spiritual beings. It has been shown that negative or lower level spirits cannot enter space where the spiritual vibrations are at a high level. The two are just not compatible. Anger, illness, or negative intent can cause the vibrational level of your sacred space to drop, which is why a circle should only be cast after you are purified in mind and body and are focused solely on the purpose of your ritual.

If you are in a group, decide well ahead of time if you want to invoke deities or not. Some people are uncomfortable with this process, and it should not be required for anyone. The ritual will work as well without invocation, though you will miss out on some deeper interaction between deities.

There are numerous ways to invoke a deity,[5] and you may need to experiment both to find the one that works best for you and to build the relationship with the divine that allows full merging of energies. Three of the methods you can use to begin your experimentation are:

Directing a Wand or Blade to the Point of Origin
This is the same method usually used for Drawing Down the Moon, in which a projective ritual tool is aimed at the place where the Goddess is imagined to be. The energy is invited into the tool, then transferred through visualization and will into the body via a chakra point such as the forehead, solar plexus, or navel.

115

Mental Merging

This method involves the eyes-closed visualization of the Goddess coming toward you from the Otherworld. When you are face to face, turn your back to the Goddess and allow her to step into your physical self.

Drawing the Energy Up or Down

While standing straight, visualize the energy of the Goddess as dwelling either in the upperworld directly above you or the underworld directly below you. Visualize a beam of pure light energy coming from that place and entering you, engulfing you with its power. Invite the Goddess along that beam of light and into yourself.

Groups often like to have one or more persons assist the one who is invoking, either by drawing in the energy through their own tools or by verbally directing the course of the merging visualizations.

For best results, whether you are alone or with a group, make sure to pre-plan certain aspects of your ritual drama. You do not have to follow a blow-by-blow script but you do have to have some markers for what you will be doing. If people are wondering what they are supposed to do next, they will not be participating in a spiritual rite as much as trying to "upstage" others.

If you are in a group, give everyone who will be present a part and decide who will lead the drama. Call this person the director if you like; she will be the one who keeps things going, cues the actors for their parts, and gets things back on track after they have taken off on tangents.

Both solitary and group ritual dramas should allow for tangents. This is not a stage play, where the floor beneath you is marked with tape to lead your every step. There are no drama critics around the circle. You should certainly allow for flexibility and spontaneity, for this is when you are most likely to learn how the deities interact with one another. These tangents will happen most often when you are in a group and have invoked a number of deities. They are *real* beings, not stage characters, and they will not hesitate to take things in a new direction if they feel it is needed.

It is most important to carefully choose the myth you wish to work with. In a ritually cast circle, all energies are naturally magnified, and you don't want a random negative aspect creating havoc within your circle. If you are in a group, you all need to agree beforehand on which version of the myth you want to work with: old, new, revisionist, or some other text. This is why some preplanning is necessary—to keep each individual from trying to force her own interpretation of the myth to come into the foreground.

Some of the myths that make good beginning ritual dramas for Celtic women are those surrounding Brighid (the creation of keening), Blodeuwedd (her trickery of Llew and her transformation into an owl), and Rhiannon (her being accused of killing her son, and her punishment as servant outside the gates of her husband's kingdom) and in the heroic tales of warriors such as Boudicca (who fought and won against the Romans). These tales are easy to find in almost any book on Celtic myths or folklore. (See the Bibliography for some specific titles.) You might want to look into several of these to compare versions and interpretations.

If no one wishes to take on a male role, you should feel free to rewrite the myths or arrange the scenes so that all women get female parts. Talk about the events in which men participated, rather than acting them out, and you may find that the feminine viewpoint on them becomes much clearer.

Allow your feminine intuition to guide your ritual dramas. Recall once more your inner child, who could practice this art so well. When you work alone you will find this easy, but it can also be achieved in group efforts. When I was thirteen I often played at dramas with three best girlfriends. Many of these were based on our personal fantasies and dreams for the future, or involved either famous actors or local boys on whom we had crushes. Sometimes we used the dramas to deal with problems at school that seemed insurmountable. Often the dramas showed us solutions we might not otherwise have found. We knew our basic storyline beforehand, and we allowed our inner selves to guide the direction of what became very complex "soap operas." So vivid and real did these become that when I look back on them today, I can recall entire sequences, and admit to having trouble separating the three of us from the many imaginary figures who populated our dramas.

When your ritual drama is complete, release the invoked energy by reversing the process you used to invoke. It is best to use the same process coming and going to help keep the conscious mind, which loves logic and often resists the spiritual, happy with the process. After the invoked energy is released, you may dismiss the quarters and close the circle.

Notes

1 *Celtic Folklore: Welsh and Manx* (Oxford: Clarendon Press, 1901).

2 VonFranz, Marie-Louise. *Creation Myths* (Boston: Shambhala Publications, Inc., 1995; originally published 1972).

3 For a detailed ritual script of a Drawing Down the Moon ritual, please see my earlier work, *Lady of the Night: A Handbook of Moon Magick and Ritual* (St. Paul, Minn.: Llewellyn, 1995).

4 I refer you to my earlier work, *Celtic Myth & Magick*, which gives detailed instructions for creating guided meditations with divine archetypes, and provides three pre-written paths with which you can begin to experiment.

5 I wrote in detail about both invocation and evocation (the art of inviting the presence of the divine without bringing it within you) in *Celtic Myth & Magick*.

THE DIVINE SOVEREIGN

The Goddess as the personification of the land, who is wedded to the sacred king who rules over it, is at the heart of the Celtic concept of the divine. The land was the true sovereign. It provided everything needed by humanity. It nurtured and it taught. The land was ever faithful. It was only when people failed to remember to honor the land that nature appeared to turn against them.

Unfortunately, this ancient belief, one of the few unifying elements among the Celts, took a beating in the intervening centuries and is only now being restored to its rightful place as a central feature of Celtic Paganism. But even among those who seek to restore this aspect, it occasionally remains misunderstood.

One of my first exposures to this concept and its perversion came when I was only fifteen, reading Thomas Tryon's bestselling novel *Harvest Home*,[1] about an old fertility cult in modern New England. The cult members kept alive the practice of hallowing and sacrificing the sacred king by forcing unwilling young men to play this role. The result was something of a horror novel that kept all the death imagery but failed to show the eternal rebirth aspects of the sacred king.

Shortly after I read this book, the movie version of the stage musical *Camelot* was released, a show about King Arthur and Guinevere. One man who had seen the show remarked to me, "See that? It was a woman who brought down the perfect kingdom." The comment stung. More than that, on some intuitive level I knew that was not the message I was supposed to be getting from this legend. Here was Guinevere, married to an aging king, yet wanting the strong, youthful knight. Her reward? Charges of treason.

Treason? It just didn't quite make sense. There was definitely something amiss in both the book and the musical, but it would be many more years before I could figure it all out.

The idea that the land is the Goddess, sovereign and supreme, and that there was a king who was wedded to the land, is an ancient one that still echoes through the lands the Celts inhabited. Over the centuries the process by which the king has been wed, or hallowed, has altered, but the concept remains the same. The king becomes the God incarnate, marries the Goddess and, like her consort, must die so that she may give him rebirth and begin anew the cycles of life. It is through her gift of sacred marriage that consent is given to him to rule. When she withdraws from the marriage, as Guinevere did with Arthur, then he is no longer able to remain king. A new, younger, stronger king must be chosen to replace him so that the land and its people can remain strong and healthy.

So intricately wedded to the land was the king that, in old Ireland, it was decreed that the king must be *"blemish free."*[2] Any weakness, scar, or disfigurement, no matter how small, disqualified one for kingship. This was because the king so deeply represented the land that what befell him would befall the land. If he was blighted, so would be the land, its people, and its animals.[3] It was the duty of the Goddess/queen, who was the land, to do what was best for it by mating with the new, younger king, and discarding the old.

It is only within this framework that the charge of treason against Guinevere makes any sense. Can you imagine a queen today being accused of treason because she chose to sleep with another man? Guinevere's "crime" was not her infidelity to a man but her fidelity to the land she represented. When she turned to another man she was, in fact, granting him the right to rule Camelot, to replace the old king, Arthur. A woman did not bring down the perfect kingdom but saved it by granting her sacred marriage to the one best suited to represent the land. Guinevere was accused of treason only because, through her, Arthur would lose his throne.

A similar glitch in interpreting Celtic history dates to first-century Britain when the woman warrior and chieftain Cartimandua left her chieftain husband and made another man her lover. The result of this was an inter-tribal war similar to that presented to us in the Camelot legends.[4]

Since when do people go to war because the wife of a head of state chooses to sleep with another man? If this were common practice, the world would be even more constantly at war than it is now. This dissension among Celtic tribes can only be adequately explained when the leaders are assuming the ancient roles of sovereign Goddess and sacred king. The Celtic myths clearly show us that troubles in paradise ensue not when the Goddess/queen takes another lover, but when the old God/king fights the inevitable change in leadership.

That this concept was perverted by the patriarchy is not surprising.[5] In many cultures, women's mysteries and power cycles suffered similar blows. Most notable is the use of the menstrual lodges of the tribes of the Native North Americans. The menstrual period was once viewed as a time when women were at their most powerful and it was for this reason only that they separated from the men of the tribe during this time, to enter a sacred space in order to take part in the women's mysteries with other women.[6] Over time the separation began to be viewed as something to protect men, not from the Goddess-like power of women, but from the "evilness" of their blood.

Celtic myths are rife with references to sacred kings, though many have been buried under centuries of patriarchal debris that paint the woman/God-dess in the role of temptress or whore who leads her mate to destruction due to her infidelities. Again, this fear goes back to the image of woman as the de-vourer, the one who consumes life as freely as she gives it. From blood men are born, and in blood they die.

Such triangular arrangements are popular features in Celtic myth. Some-times it is two male lovers who fight for the sovereign Goddess; at other times it is a father who is fighting with a son or a potential son-in-law, the new God/king destined to replace him. But in all the myths two themes remain: the concept of the sacred number three as being one of action and creation, and the concept that the Goddess is supreme and that only she can grant a God/king the legitimacy of his kingship.

The Irish *seanachai*, or storytellers, differentiated between love stories of wooing and elopements and love stories involving these sacred trios. These latter were called *secra*, or tales of "Loves" in which two men eternally con-tested over one woman and the powers she brought to the victor. One uniting feature of these *secra* is that most of them take place in May, the month of the Bealtaine festival when the sacred marriage of the God and Goddess is cele-brated. Often the culmination of the tale was made to fit the season. The man who represents the dark lord aspect, or underworld, is victorious at Samhain, the point in autumn when the dark part of the year begins and the land lies barren. The dark lord takes the sovereign Goddess to his underworld realm where she cannot bless the land with her fertility until she is won or stolen back by the light or bright lord in the spring (or at the festival of Bealtaine, the point opposite Samhain on the Celtic solar calendar).

Among these sacred Celtic trios are:

- Isolde with King Mark of Cornwall and Tristan (uncle and nephew)

- Guinevere with King Arthur and Lancelot (king and warrior)

- Morgan LeFay with King Arthur and Modred (father and son)

- Creiddylad with Gwythyr Ap Greidawl (a solar deity/warrior) and Gwyn Ap Nuad (an underworld ruler and leader of the "Wild Hunt," a nighttime quest for souls for the underworld)

- Grainne with Fionn MacCumhal and Diarmuid (old warrior and young warrior)

- Olwen with Ysbadadden and Culwch (woman's father and his potential son-in-law)

- Queen Maeve with King Ailell and several other men (king and warriors of their kingdom)

- Blodeuwedd with Llew and Grown (uncle and nephew)

- Deirdre with King Cormac and Naoise (older king and young warrior)

- Dubh Lacha with Bradubh (an Ulster king whose name means "black raven" and who represents the dark half of the year and death) and Mongan (a warrior who represents the sun and the light half of the year)

- Blathnat with CuRoi (a Fianna warrior) and Cuchulain (an Ulster warrior who took many wives and lovers)

- Rhiannon with Gwawl (a warrior whose name means "light) and Pwyll (a king of the underworld), representing two halves of the year with "ownership" of Rhiannon as their turning point

- Branwen with Mathowch (a Welsh king) and Bran (a war chief and a deity who represented protection and divinatory powers)

- Edain and King Eochaid (a mortal king) and Midhir (a "faery" king who represents the underworld)

- Goewin with Math Ap Mathowch and several other men (king and warriors of his kingdom), and with the twins Gwydion and Gilfaethwy.

Not all sacred kings fought the inevitable change in kingship. In numerous fairy tales, many of which are Celtic in origin, we see kings who offer their daughters to men in their kingdom for some display of great bravery. This offering has been interpreted by modern feminists as showing the man's ownership of the women of his household when, in truth, it is the king's way of selecting his own successor. By giving a royal woman, he was offering not just a mate but the gift of sovereignty, the right to rule the land.

When the king was wed to the land he became a God of fertility, able like the Goddess to pass along his powers of fruitfulness to his people. This is likely the rationale behind an old Irish law known by the French term *droit de seigneur*,[7] allowing the king first right to bed a new bride on her wedding night.

This image of the old God/king being replaced over and over again is echoed in the myths concerning the turning of the wheel of the year. At the two solstices we are presented with the symbolic struggle between two forces, one representing waxing energies and another representing waning energies. At these turning points in time, one aspect is victorious and the other "dies," then the battle is picked up again in six months with the former loser becoming the victor. The Oak King (waxing year) and Holly King (waning year), the Red Dragon (waxing year) and White Dragon (waning year), and the eternal battle of Gwythyr (waxing year) and Pwyll, Lord of the Underworld (waning year), are prominent examples whose battles are often reenacted in Pagan circles at the changing points of the year. Whenever a woman is involved in the battle myth, she is undeniably representing the sovereign spirit of the land. She does not choose the younger, stronger man for selfish reasons but because it is her duty to select the best ruler to be joined with her in sacred marriage. The most fit ruler makes the most fit land.

In many Celtic myths the older, outgoing king does not struggle physically with another man but against the inevitable tide of time, and puts up a fight to keep his sovereignty. One example of this is in the Welsh myth surrounding Olwen. Olwen wants to marry Culwch, but her father, King Ysbadadden, sets up obstacles of nearly insurmountable proportions because it has been foretold to him that a grandson of his would slay him and take his throne. This is clearly meant in the context of the sacred king, yet the old king fights to keep his place. Another grandfather and grandson sacred duo of battlers are Lugh and Balor, both sun Gods. Lugh slays Balor and represents not only a change in sacred kingship but the turning of the wheel of the solar year from dark half (waning sun) to bright half (waxing sun).

Hallowing the Sacred King

Unlike the hapless young man called Worthy in Tryon's *Harvest Home*, the sacred king of Celtic lore meets his sacrificial death willingly and with full awareness that it is for this duty that he was born and to this end that he took his vows of office. Even in the modern-day British coronation ceremony, many aspects of hallowing, of wedding the monarch to the land, remain intact.

One did not become a sacred king by accident. The best man for the land got the job, which may be one of the reasons why the early Celts did not adhere to the custom of primogeniture, where the eldest son inherited everything, including a throne. One had to prove one's worth and then be made sacred through symbolic wedding of the Goddess of the land. At various stages in Celtic history, and in different parts of the Celtic world, this process was handled in slightly different ways.

In general, all the Celtic legends involve the *hallowing* of the king, or making him sacred by giving him an object or talisman of empowerment that he is to use and guard.[8] This item most often—but not always—has its origins either in stone, which is symbolic of the earth element, or in water. Both water and stone, as representatives of the earth element, are symbols of the divine feminine and of the sovereign essence of the earth itself.[9] At other times, the object is a gift from the sovereign Goddess herself.

Symbols of hallowing found in Celtic myth include banners, shields, cauldrons, chalices, grails, cloaks, mantles, crystals, stones, spheres, scepters, drums, blades, swords, game boards, harps, lances, spears, lamps, crane bags (magickal pouches similar to Native American medicine bags), runes, scabbards, staves, and wands.

Weapons are the most often seen hallows, and are among the most widely known in terms of popular legends. Ulster's greatest hero, Cuchulain, though not a king, was hallowed by the gift of an invincible spear from his teacher Scathach of the Gae Bolg. When thrown at an enemy, its barbed edges dealt a painful death. Like the sacred kings, Cuchulain was impervious to many spells and other maledictions impressed upon others. In his case, he was immune to the curse of Macha (discussed in Chapter 10) that affected the other Ulster warriors. He died at the hands of the forces of Queen Maeve, and his blood was spilled on the earth.

Bran the Blessed of Welsh mythology is given a cauldron that gives life, one of the most pervasive and important of the Celtic hallows, and one intimately associated with the Goddess. Also from the Welsh tradition is Gwyddiw Garanhir, who has a cauldron, or basket, that provides a neverending supply of food. Nuada of the Silver Hand is given a sword that, like the Gae Bolg, never fails to kill the enemy.

Probably the most famous of the hallows is Excalibur, the sword of sovereignty given to young King Arthur. Thanks to the book *The Once and Future King* by T. H. White[10] and to Walt Disney's animated movie *The Sword in the Stone*, most people are aware of the legend telling of the young Arthur being able to extract the sacred sword from a large stone after all the warriors of the kingdom had failed. Though these two presentations preserve the essence of the legend, they carefully worked around the Goddess's role. It is doubtful that this was intentional, but was merely the result of their creators using medieval texts, such as those of Mallory and Geoffrey of Monmouth, which had already created popular versions of the ancient legend that either eliminated, downplayed, or diabolized the Goddess.

In these "Christianized" versions, the stone from which Arthur pulled the sword was found in a churchyard. The idea is still that a divinity granted sovereignty, but in this case the focus has shifted from the ancient Goddess who was the sovereign of the land to the Christian God. This is where the modern concept of the "divine right of kings" comes from. In the original Arthurian myths, Excalibur was presented to Arthur by the Lady of the Lake, a Goddess who embodies the spirit of the land and the essence of the water element. Excalibur was embedded in a stone that either rested in her lap or floated on her lake, and it was from this that Arthur extracted his hallows.

The belief that a stone can be sovereign and has the right to bestow legitimacy of rulership is ancient. The most famous sovereign stone is without a doubt Ireland's *Lia Fail*, or Stone of Destiny, that was said to roar when the rightful ruler stepped onto her.[11] Another Lia Fail (or perhaps the same one, only stolen) was used in Scotland until the thirteenth century, when it was in turn stolen by England's Edward I. In London's Westminster Abbey, the stone that sits under the throne of the British monarch is said to be the same Lia Fail, still granting the gift of sovereignty to kings and queens.

Another famous stone that once had spiritual links is Ireland's Blarney Stone. If one can kiss the stone while leaning over backwards, it will bestow the gift of glib speech.[12] This was once likely a sovereignty stone that "gave life" to rulers the same way other cauldrons took away speech when used as a portal between worlds. This is seen in the myth of the battle between Ireland and Wales, in which the Welsh used the Cauldron of Rebirth to restore life to their warriors, though they came back to life minus their powers of speech.

All over the Celtic lands table-like stone formations, called dolmens, exist that likely served as altars in the past. Again, the symbology is that of earth/Goddess/female as the grantor of sovereign power. It was the use of stone as embodiment of the Goddess that gave rise to the use of human women—priestesses—as altars. Several references to old Pagan practices talk about using the body of a woman as the altar, a practice that has been perverted by those who do not understand its sacred significance and see it only as another opportunity to degrade the female body.

In some myths and legends, the hallows are known as the "four hallows." They relate to the four elements central to Pagan practice: earth (stone), water (chalice), fire (spear), and air (sword).[13] Sometimes only one element is present, such as that of air (or fire by some interpretations) symbolized in the Gae Bolg or Excalibur; at other times there are two or more hallows, each representing a different element. One excellent example of a four-fold hallows given to one man is the Four-Sided Cup of Truth presented to Ireland's High King Cormac MacArt. Myths vary on exactly who presented this cup to him, but at least one cites an Otherworld Goddess on one of his many trips there. In still other myths, there is a "palace" of the four hallows, either implied or actual, through which a potential sacred king must navigate and prove his worth while attaining his hallows and healing the scarred land.[14]

Sometimes the marriage of king to land is more sexually symbolic than the mere acceptance of a hallowing tool. The Irish kings at Emain Macha, the stronghold of the Ulster kings in present-day County Armagh, were at one time required to symbolically mate with the Goddess in her white horse guise.[15] We have already discussed the many Goddesses who took a horse form and, as such, symbolized the power of the sovereign. In Gaul they were important both in the economy and for war, as well as in a religious context.[16] When a king ritually mated with a horse who was a representation of the sovereign Goddess, it made him the sacred king, the mating act taking the place of his being offered a physical hallowing symbol. This union of Goddess and God is irrevocable, ending only with death, which is why a symbolic commemoration of this union, known as the Great Rite, is an integral part of modern Pagan practice. In the Great Rite symbols, or hallows, of the Goddess and God are united in ceremony to reenact their eternal sacred marriage. This is usually done by ritually placing an athame, or ritual blade (representing the phallus) into the chalice (representing the womb area of the Goddess). The ceremonies are quite moving and, when performed correctly, the energy they produce can be a tangible presence in the circle.[17]

It is not only the act of the Goddess mating with another man that removes sovereignty from the old king, but that of withholding sex as well. In a Breton legend we read of Princess Marcassa,[18] who refuses to sleep with a dying king. Only engaging in sex with her can cure his "disease." The Princess refuses and "hibernates" until the king dies, possibly a metaphor for going through a crone period until she is a sovereign virgin again in spring. When she awakens, she weds the young warrior of her choice.

The Sacred King as Sacrificial God

In keeping with the eternal cycles of birth, death, and rebirth that the Celtic God undergoes, the sacred king who accepts the role of God incarnate must also endure periodic sacrifices in order to keep the land fertile and healthy. Like a great cosmic father, his seed, in the form of blood, must be spilled on the land to fertilize it. To die a sacred death, the old king must shed his blood on the earth in a fertility rite so ancient that its origins are not pinpointable. As he performs this last act of love for his land, Goddess, and people, he dies so that his younger, more fit, self may step in and assume his place.

This concept—that it is the male who must die through a sexual act, one either symbolic or *de facto*—is part of what gave rise to the fearful myths of the devouring female examined in Chapter 2. But the symbolism is clear. After sexual intercourse, the women bears the seed of the man (sperm) and then contains within herself the potential for procreation. There are no scars and usually no outward evidence on the female body that a sexual act has taken place. For her, the process is internalized, the power taken within and turned into potential life. On the other hand, the male body shows evidence of spent sexual energy in the form of a detumescing penis that has voided itself of life-giving qualities and, to the naked eye, appears to be "dying." The same idea is present in the spilling of the blood of the sacred king on the earth which functions as the womb of the Goddess.

As time went on, the oral legends became even more perverted, casting all women in the devourer role, until much of the original meaning of the sovereign Goddess was forgotten. One such example is the Goddess Nair, a sovereign who came to personify regicide. Old Irish legends tell us that all kings who slept with Nair would die, but neglect to mention for what purpose.

The precise extent of the practice of sacred regicide, or king-killing, has been hotly debated for many decades, though in Ireland there is evidence that it may have persisted until at least the seventeenth century.[19] At the heart of the reign of the sacred king is the knowledge that he will also be called upon to die for the land in a sacred act in which his blood is spilled upon it, fertilizing the Goddess so that she can give birth anew to crops, animals, people, and—most importantly—so that she can mate with a stronger, younger sacred king.

In Margaret A. Murray's controversial book *The God of the Witches*,[20] she traces several kingly deaths to what she believed were sacred murders, thus building a case for the survival of Paganism in Britain and Ireland. That these religions have survived is a given, though her assertions that British monarchs, or their chosen substitutes, are still dying in sacred rites is open for debate. One intriguing look at this concept is presented by science fiction author Katherine Kurtz in her novel *Lammas Night*,[21] in which she builds on Murray's hypothesis to create a compelling tale surrounding ancient rites in World War II England. Though it downplays the Goddess element, it is a novel I highly recommend.

In modern Paganism we commemorate the death of the God/sacred king during the harvest season, usually at the sabbat, or solar festival known as Lughnasadh or Lammas. This coincides with the harvesting of first grains in much of the northern hemisphere, and it is in this harvest that the king is embodied. When the king weds the land, he shares its fate. When a plant gives up its fruit at the harvest, it begins to die, symbolically sacrificing itself for the good of the people. The sacred king also begins the dying process, one that is seen in many Pagan traditions as being completed in the late autumn when the last of the harvest has been taken in. In many Pagan traditions, Celtic or otherwise, the last sheaf harvested is kept and honored throughout the remainder of the year as a symbol of this sacrifice, of the living legacy of the deities. In other traditions it is woven into the form of a female, sometimes called the Corn Dolly, who represents the sovereign spirit of the land.

Even after death the sacred king's role as guardian of the land on behalf of the Goddess and her people does not come to an end. Bran the Blessed insisted that his head be buried near the present-day site of the Tower of London.[22] It was to face south to guard and warn against invasion. And King Arthur is said to be sleeping in a hidden cave with his warrior legions, awaiting the call of his people in need so he can rise again to defend them.

These legends of sleeping sacred kings are tied to the many legends of the wounded land, or wasteland, that only the restored, healthy king can cure. This is seen clearly in the Fisher King of Arthurian myths, in which a sacred king lies wounded ("blemished"), waiting to be healed by the return of his hallowing symbol. His wounds separate him from the power of sovereignty,[23] presumably because of the misuse of his power, and only the continuation of the sacred cycle of death, rebirth, and his rehallowing can restore him and the land he protects on the Goddess' behalf.[24]

Identifying the Sovereign Goddess

The Goddess of sovereignty comes in many guises, but learning to identify her is easy. In Celtic myth she is the one who symbolizes either the land or the right to rule over it. In some Celtic myths many of the sovereign Goddesses are hard for the uninitiated[25] to readily recognize, since many seem to play a lesser role than the males in the stories. Yet when examined with a knowledgeable eye it is clear that these Goddesses are at the very heart of the myths, for they represent the land and all that has befallen or shall befall it.

Not all sovereign Goddesses are involved in romantic triangles. Some simply embody the power of the land through their name, or by some action or place of association. These Goddesses belie their sovereign nature by being deities of places on earth: of streams, of stones, or of other natural landmarks. All these so-dubbed "minor" Goddesses of land features and water at one time functioned in sovereign roles for the clans or tribes that lived near them. In the Celtic traditions there are hundreds of these Goddesses, many of their names lost to us today. Occasionally male deities ruled some of these sites, but by far the female predominated.

Though she was never part of a romantic triangle, Eire, for whom Ireland is named,[26] is the supreme sovereign of that island. She has been worshiped by modern Pagans as both a sovereign and Goddess of protection. In the earliest oral traditions, Eire was created along with the land. (Though the myths do not say who or what did the creating!) In later myths, Eire was said to be a daughter of Dagda and Delbaeth, a virgin aspect of a Triple Goddess that included her sisters Banbha and Foldha, whose names are also used poetically as synonyms for Ireland. Eire's magick was so potent that she was able to toss mud balls, which became living warriors, down on the Milesian (Celtic) invaders. She won the initial battle, but still lost the island to the Milesians. Out of respect for her display of power, the bard, Amergin, agreed to name the island in her honor.

Eire's symbol was the harp, an emblem that still stands as a proud symbol of Ireland's sovereign spirit. The harp has graced Irish flags and coinage, and the Irish have defended this symbol with the same ferocity that modern soldiers display in honor of the flags of their respective nations.

Another sovereign whose fame is honored in the name of a country is the Anglo-Celtic Goddess Brigantia, also known as Brittania, symbol of the sovereign spirit of Great Britain. She was also a Goddess of fire, crafting, and inspiration, like her Irish counterpart Brighid. In 1667, King Charles II revived an old Romano-Celtic custom and had Brittania's face put back on English coinage, where it remains today.

When nations attempt to chronicle the achievements of the first human to set foot on their lands, they often look to the story of a man, a foreign explorer or warrior, whether or not indigenous people had already lived there. Columbus and his "discovery" of the Americas is one such example. The indigenous people of the Americas already knew it was there, so technically it had already been discovered many centuries earlier. Ireland's first human was a woman named Cessair, who led her people, the Partholans, through a great deluge that left only three women and fifty men alive. As such, she is considered Ireland's first ruler and sovereign. Some scholars hypothesize that she was once a pre-Celtic mother Goddess, since her myth credits her literally as being a source of life's regeneration and renewal.

Another famous sovereign of the land is Taillte, a Goddess of the earth, competition, harvest, first grains, and particularly of wheat, which is a feminine fertility symbol. She has been called "the foster mother of light," which has been interpreted by some as meaning she is the mother of the sun, indicating that she may be part of an old, lost creation myth in which the Goddess gives birth to the sun before creating anything else. Similar themes are echoed in both the oral and written creation myths of several other cultures. Many of Ireland's famous year-and-a-day trial marriages (see Chapter 1) were celebrated on the great playing field she had cleared near Tara.

One sovereign Goddess who was never directly connected with the land, yet was clearly a sovereign, was Goewin, the official "footholder" of Wales' King Math. He was permitted to rule only so long as he kept his feet planted in her lap. The only excuse for removing them was going to war. Goewin also stood up for herself when Math attempted to make her a slave, and she was at the heart of several battles and stories of rape,[27] all of which tell us she was a sovereign, and that mating with her was a must for any man who wished to rule Wales.

Queen Maeve, and the other women of legend who splintered from her myths, served many archetypal functions, including that of sovereign.[28] This Connacht Goddess, made into a queen by the transcribers of the myths, personifies the heights of feminine power. Some texts present Maeve as "promiscuous," a necessary attribute for a sovereign who must mate with the men who are best able to rule the land. Her warrior and sexual aspects are quite strong, and some legends record that she often boasted that she could sexually exhaust thirty men in a night. Both of these were part of how she protected the land.[29] Her husband, King Aillel, who plays only a passing role in his wife's myths, always seemed to understand that it was Maeve's duty to take other lovers from among their warriors. One myth records his saying that this was something she "has to do." Whether this is an open admission acknowledging her sovereignty or a casual acceptance of her infidelity is open for debate. In any case, Aillel did not try very hard to keep Maeve from taking lovers.

A Leinster queen named Maeve Lethderag, or "Half Red," likely a splintered version of Connacht's Maeve, was the wife of nine different High Kings in succession. Note here the use of the sacred three times three. This Maeve would allow no king to sit at Tara without her as his wife.

In Wales and Cornwall, an archetypal guardian of the feminine mysteries and Goddess of sovereignty is Condwiranmur, wife of Sir Percival of the Arthurian myths. After he marries and has sex with her, he returns to the sealed Grail Castle for the second time, and this time is admitted. When blessed by her sovereignty, he becomes one of the three knights who achieves the quest of finding the grail, another feminine symbol of sovereignty.

The search for the grail is ultimately a search for the sovereign. Only when she is brought back to the "wounded land" can it be healed and made whole again. Like the Goddess in the underworld, the missing grail represents a people cut off from the fertile and life-giving powers of the sovereign Goddess of the land. The grail myths serve as a warning of what happens when we forget to honor the land, and nature turns against us, as it has in our modern world.

Goddesses who return to a virgin state upon having sexual relations with men are also sovereigns. In Chapter 6 I mentioned Flaithius, who made this transformation, decreeing that her lover, Niall of the Nine Hostages, would become a great High King. Since many of the Goddess myths have been devalued into "faery tales," a great many of these transformative deities are found within Celtic folk legends surrounding faery women. Nearly all of them involve female figures who are intimately associated in some way with the land, making their identity as sovereigns unmistakable.

One of these faery tale women is the Irish Goddess Becuna, who became the faery mistress of High King Conn. She felt she was not being treated with the respect her station deserved and decided to seek vengeance by bringing mass infertility to Ireland's people, animals, and land. In this aspect she represents the crone of winter, a time when the land lies fallow and the animals rest. In the myth, another faery woman of the same name, representing Becuna's virgin/spring and sovereignty aspects, banishes the crone faery aspect and restores the fertility to Ireland.

131

Numerous other heroines and Goddesses have sovereign attributes, and the old myths need only be read to ferret them out. Many times the imagery is quite evident, but at other times it must be looked for more closely.

Building on these legends, many modern Celtic Pagans still hallow sacred kings in the form of their priests, and it is still women who hold the key to his leadership.

Using Modern Ritual to Hallow the Sacred King

Rituals in which a woman is made the earth sovereign who hallows a man as sacred king are fairly common in modern Celtic-based covens. My mixed-gender Irish coven in Texas did this each August. We would select one woman to act as sovereign. Then the eight female members of the coven would do a private ritual with her, in which we established her connection to the earth through meditation and symbolically invest her as the earth's queen. This was done by having her lie prone on the earth and guiding her through a meditation in which she melded her energies with the earth's. She was directed to visualize the condition of the land, to allow its spirits to speak with her, to watch them acknowledge her as a holy part of itself. We would anoint her as one would a queen, and we would remind her of her responsibility to the coven in the coming year. It would be her duty to look out for the land on which we met, to protect it and make sure it was being used in a fitting manner. She would also be called upon to serve the coven at times when gaps in leadership or communication had to be filled.

After we had created our sovereign we would meet with the rest of the coven: the four men. Together we selected a willing man to be our sacred king. Remember that to be valid the sacred king must take on his responsibility willingly.

With the women assisting the sovereign and the men acting as pages to the sacred king, we offered him the hallows of the four directions that formally connected him with the spirit of the earth. During the year to come he was required to serve the coven in any reasonable way needed. At the end of his year he would offer a symbolic sacrifice to the earth, usually a gift of food or a ritual object, and then we would mourn his symbolic death and hallow our new king.

I have known of women's covens who use a stalk of ripe grain, such as a corn stalk, to represent the king. They first seek out a stalk that seems willing to perform this task for them. If possible, the ritual is done in the field where the stalk is growing. They perform the hallowing ceremony in the same way as they would if a human man were present. After this is done it is easy to sacrifice him by ritually severing the stalk from the earth.

Even if you are working alone you can use a grain stalk or small patch of garden to represent the sacred king. The important thing is that the item you select feels to you as if it truly represents the spirit of the land. Spend time meditating with the earth and its spirits, and feel yourself sovereign over your own area of land. Then do the same for the grain you have chosen to be the sacred king. Offer it the hallows, the symbols of the four elements. The traditional Celtic hallows are listed below, but feel free to substitute where needed:

Earth: Stone

Water: Chalice

Fire: Spear

Air: Wand

When the ritual is done, sacrifice the willing sacred king to the good of the land and its people.

Notes

1 New York: Knopf, 1973.

2 Matthews, Caitlin. *The Elements of the Celtic Tradition* (Longmeade, Shaftsbury, Dorset: Element Books, 1989), 29.

3 Ibid., 26.

4 King, John. *The Celtic Druids' Year: Seasonal Cycles of the Ancient Celts* (London: Blandford, 1994), 50.

5 Green, Miranda J. *Celtic Goddesses: Warriors, Virgins and Mothers* (London: British Museum Press, 1995), 70.

6 One book that looks in depth at this practice, and includes practical information, is Kisma Stepanich's *Sister Moon Lodge* (St. Paul, Minn.: Llewellyn, 1992).

7 Power, Patrick C. *Sex and Marriage in Ancient Ireland* (Dublin: Mercier Press, 1976), 23.

8 Matthews, Caitlin (1989), 30.

9 Mann, Nicholas. *The Isle of Avalon: Sacred Mysteries of Arthur and Glastonbury Tor* (St. Paul, Minn.: Llewellyn, 1996), 130–31.

10 New York: Berkeley Publishing, 1966.

11 Ellis, Peter Berresford. *Dictionary of Celtic Mythology* (Santa Barbara, Calif.: ABC-CLIO, Inc., 1992), 142.

12 Walker, Barbara G. *The Crone: Woman of Age, Wisdom, and Power* (San Francisco: HarperCollins, 1985), 54.

13 For a more detailed look at each of these hallows and how they relate to the Arthurian myths, please see Caitlin and John Matthews' *Hallowquest* (Wellingborough, UK: Aquarian, 1990).

14 Matthews, John. *The Elements of the Grail Tradition* (Longmeade, Shaftsbury, Dorset: Element Books, 1990), 25-26.

15 Matthews, Caitlin (1989), 19.

16 Green, Miranda J. *Symbol and Image in Celtic Religious Art* (London: Routledge and Kegan Paul, 1992), 23.

17 For more on the Great Rite, and for detailed rituals, please see any of the books on modern Wiccan/Pagan practice currently available. Virtually all of them discuss this rite and its meanings in detail.

18 Much Celtic folklore calls these women of power "princesses" when the original title was closer to "chieftain." In this case it was likely *pennsvierges*. In Brythonic languages the root word *pen* means "head," as in "the head of something," like a clan.

19 Green (1995), 72.

20 London: Faber and Faber, Ltd., 1952.

21 New York: Ballantine, 1983.

22 Matthews, John (1990), 19.

23 Wolfe, Amber. *The Arthurian Quest: Living the Legends of Camelot* (St. Paul, Minn.: Llewellyn, 1996), 191.

24 A king could be rehallowed if a willing substitute first died in his place.

25 In this case the term "uninitiated" has nothing to do with formal declarations or ceremonies, but with personal knowledge of the subject at hand. It is used this way in several places throughout the remainder of this text.

26 Eire is the Gaelic word for Ireland. The popular appellation Erin for Ireland is merely another form of Eire's name.

27 Green (1995), 62.

28 Matthews, Caitlin (1989), 27.

29 Green (1995), 40.

MAGICK AND WITCHCRAFT

Belief in magick is one of the defining tenets of Pagan faiths, the Celtic ones included. By "magick," we mean that we recognize in ourselves the ability to alter our reality as we will. The methods and catalysts used to make these changes—or spellcrafting, as it is often called—are many, and each one is a particular favorite of someone. But no matter which outside sources are tapped—oils, herbs, stones, or other materials—the true magick remains within. Only by our will, visualization, and effort do we find our success.[1]

The power of magick was recognized but denied by the early church which thoroughly condemned it and those who practice it. On the one hand, they claimed there was no magick; on the other, they were swift to punish those caught doing it. If there was no power in magick, the grand effort to eradicate it would make no sense. To overcome this problem, the church decreed that no human could possess magickal powers, only supernatural beings. Therefore only God or his anti-self, Satan, could work magick or grant the power to do so to others.[2] And since God was unlikely to do this—with the exception of a few church-approved miracles here and there—then those who made magick must be in league with Satan and should be destroyed for the good of the entire community.

The name applied to these magickians who worked outside the bounds of church approval was *Witch*. Even today the words "Witch" and "Witchcraft" are what we might call "loaded terms," even among many Pagans. Tossing them out into a conversation is sure to create havoc, no matter what the venue. The route by which "Witch" came into the English language has been argued ad nauseum, but it is likely that it came from one of two sources, or a blending of both. One source is the Old English word *wyk*, meaning "to bend or shape," a term that speaks clearly of a Witch's magickal abilities to create change. It is also where the word *Wicca* comes from. Originally the religion known as Wicca was an Anglo-Welsh version of Paganism, codified in the early part of the twentieth century, but the term is now liberally applied to a variety of Pagan traditions with roots in western Europe. The other source of "Witch" is the Anglo-Saxon *wit*, meaning "to have knowledge or wisdom," which is where the country term for Witch, "wise woman," came from.

Today a Witch is a follower of one of the old Pagan religions of western Europe, and Witchcraft is both her religion and her art.[3] Many Pagans are not Witches, and it is a label they do not like for a variety of reasons. When it comes to Celtic Paganism there seems to be a fairly even split in this preference. Many women who have found their way back to religions where the Goddess is supreme have reclaimed the word *Witch* as a title of honor, using it, along with *hag, harridan, virago,* and others, to make statements about ourselves and our beliefs that are truly positive, even though the rest of the world conceptualizes them in a negative way.

The diabolization of the word *Witch* came during the Middle Ages, when the church sought to tighten its grip on the lives of Europeans by formally condemning anyone who practiced any art that could be construed as Pagan. Considering that vestiges of the old faiths are still with us today, and that many modern church and synagogue celebrations were forced to adopt elements of Pagan practice to make them acceptable to the masses, this must have been a daunting task for the churchmen. Among the offenses that were considered evidence of Witchcraft were any form of natural healing, taking walks in the woods, harvesting non-culinary herbs, and celebrating any part of the old cherished festivals.

The traditional healers at this time were the women who used herbs and plants to make their curatives. Healing became a crime under church law, a deliberate attempt to thwart the will of God. Using a mistranslation of an old

Hebrew word, the churchman labeled these women Witches and, using a host of fabricated or ridiculous bodies of "evidence," condemned them to die. The Biblical authority they cited for this right to break the "thou shalt not kill" commandment was a passage in Exodus that said, "Thou shalt not suffer a Witch to live."

It is popular knowledge among Pagans today that this is a mistranslation. The original word in the old Hebrew texts was *m'ra-ay-lah*, meaning "poisoner." Poisoning was a dreadful crime in the centuries before forensic medicine could ferret out even the faintest traces of toxins in the body, and history is littered with the names of famous people thought to have been poisoning victims, but whose murders cannot be proven. It has been assumed that this mistranslation was done during the reign of England's King James I (1603–1625), simply because he had many other subtle alterations performed on his Bible (the ever-popular King James Version) to make points he wished to make, or to authorize aggression against vestiges of the old religion.

As I was writing this chapter I asked my husband, Mark, to look up this passage in a Hebrew Bible and tell me what word he found there. I was so sure he would find *m'ra-ay-lah*. He came back from his search with a puzzled frown and told me the word he found was *m'khashayfah*, one that means sorceress, but is often translated as Witch.

By then I was upset. I had always trusted in the original Hebrew and in what I had been told my whole life—that the original Hebrew word was "poisoner." What could have happened? At first I simply assumed that the acceptance of this translation was so widespread that it had somehow found its way into the Hebrew texts, but that just didn't correlate with the care I know had been taken by Hebrew scholars in translating and commenting on their Bible. I managed to find a few commentaries, mostly in very recent sources, that alluded to the fact that this passage had undergone some alterations over time, but still could find no source that would make a definitive statement.

Finally Mark sat down with a piece of paper and began doing some enlightening manipulations with the Hebrew alphabet. This manipulation is an old Kaballistic art known as *gematria*, usually a practice linked to numerology, but many variations on the manipulation exist. Mark did graduate work at the Jewish Theological Seminary, and is an amateur Kaballist, who remembers being in a class where he had learned how some of the old Jewish laws were derived through gematria. One he specifically recalled was how the early Jewish leaders had disliked the bloody sort of justice they found in the "eye for an eye" passage, so they took the Hebrew word for eye and scrolled down one letter in the alphabet and found the word for money. This was how the idea of monetary compensation for injuries began. When Mark used a similar gematric maneuver on *m'ra-ay-lah* he got—surprise!— *m'khashayfah*.[4] We can only surmise that, caught up in the same frenzy to diabolize the old ways as the church, some Jewish scribe once felt free to manipulate m'ra-ay-lah into a sorceress and then into a Witch.[5]

There is no more evil in Witchcraft than there is in any other religion. Its followers are just people, vulnerable to human failing. Like all other religions, Paganism/Witchcraft is based on a set of ethics, one that teaches us that we may do as we like so long as we harm no living person or thing.[6] We can only do our best to live up to that tenet, and I think more Pagans/Witches make a conscious effort to do so than the followers of many other faiths who are offered weekly absolution for their transgressions. Pagans/Witches know that they must assume responsibility for their own failings, and that no absolution (short of having their harm come back to them threefold) is possible.[7]

Most people today, Pagan or not, are well aware of the flimsy evidence once used to convict Witches. In almost all cases, merely an accusation was the same as a conviction. Very few escaped the charges with their lives. In the Middle Ages, when true justice was a rarer commodity than it is today, the Witch trials were deliberately created so that it was impossible to get an acquittal. As in much of Europe from the thirteenth to the eighteenth centuries, Witch hunts and trials were a common occurrence in the old Celtic lands. These communal purges served four major purposes. First, they asserted the authority of the church over the people. Second, the fear they engendered helped keep people living and acting in church-approved ways. Third, they increased the wealth of the church since, in most cases, the property of one convicted of Witchcraft reverted to the church. Finally, they allowed a community to eliminate drains on its charity, particularly elderly women, or the independent woman who was perceived as a threat to family structures. It was these women who became the primary targets of the hunts.[8]

A Legacy of Celtic Witches

Most of the well-known Celtic Witches of both history and legend were healers in the old country tradition. They were the wise women, the midwives, and the herbalists to whom their neighbors turned for medical assistance and, occasionally, for a love spell or protection charm. An amazing number of these women had links to the faery realms.

In Celtic terms the word *faery* carries the burden of multiple levels of meaning. On the one hand, the faeries are the nature spirits of the land; on the other, they are the vestiges of the old Gods and Goddesses who, according to legend, went underground to live when they could no longer dwell side by side with the humans. For the modern Celt, the world of faery is both the Otherworld and the underworld, the natural world and the inner world. These apparent dichotomies create a rich, though often confusing, backdrop for magickal exploration.[9]

One of the famous Celtic Witches of legend is Scotland's Meg the Healer, who was so adept at her craft that it is said the faery folk came to her when faced with illnesses they were unable to cure. If we perceive the world of faery as being an unseen part of the natural world, Meg was one of the very few humans allowed to walk freely into the realm of faery and back again. If we choose to think of this world as an Otherworld inhabited by other spirits, then Meg became a shaman, able to travel between worlds and bring back the knowledge of one realm to aid those dwelling in the other.

Scottish folklore tells us that Meg would occasionally come across humans held captive in faeryland, and would ask a local wizard to help her release them. Again, the concept is a cloudy one. Were these trapped souls merely metaphors for those caught in an altered state of mind from which they could not escape, or were they spirits of the dead who were unable to reincarnate? A case for both Celtic concepts of faery can be successfully made here. The crafters of this bit of folklore may have meant for us to view this faery world as an Otherworld of the dead and deities because it says that when Meg died, she went there to stay permanently.

Another Scottish Witch was Stine Bheag O'Tarbat, an old woman from Tarbat Ness who was believed to possess the secrets of weather magick. Control of the weather is both a power given to many faeries and to the crone as well. In some of her legends she is referred to as "Mother Tarbat," indicating that she may have once been a mother Goddess or priestess of some sort.

In Innishark, Ireland, midwife named Biddy Mamionn had a gift for healing. It was said that the faeries took her into their world to heal a sick child. After that, the faeries and Biddy were believed to be on good terms, and exchanged much healing lore.

This idea that Witches were on good terms with the faeries was a strong aspect of Celtic Witch lore, and in Celtic countries, seeing a woman approach a faery rath or burgh[10] was admissible evidence against her in court. Old Celtic legends say that the faeries shared their healing knowledge with those who honorably interacted with them,[11] a thread that runs through almost all the legends concerning famous Celtic Witches.

Probably the most famous of all Celtic Witches is Biddy Early, a woman who lived in the mid-nineteenth century in Ireland's County Clare, who has been the subject of several books by those seeking to separate fact from fiction. Biddy was allowed to practice her craft with little harassment from authorities, though several entertaining stories exist about how she routed angry priests. The anti-Witchcraft laws of Ireland, drafted in 1586, were still on the books and quite enforceable at the time Biddy lived,[12] yet no one ever made a move to arrest her. Her neighbors appear to have looked upon her with a combination of fear and pride, and both highborn and low beat a path to her doorway seeking cures and spells.

Biddy's claim to fame was a blue glass bottle that was supposedly a gift from the faeries, though just why they gifted her in this way is open for debate. To find a cure or spell, or to divine the future, she needed only to peer into the depths of the bottle and report to the seeker what she had seen.[13] This method of scrying for magickal answers found its way into Irish folk practice. If a woman wants to find a missing person or object, she will make a cylinder with her hands and peer into it for answers. Clare legends say that before Biddy died, she tossed her famous bottle into a nearby lake, where it still rests.

Another interesting account of an Irish Witch, one that shows that the accused may have actually had some working knowledge of the old Religion, or at least of folk magick, is that of Dame Alice Kyteler. Alice was a four-time widow who lived in fourteenth-century Kilkenny. Very late one night, a neighbor man saw her outside her home, sweeping the dust from the street into her home. As she swept she chanted a rhyming couplet, something to the effect that all the wealth of the town would come to the home of her son William.[14] The use of the broom, or besom, for magick is well known, and is a popular device today. The image of sweeping toward her home while chanting a spell for wealth is a very accurate folk magickal practice.

The neighbor reported the incident, and then the local bishop took up the case. Before it was over, Alice's children had all accused her of using sorcery to kill their fathers,[15] and the various eyewitnesses claimed to have seen her cavorting with demons, divining with entrails, and making living sacrifices.[16] Alice was able to escape to England, and the wrath of Kilkenny fell upon her maid, Patronilla, who died in her stead.

During this period, the folklore surrounding Witches became increasingly vicious, always allying the Witch with Satan, an entity who is wholly a construct of Christian theology and not accepted by Paganism. The physical image of the Witch grew ugly as well, the result being the modern crone-like Halloween Witch who eats children and brews noxious potions in what was once the great cauldron of life and wisdom.

Hallmarks of Celtic Magick and Witchcraft

Celtic-style magick has several distinguishing aspects. You might want to think of it as folk magick and spell-casting with a brogue. These aspects are:

- The use of the sacred number three
- Using the power of places "in between"
- Power raising through traditional dance and music
- The use of magickal positions, gestures, or actions
- The unbinding of hair (for women) when casting a spell
- Traveling to and from the Otherworld

The last aspect, traveling to and from the Otherworld, is more a practice of Celtic shamanism than it is of any single Celtic Pagan tradition, and it will be discussed in detail in Chapter 17.

The number three as a special and sacred number to the Celts has already been discussed. It appears frequently in Celtic spells, either in the number of times a chant or gesture is repeated, in the number of catalysts used, or in the number of deities called upon. In many "modern" folk spells, especially from Catholic Brittany and Ireland, the old evocation of the Triple Goddess to seal a spell has been replaced by the summoning of the Christian trinity of Father, Son, and Holy Ghost. This Celtic reliance on the number three is also responsible for the popular saying, "Three's the charm," meaning it takes three workings of a spell to make it "take."

The power found in "in between" places or times is another hallmark of Celtic magick, and is reflected in the casting of our circle, which puts us in a place that is neither fully in this world nor fully in another. It is also seen in the popular term for midnight, "The Witching Hour," a moment in neither day, yet in both. In-between times and places are many, and include midnight and dawn, sunset and year's end, seashores and cave mouths, burial grounds and tree tops. All are fluid places, whose exact locations in time and space are indefinable, and contain mutable energies that we can tap into for magickal purposes.

Music was also a form of magick itself, used by poets to level curses, create satires, or sing praises. All of these things produced magickal consequences in the lives of the ones to whom the music was directed. An example was when the bard Cairbre MacEtan sought to remove Bres from the High King-ship of Ireland, and did so by creating a satire so biting that it caused the king to become blemished and, under old Irish law, unable to remain king. Another king blemished through music was Connacht's King Caier, who was deposed musically by his chief bard, Nede MacAdnai, when he was unable to keep a promise.

When we make magick we attempt to manipulate and shape the energies surrounding us. We do not want to expend a great deal of our own precious energy. These in-between times and places are great sources of magickal ener-gies because they are on borders where worlds collide and we have access to the universal flow of power that we often see as ultimately coming from the Otherworld.

We can also raise energies to use for magick, and a favorite way of doing this for magical peoples the world over is through drumming, dance, and music. Celtic music is regaining popularity today, and the traditional goatskin drum, known in Irish as the *bodhran*, is more readily available than ever. Recorded and printed Celtic music is also easy to find. If you cannot find ex-amples in your local music store, see Appendix C for places from which in-struments and music can be ordered, or Appendix G for scores of some tradi-tional Celtic music.

If I were to tell you to "assume the position" in a magickal sense, I would not be asking you to bend over to receive corporal punishment, I would be asking you to make a gesture/posture associated with the transference of mag-ickal energy. Such gestures/postures have been known in other cultures as well, particularly in eastern mystic schools, and they are also known in the Celtic traditions.

Magickal gestures for releasing positive energies include the famous salmon leap used in battle by Cuchulain, a technique perfected under his tutor, the Goddess Scathach, and the cross-legged sitting position seen in old Celtic renderings of poets[17] and of the Horned God on the Gundestrap Cauldron.[18] This latter position would be an acceptable posture to use for teaching, bless-ing, or sending out other positive energies to someone who is with you at the time, such as a student.

There is also a Celtic tradition of women unbinding their hair in ritual or when sending out magickal energy. This image is seen in the original texts of several myths and legends, and it is an accepted part of Celtic women's oral traditions. I have been personally acquainted with covens, some Celtic and some not, that ask their female members to wear their hair loose when com-ing into the circle.

One of the more curious magickal postures is that of closing one eye, and placing one arm and leg behind you so that it is unusable. This is a posture that has been associated with the leveling of curses, or the transference of negative energy. Experienced Pagans know that negative energy can have positive consequences if that which you seek to destroy is negative, such as a bad habit or illness. But in this case, the uses for which we have extant mythic reference do not seem to have this end, or else the end result is neither clearly positive nor negative, such as when the Formorians fought the Partholans in early Ireland, or when a woman who was refused hospitality cursed the Da Derga's household.[19] A disagreeable Scottish faery, called the Fachan or Peg Leg Jack, has one eye, one arm, one ear, and one leg, aligned straight down his body, and may be a vestige of the old magickal cursing posture.

One Pagan I knew hypothesized that this posture was meant to emulate a tree, to stretch the self from underworld to upperworld and everywhere in between to act as a channel for magickal energy. This theory is a good one, especially since it has a history of similar use in ceremonial magick for a protection ritual known as the Lesser Banishing Ritual of the Pentagram. But the telling aspect of this posture really comes through when the sun God Lugh uses it in his battle against his grandfather Balor. The original myths tell us that when he assumed this posture he resembled a bent, old woman. Ah ha! Crone power! It doesn't take too much reading between those proverbial lines to see that the power of the crone is being emulated here.

A Sampler of Celtic-Style Spells

The following spells all employ some distinguishing aspect of Celtic magick. I make no claim for their antiquity. Like most spells found in print today, they are modern in origin, but contain ancient concepts and imagery and work very well.

Making a Biddy Bottle

I made a scrying bottle in the style of Biddy Early's, and though crystal scrying has never been one of my strengths, I find it works very well. To repeat my efforts you will need a small blue glass bottle, preferably with some type of stopper-style cap (like a cork). These are fairly easy to find in gift shops, or shops that sell country decorations or antique reproductions. Mine is small, only six inches high, and cost about $2.50. You will also need a "faery oil," a scent that is traditionally one that the faeries like. I recommend trying lilac, primrose, tuberose (a costly one!), or cedar. If you have already had experience with the faery world you may have your own ideas about this and should use them. Blends that combine faery-related elements in oils are also nice.

Take the blue bottle and psychically cleanse it by holding it under clear, running water, all the while visualizing all the previous programming that might have come into contact with it being washed away. Spend at least three nights with the bottle, holding it, stroking it, allowing your own energies to merge with it as much as possible. Many feminine mystery schools advocate mixing a few drops of your menstrual blood into any anointing mixture, if it is possible and practical. This symbol of power is linked both to you and to the Goddess and, done with the proper attitude and visualization (i.e., not seeing it as "yucky"), it can be a great spell booster for you.

On the fourth night, begin visualizing the new programming of the bottle—that of it being a scrying tool for you. At this point you should ask the blessing of the faery world on your endeavor, regardless of how you visualize these beings. Anoint the bottle with the faery oil, stroking from the outer edges in to symbolize your bringing power into the bottle.

Wrap your bottle in a white cloth and bury your bottle on a hill, set it in a garden, or put it in any other place that you feel faeries would enjoy, for three nights. The white cloth will prevent the bottle's new energies from being grounded and lost while it connects with the world of faery. It is also customary, and courteous, to leave the faeries a gift of food. Milk, honey, and bread are favorites.

After you retrieve the bottle, discard the cloth and unstop the top. Think of a question or issue you have, and peer into its depths for the answer.

The Wishing Stone

Stones have played a large role in the spiritual life of the Celts. The pre-Celtic standing stones, the dolmens, and the Lia Fail (see Chapter 12) are all examples of this. Stones have also been used in wishing magick, which is essentially how the Blarney Stone is used today.

Another interesting wishing stone, known as the Deer Stone, can still be found at the Christian pilgrimage site of Glendalough in Ireland. Though this site is sacred to the new religion's St. Kevin, its Pagan and Goddess origins are clear. To activate the power of the stone (related to the feminine earth element), you sit on it facing west (the direction of the Celtic Otherworld) and lean backward until your hands touch the water (the other feminine element) behind you.[20] Thus you are facing the home of the Goddess, while connecting yourself simultaneously to her two manifest elements. If you can manage this feat you may make three wishes.

To make a wishing stone of your own, take a long walk in a wild place and find one that speaks to you. Take it home and place it in a glass jar with earth and water. Leave it there for three days. Every day spend some time projecting your desire or wish into the jar, toward the stone. After three days, release the stone backwards into the wild so that it can carry your wish to the Otherworld.

Song Spells

Songs play a huge role in Celtic magick. They have been used so frequently to preserve history and to pass along teachings that the Irish word for teach actually means "to sing over." They have also been used to satirize someone in power to the point of abdication, as was mentioned earlier in this chapter. Today, as in the past, we have leaders whose blemishes need to come to light. We've all had a boss, club president, committee chairperson, or local politician whom we sometimes realize is a problem. If you have such a person in your life, composing a song in satire will expose his or her weaknesses, and then the natural law of "what goes around comes around" can take its course.

Making a Protection Charm

The Celts were big on offering blessings, a custom that has persisted into the modern era in rural Scotland and Ireland. Several collections of popular blessings are in print now, many of them copyright-free because they are of unknown origin and age.[21] In modern Celtic Pagan traditions these are often used in conjunction with talismans to increase their efficacy.

To make a protective charm for yourself, take three leaves from trees that speak to you of having protective energies. Oak and other hardwoods or trees with prickly spikes are always good choices. Wrap these up in a cloth of gold or white (colors of protection) and tie them with a red thread (a color of warning and defense). Bless the charm in the name of the Triple Goddess, employing a traditional Celtic blessing or one you have adapted from another source.

To make the charm more Celtic, and to further imbue it with your personal energies, you may want to write or embroider a traditional Celtic or Celtic-style blessing on the cloth before wrapping it around the leaves.

Irish Folk Healing

The Irish shared a belief with many ancient people that the creator put no illness on the earth for which there was not also a cure. It was the job of healers to find these cures and pass them along for the good of the people they served.

The Irish have a plethora of Goddesses related to healing. The most well known is Airmid, daughter of the Tuatha De Dannan's God of medicine,

Diancecht. She and her brother, Miach, crafted the silver hand of the Tuatha king Nuada of the Silver Arm so that this blemish would not keep him from ruling. After this, Diancecht killed Miach in a fit of jealousy. Airmid tended her brother's grave by harvesting on it all the world's herbs. There she "spoke" with the herbs to catalog their healing properties, and they told her the cures for all the earth's illnesses. One by one, she placed them on her spread cloak, in an order that would cause her to remember their properties. When jealous Diancecht saw this display, he shook out the cloak and scattered away the healing knowledge. Legends tell us that there was no illness for which Airmid had not found a cure, and that those cures for all our ills are still out there somewhere, waiting to be rediscovered.

Goddesses who are linked with the imagery of regenerative symbols of snakes or eggs are also good candidates for healing Goddesses, as well as being fertility deities.[22] The two functions are closely linked. What was the replacement of Nuada's arm but a healing that involved regeneration? One such Goddess who embodies all these images is Sirona, an earth Goddess often depicted with snakes and eggs.[23]

Before attempting any self-healing regimen, it is wise to seek the advice of a physician. With some effort you can find a good one who practices a holistic form of medicine and is sympathetic to including natural remedies in her prescriptions. Make sure both you and your doctor are aware of how any substance(s) will react (interact) with your body chemistry or other medicines you are taking. Unfortunately, most members of the modern medical establishment are something like Diancecht, outwardly scorning the use of the old natural medicines while instinctively recognizing their worth. Until they can find a way to patent these natural remedies and make a vulgarly large profit from their use, don't count on them being found on pharmacy shelves any time soon.[24]

Many popular Irish healing charms show links to the old religions with their emphasis on the number three, the evocation of a triple deity—though usually now the Christian trinity rather than the Triple Goddess—and elements of animals and the earth. Following are some of the more interesting, or, if you prefer, more entertaining of these healing charms, which were in active use until at least the early twentieth century.

- Toothaches can be cured by crawling to a holy well on your knees while praying to the Goddess. Once at the well, immerse your face three times, then leave a small white stone at the well before you leave.

- To help heal a broken bone, take a black thread and wrap it fully around the break three times. Sprinkle the tie with holy water—one Pagan version of this is lightly salted blessed water—in the name of the trinity of your choice. Do this every morning upon waking for three days, then discard the thread.

- To break a fever, write the name of a deity on a piece of paper nine times and feed it to a wild animal who will carry it away.

- Cramps of all sorts can be cured by taking three hairs from the tail of a black cat and three from the tail of a white horse, and weaving them into your belt. Wear this until the pain subsides, or wear it overnight to prevent midnight leg cramping.

- Remove warts, moles, blemishes, and other skin abrasions by rubbing them with mud made from the earth under which an unburied coffin has lain.

- Any pain can be removed by rubbing it with a turnip that has been cut in half. Chanting a prayer to the Goddess may be done in tandem with this. When the pain is in the turnip, pin the two halves back together and bury it. Make a large 'X' over the spot where it is buried and the pain should be buried with it.

- To cure a stomachache, take some scrapings from the horn of a black cow, and some from a white cow, and put these into a tea.

- Passing your body nine times through a large hole in a stone is supposed to cure a large number of ailments, including infertility.

Augury and Divination

Divination is the art of reading either the future or the unknown past with cards, crystals, stones, sticks/wands, or other objects. Augury is the art of using nature's signs—birds' flight, cloud formations, tree limb movements, and so on—to do the same. More precisely, augury was a method of deciding a specific course of action that would be revealed through these signs, and was an art at which women were believed to excel.[25] Augury was popular among the early Celts, who had a priestly class of men and women who eventually mastered these arts. Divination is probably the more popular of the two today among Pagans, thanks to the easy accessibility of tarot cards and rune stones.

Celtic priestesses were thought to possess prophetic gifts, which made augury come naturally to them,[26] and several myths show us women who gave word of impending battles or death, such as the women/faeries who foretold for Queen Maeve her victory over Ulster and her own demise.

Anything in nature can be taken as a sign that foretells the future, speaks of the past, points us in the right direction, or underscores a current concern. There are no set ground rules for any of these signs, which is what makes augury a personal art that can only be mastered with time and careful cataloging of results. While many symbols can be called archetypes, universal patterns that have similar meanings for all people, a great many others can only be accurately interpreted by the person seeing them.

To begin your study of augury, select a part of nature you wish to study more closely. Some suggestions are:

> Cloud formations
>
> Birds in flight
>
> Tree movements in the wind
>
> The behavior of burrowing animals
>
> Animal tracks in the wild
>
> The growth pattern of your own garden
>
> The nighttime sounds of animals

Get a spiralbound notebook and, each time you go out to gaze at your chosen natural phenomenon, make notes about what you see and how you think this ought to be interpreted. Sometimes these associations will be readily apparent, but at other times they will take closer examination.

For example, reading cloud formations, an art known as nephomancy, is as popular today as it was in the past. People simply enjoy having time to lie about gazing at the clouds and looking for symbols within them. The movements, coloring, and changes in the clouds can also have meanings. I find that the sudden silvering of a dark cloud is a sure sign of impending victory or success, while rising clouds mean that the situation I am concerned about has moved out of my hands.

Lots of Celtic lore surrounds animals. Their movements, noises, and appearance can be taken as omens about the future. Howling dogs at night have always been seen as harbingers of death or illness, and owls, once sacred as birds of the crone Goddess, are viewed today as omens of bad luck. Carefully making records of your own observations will show you how these sounds and movements are to be interpreted by you.

Whichever nature sign(s) you choose for your own venture into augury, you will notice that over time, and with consistent effort, you will have written in your book the causes and effects noted after each observation and will be able to compile a detailed listing of what each symbol, movement, formation, or other occurrence means. If you need a jump-start for doing this, try glancing through a book on symbolic dream interpretation, but please don't rely on this for the long term. These books are just too general to do you much good.

In terms of general divination, or of using non-naturally occurring formations to foretell the future, one of the most controversial among the Celts is that of using entrails or blood ritually taken from an animal. The most likely uses of these types of divination were to predict the outcome of battles, or to help judge the guilt or innocence of someone. That the Druids practiced some forms of divination using living sacrifices is pretty much a given; that we modern Pagans do not want to use living sacrifices is another. We can use the form of these old divination practices without actually harming living things by making creative alterations—that's what we women are best at!

For blood we can substitute water. The water can be dyed red with food coloring or wine if you desire so that it has the appearance of blood. This divination works best when attempting to reveal the identity of an unknown person who has done some known harm to someone you care about. While it can help you discover the identity of an offender, it should not replace the criminal justice system. If you have been the victim of a criminal act, consult a lawyer or call the police. Never attempt to right these matters on your own or you will only make the situation worse. Magick can certainly help assist you in gaining justice through the proper channels, but it is not a cure-all.

For this divination you will need to be outdoors, in a dry area where you will be able to see your water markings. Dry soil or sandy areas are both good, but don't discount using the ugly and toxic blacktop of your driveway. While the surface isn't very magickal, it makes a good background for reading water spots. You will also need a shallow bowl a little larger than the palm of your hand, and some sidewalk chalk or water-soluble paint.

When you have chosen your working surface, draw on it a circle about three feet in diameter. In the center draw a smaller circle about four inches in diameter. The smaller circle represents the person whose guilt or innocence you are trying to determine, and the larger circle represents the complete situation, both the known and unknown elements. Further divide the circle into quarters to represent the divisions of truths, lies, the self, and others. Finally, around the outer perimeter make several more four-inch circles to represent others who may be guilty and are unknown. Feel free to name one or two of these if other suspects are known to you.

Sit in front of this circle with the bowl of water held in front of you, resting in the palm of one hand. Hold the other hand over the water and focus on the water being the catalyst for finding answers. When you feel you are properly focused on the issue, take your free hand and slam it down into the water, allowing it to splatter where it may. This is as close as you can get to mimicking the action of slicing the jugular vein.

When the spray settles, set the bowl to the side and examine the water droplets: where in the area they land, how many drops there are in each section, and how big the drops are. All these details help to form a picture of the truth. For example, if the majority of the water lands in or near the suspect's circle, it may indicate guilt. However, if a large amount of water falls in the "truth" quarter, it could just as easily indicate innocence. When the drops land everywhere but on the suspect, it likely signifies innocence. However, if a copious amount of water is also sitting in the "self" quarter, it may suggest complicity or foreknowledge in the incident in question. Water concentrated principally inside the three-foot circle probably means that you are on the right track with your general suspicion. If most of the liquid lies outside the perimeter, then it is an excellent sign that none of those you suspect is at fault in the matter at hand.

Notes

1 There are many good books on the market that discuss magickal theory and physics in detail. Marion Weinstein's *Positive Magic* (Custer, WA: Phoenix, 1981) is almost a modern
classic. I also wrote a detailed book on natural magick called *Making Magick* (St. Paul, Minn.: Llewellyn, 1997). Many of the books by Scott Cunningham, Raymond Buckland, and Doreen Valiente are also good for beginners of magick.

2 Condren, Mary. *The Serpent and the Goddess: Women, Religion and Power in Celtic Ireland* (San Francisco: Harper and Row, 1989), 80–81.

3 A Witch may be either female or male. I use the feminine here, as I have tended to do throughout this book, because I am primarily addressing women.

4 The twenty-two-character Hebrew alphabet does not include vowels. Vowel markings that indicate what sounds the consonants are linked to are inserted above or below the characters in modern Hebrew. Biblical Hebrew does not use these markings at all, which accounts for the discrepancy in character count between these two transliterated words.

5 Modern Pagans usually draw a distinction between Witchcraft and sorcery. Witchcraft is a religion and a magickal art form that seeks to be positive in nature. Sorcery is not a religion, but a magickal practice that usually seeks to be negative in nature.

6 In modern Paganism this ethic is known as the Wiccan or Pagan Rede that states "As it harms none, do what you will."

7 In modern Paganism this is known as the Threefold Law, a karmic principle that tells us that the energy we send out, both the positive and the negative, will return to us in meaningful ways.

8 For a more detailed discussion of the crone's demise, see Barbara Walker's *The Crone: Woman of Age, Wisdom, and Power* (San Francisco: HarperCollins, 1985), Chapter 5, "The Crone Turns Witch," 125–144.

9 Two books that present divergent viewpoints that occasionally overlap are Hugh Mynne's *The Faerie Way* (St. Paul, Minn., Llewellyn, 1996) for the deity/faery concept, and my own *A Witch's Guide to Faery Folk* (St. Paul, Minn.: Llewellyn, 1994) for the nature spirit/faery concept.

10 A rath is a stone formation, and a burgh is a hillock usually covered in grass or trees, under which faeries were believed to dwell.

11 Mynne, 41.

12 Unlike the English anti-Witchcraft laws that were repealed in the early 1950s, Ireland's may still be on the books. No source seems to be able to give me a definite answer on this one, and I would greatly appreciate whatever information anyone has on this matter.

13 If you are interested in reading more about Biddy, I recommend Edward Lenihan's *In Search of Biddy Early* (Dublin: Mercier Press, 1987).

14 Ashley, Leonard R. N. *The Complete Book of Magic and Witchcraft* (New York: Barricade Books, Inc., 1986), 84.

15 Seymour, St. John D. *Irish Witchcraft and Demonologie* (New York: Dorset Press, 1992), 28.

16 Ibid, 27–29.

17 Matthews, Caitlin. *The Elements of the Celtic Tradition* (Longmeade, Shaftsbury, Dorset: Element Books, 1989), 50.

18 A gold cauldron discovered in a Danish bog near the town of Gundestrap that is clearly Celtic in design and bears the image of a horned animal/nature deity.

19 Matthews, 50–51.

20 Rodgers, Michael and Marcus Losack. *Glendalough: A Celtic Pilgrimage* (Blackrock, Co. Dublin: The Columbia Press, 1996), 77.

21 The *Carmina Gadelica*, a collection of Christo-Celtic blessings collected by a musicologist and folklorist named Alexander Carmichael in the late nineteenth century, is a treasure trove of ancient blessings. Also look for various Irish blessing books to appear in bookstores around St. Patrick's Day (March 17).

22 Green, Miranda J. *Symbol and Image in Celtic Religious Art* (London: Routledge and Kegan Paul, 1992), 43 and 61.

23 Ibid, 63.

24 I want to amend this statement by saying that a growing number of modern physicians are recognizing the importance of mental outlook to recovery. Many are employing techniques of positive visualization and total body relaxation, but most are a long way from actually prescribing so-called "new age" cures, such as herbal medicine, auric cleansing, or healing touch.

25 Jones, Noragh. *Power of Raven, Wisdom of Serpent: Celtic Women's Spirituality* (Edinburgh: Floris Books, 1994), 120.

26 Green, Miranda J. *Celtic Goddesses: Warriors, Virgins and Mothers* (London: British Museum Press, 1995), 147.

FEMININE CELTIC SHAMANISM

Shamanism is not a religion, but a spiritual practice that has been a part of all ancient religions. In fact, it is likely the oldest of all spiritual disciplines.[1] That shamanism is universal often comes as a surprise to many people who tend to think of this term only within a Native American framework. The word itself comes from an extinct Asiatic language called Tungus and means, roughly, "one who walks between the worlds."

A shaman was the tribal healer, seer, visionary, and intermediary with the deities, a role modern-day shamans fulfill in today's tribal cultures. Pagans of all traditions are rediscovering these powerful roots of their own cultural heritage, and are actively reclaiming them as a valid part of modern spiritual practices.[2]

The shaman has to have a special vision, one that can recognize the interconnectedness of all things. She does not balk when an animal often considered lowly by other people comes to lead her on her way. She not does hesitate to send her consciousness into unknown realms to help reclaim a lost soul, and she knows how to navigate the Otherworld and return with new knowledge that she is not afraid to implement.

She does these things by learning to enter an altered state of consciousness almost at will, a talent expected of priestesses past and present.

The shaman knows that occasionally a sacrifice will be asked for in exchange for her skills. In the Celtic tradition, we see this thread in the stories of the wise woman Biddy Early. Though she was a famous healer and seer in her native County Clare, she was said to be tormented often by the faery beings who had reputedly given her the gift of prophecy and healing in the first place.

Shamanism is not an area into which all women wish to travel, simply because the practice has been associated with cults of male priests. Yet women also functioned as shamans. In some cultures, the word for a female shaman is *shamanka*, but this term is in disfavor among modern women who tend to find it sexist.

Female shamans frequently journeyed into the Otherworld, a deeply woven theme in Celtic shamanic practices. With the coming of patriarchy came a repression of the crone. She and other dark images of the feminine, which are an inherent part of the Otherworld, were deemed unhealthy, even dangerous.[3] Men were taught to fear them and, as a result, certain Otherworld adventures fell into the hands of women—when they were still allowed to openly practice this art. Where women were cut off from practicing this art, the memory of the Goddesses slowly died, replaced by male Gods or, in some cases, one supreme male deity.

Throughout history, shamans could defy time. They could work their wonders in the future or in the past to affect the present. They could do this because ancient people knew what modern Pagans and scientists have only recently rediscovered: that time is not a linear event, but an omnipresent now, a concept also understood by the Celts. The acceptance of omnipresent time does not mean that you will suddenly experience your life in a non-linear framework, but that you will find traversing the wheel of time easier. This is the essence of the shaman's journey.

Aspects of Celtic Shamanism

Celtic shamanism has its own cultural hallmarks that make it stand out as having a unique perspective. Some are shared with other forms of shamanism, but are accented with a unique Celtic voice. This is due in part to the fact that the Celtic culture was flourishing well into the period when history was being recorded, and to the efforts of modern Celtic Pagan researchers, who have been making efforts to piece together the special parts of our spiritual past. Celtic shamanism features the following concepts and practices:

Otherworld Journeys

Journeying into the Otherworld to retrieve information is a basic shamanic art for which the Celts had their own unique twists. Above all else, the Celts saw the Otherworld as their original or spirit home, a place to which they would return upon death.[4] While there, shamans could meet with ancestors, commune with deities, take personal challenges, mend broken souls, gather healing knowledge, or correct problems in the physical world. The many facets of the Celtic Otherworld will be discussed at length later on in this chapter, and in Chapters 15 and 16.

Soul Healing

In no Celtic language is there a native term for "soul" as we generally define that word today, yet there was a belief in the eternal aspects of a spiritual essence. All Celtic languages have words for ghost or spirit, parts of the whole person that can be lost before death, and that need to be reconnected in order for wholeness to continue. The idea that illness of the body or spirit can be caused by soul matter that has escaped the body is a common feature of worldwide shamanism. This is often called the "shattered soul."[5]

One of the shaman's medical duties is to retrieve these shattered soul parts from whatever Otherworld realm they have flown off too, and to bring the soul back to reintegrate with its earthly host. This is done only at the request of the ill person. Paganism acknowledges the free will of all and the right of every individual to live as they choose, as long as their choices do not impinge on the freedom of others. The Celts were great lovers of personal freedom, and took great pains to identify their freeborn people.

Sometimes the person in need of healing is near death, and the lines of free will versus manipulation are unclear. In the old tribal societies, the shaman would still try to make this effort to retrieve the soul, but would let go if the soul made it clear to the shaman that it wanted to move on.

Use of Animal Spirits as Catalysts and the Art of Shapeshifting

Where most shamanic practices rely on animal spirits as allies and assistants, the Celtic focus is more on using the animals as catalysts for a specific practice, or as transportation to a specific Otherworld realm. For example, rather than expecting a bird to show up as a guide to take you to the Otherworld, you would be more likely to transform into the bird and travel there yourself.

This is part of the art of shapeshifting, another universal shamanic practice that has its own Celtic flavor. Often the shifting occurs in order to achieve some personal task, such as an initiation rite or to celebrate a change in the seasons, or to serve a communal purpose.

The Celts saw their women/Goddesses as natural shapeshifters. The majority of the Celtic myths about shapeshifting involve women (Cerridwen, Blodeuwedd, Liban, and others), while a few involve male-female couples (Edain-Midhir, Saba-Ossian, Cerridwen-Taliesin, and so on). The fewest myths depict men alone as shapeshifters, though these stories do exist.

Shapeshifting can be done through visualization while in an altered state of consciousness, or by taking on the attributes of a spirit or animal while in the ritual circle. Both methods are employed today, and both work equally well. Which one you choose depends on your ultimate goal in taking on another shape. For instance, if you are seeking entrance to the Otherworld, visualization will work best, while if you want to take on the spirit power of a certain animal to use in your physical reality, then the ritual alignment would be your best choice. Animals one works with on a regular basis, who seem to share attributes with you, are known as your totem animals. *Totem* is a Native American word Celtic Pagans often use because it fits the concept so well, and is readily understood by most westerners on magickal paths.

Taking on an animal attribute was part of the famous Celtic ceremony known as the *tarbh feis*, or "bull contest," in which the magickians of the community would feast on a ritually slaughtered bull, after which one member would wrap up in the skin and allow visions to come via the bull's spirit.[7] This was one way in which kings were selected by communities.

In the Celtic world, certain animals are considered the "oldest animals." They are highly sacred and were believed to have once been in the sole possession of the deities in the Otherworld. Their meats were featured at Otherworld banquets such as the Feast of Age. When one consumed the pork served there, it would prevent aging.

The Welsh mythic poem known as *The Battle of the Trees*, or *Cad Goddeu* in Welsh,[8] relates how these sacred animals came to earth through a war. Some deities felt that humans needed four animals: the dog, the deer, the pig, and the lapwing, all animals said at one time to be in sole possession of the Otherworld inhabitants.

Specific Tools Native to Celtic Culture

Each culture or tradition has its own variation on ritual tools. Some are specific to shamanic practices. In Celtic culture, the basic shaman's tool is the silver branch.[9] The branch, a wand cut from an ash or yew tree, is painted silver, and apples that ring like bells are tied on it. Celtic myth refers to these as "chiming fruits."[10] They were believed to have come from the orchard known as Emain Ablach,[11] which serves as a portal to the Otherworld.

The branch was jingled in a rhythmic beat that could help lull the shaman into an altered state of consciousness, very similar to the way drums are employed in most other shamanic cultures. The Celts also used this branch to bless and protect.

Finding chiming apples to make your own silver branch might at first seem like an impossible challenge—the sort of Otherworld challenge that Celtic myth is famous for—but if you look around at Christmas time you can easily find silver and gold bells shaped like small apples that seem custom-made for making the silver branch.

Union with the Shadow-Self or Co-Walker

The Celts believed that a part of themselves dwelled within each world. The Otherworld self was known as the shadow-self or co-walker (*coimimeadh* in Irish), and was a double of the living person. This belief gave rise to the concept of the "fetch," or spirit-double, who appears to people a few weeks prior to their death in order to fetch them to the Otherworld for union with the rest of the selves.

The shadow-self is not a polar image of the physical self, bad where the physical self is good, and good where it is bad, but rather an accurate mirror of the true self. Union with this shadow-self can immediately show us our good traits and bad, and can help us find ways to overcome fear blockages that hold back our spiritual progress. In this respect it is also a guardian spirit.

The shadow-self is intimately linked to the crone Goddess and to her cauldron of transformation in the Otherworld. Only by union with the self, and willingness to enter the cauldron, can we hope to become whole beings while still in an earthly incarnation.

Seeking the Ancestors' Assistance

The Celtic spin on approaching ancestors for assistance is that many of the deities themselves were seen as ancestors, or as beings with special connections to the divine. The art of seeking the assistance of the dead, known generally as necromancy, was usually practiced near a burial site.[12] Celtic burial sites tended to be lavish stone edifices with doors that symbolized the portal between worlds. The door was closed when the two worlds needed to be separate, and could open wide to allow for free travel between them. Standing on or in one of these cairns was a right reserved for shamans and priestesses, and many folk legends tell about people who did so, with a variety of interesting results. Some came away blessed with powers of dubious worth; others were attacked by protective faery spirits. Others, like the famous Irish harper O'Carolan, were given the gift of music.

The human head was often the focus of Celtic necromantic activities. The head assumes great importance in many Celtic myths; it was a trophy to be taken when the Celts did battle, and an object of battle games that involved beheadings. It was believed to be the seat of the animating spirit, a connection to the wisdom of the Otherworld.

Use of a Crane Bag

Medicine bags, or power pouches, are a feature in virtually all tribal cultures. The Celts called these "crane bags" because they were made of the hide of a crane, a bird who, in myth, freely travels between the worlds. There are even myths of Goddesses who can transform themselves into cranes, such as Scotland's Corra and Ireland's Munanna.

Today, many Pagans balk at the idea of killing an animal for magickal purposes. They feel that people not living off the land, and in total harmony with it, do not have this right. They substitute cloth pouches for the crane bag, perhaps made of silk. Whichever way you choose to make your crane bag, you should place inside it objects you wish to wear near you at all times: amulets of protection, a small magickal tool, a special stone, or similar precious items. These objects help connect you to the power of the Otherworld and its deities and totems. Many believe that being separated from your crane bag will lessen the quality of your magickal efforts.

The Otherworld Challenge

A test or trial, in which the shaman must prove her worth to enter the circles of the sacred, is a feature of the Otherworld journey that makes up a great part of a shaman's experience. She will be given guidance, or perhaps warnings, by allies and enemies alike, but the path must ultimately be treaded alone.[13]

Fear is one of the greatest impediments to spiritual progress, especially in the fluid Otherworld, and its banishment is essential to being able to move on and grow. This blockage, which can occur at any stage of spiritual development, is usually called by the generic term "Terror of the Threshold." Usually it stops you until you can either face up to the fear, meet some challenge, or fight off the terror with your warrior self. Only after the challenge is overcome will you be allowed to venture further into the mysteries of the Otherworld.

An example of an unusual challenge is seen in the myth of the Irish Otherworld Goddess-come-faery queen, Creide. She lived all alone in the Otherworld, vowing never to sleep until she found a man who could create for her a special poem. That man would not only be admitted to her heavily guarded Otherworld home, but would become her mate. The poem had to be perfectly crafted, and had to describe in minute detail her home and all its contents. Coll, one of the Fianna warriors, was able to achieve this miraculous feat and was taken into Creide's Otherworld home as her mate.

Seeking Union with the Divine on Behalf of a Group

In any culture, the ultimate role of shamans was to impart divine favor on the people they served. Though all these shamanic arts took the practitioner along different roads, all paths eventually led to the deities. Sacrifices, gifts, and knowledge-seeking were done more on behalf of the community than for the individual. Modern Celtic shamanism has put more emphasis on the role of the individual, but the type of knowledge gained can be used to help others as well as the self.

The Land of Women

Unlike most cultures, which have only one name for their Otherworld, or Land of the Dead and Deities, the Celts have many. The Otherworld is not just Heaven, Paradise, or Hell, but is a multi-faceted realm divided roughly into three parts: the upperworld, the middleworld, and the underworld. Each section contains a host of special worlds with their own unique claim to the Otherworld experience. These areas are called by literally dozens of names, including the Land of the Ever Young, The Land of Promise, Land Under the Waves, Land of Mirrors, The Castle of Glass, and so on. All represent specific aspects of the Otherworld, a rich repository of archetypal power virtually unequaled in any other spiritual system.

One of the most intriguing of these realms is the one known as *Tir na mBan*, or the Land of Women. This world has been the destination of three separate mythic voyages, two that are Pagan, and one Christian, adapted from these older sources. The Voyage of Maelduin and The Voyage of Bran MacFerbal are the two Pagan versions. The story of Bran is the newer of the two, and formed the basis for the Voyage of St. Brendan in Christian times. The written transcripts of these ancient myths, at least the parts that still exist, serve a similar function for Celtic people as the Egyptian and Tibetan Book of the Dead serve in those cultures. They provide a framework for understanding the afterlife and knowing what to expect. The primary difference is that no "final judgment" aspect, in which a supreme being passes sentence or hands out rewards to the soul based on the events of one lifetime, is present.[14] This absence highlights the Celtic Pagan belief in both self-responsibility and the cycles of rebirth.

In both of the Pagan myths, the adventurers and their ships' crew venture to thirty-three separate Otherworld islands, but in each story it is the Land of Women that stands out as one of the most challenging and detailed. This fascination with the Land of Women hearkens back to ancient beliefs in the all-powerful mother Goddess, and an acceptance that one would go to the home of an ancestor deity after death.[15] Because the Celts were originally a "mother blood" society, one in which clans were identified by their descent from the same woman, this ancestor deity was also a woman. Celtic mythology further teaches that all dead souls must go back to their source at death, and this is sometimes portrayed as the bottomless Cauldron of Rebirth, a symbol of the womb of the Goddess. Upon physical death, a soul was reabsorbed into the womb of the Great Mother, or into some other woman form, to await rebirth.

In the story of Bran and, later, of St. Brendan, the part of the voyage that takes them to the Land of Women has a slightly sinister cast. The queen of this island literally reels Bran's boat into her harbor by casting out what amounts to a web, which catches them and draws them in. The men are feasted and petted, and for all the years they stay do not age even one single day. They are allowed to remain there, enjoying themselves, until they literally forget time has passed and that they had another life somewhere else. In this respect the women are depicted as duplicitous, deceiving the men for their own selfish aims of keeping them in the Land of Women. The men finally have to escape by trickery and violence to return to the earth.

This aspect of fighting to leave the Land of Women is at odds with what we know the Celts believed about rebirth. One did not have to fight his or her way back to life. Rebirth was offered by the Goddess and taken as one willed. The traditional Otherworld challenge is, after all, one of admittance, not of escape. It also begs the question of why Bran and his men would want to leave a perfect existence to return to an earthly realm where they would only age and die. One of the most popular names for the Celtic Otherworld is *Tir na nOg*, or Land of the Ever-Young, referring to the belief that, in the Otherworld, no one grows older. It is also telling that on this voyage, when a perfect world was sought, it was to a land of women that they were taken.[16]

Working with the Land of Women

This realm is special to women, a place in which our power is never questioned and the challenges to us only make us stronger. The next two chapters will explore these archetypes in greater detail, teaching you how to venture safely there and back, able to return with the knowledge you need for spiritual advancement.

Some women believe that the Otherworld is also the land of dreams. For women seeking to work with dreams, getting to know this world can be especially important. And because there is little as frustrating to the growing spiritual self as a dream that cannot be remembered or cannot be completed, the guided mediation in Chapter 16 will give instructions for dream retrieval.

Notes

1 Matthews, John. *The Celtic Shaman* (Shaftsbury, Dorset: Element Books, 1992), 1.

2 Conway, D. J. *Falcon Feather and Valkyrie Sword: Feminine Shamanism, Witchcraft and Magick* (St. Paul, Minn.: Llewellyn, 1995), 23.

3 Eliade, Mircea. *Shamanism: Archaic Techniques of Ecstasy* (Princeton, New Jersey: The Princeton University Press, 1964).

4 Matthews, Caitlin. *The Elements of the Celtic Tradition* (Longmeade, Shaftsbury, Dorset: Element Books, 1989), 63.

5 Conway, D. J. By *Oak, Ash and Thorn: Modern Celtic Shamanism* (St. Paul, Minn.: Llewellyn, 1995), 169.

6 Matthews, John, 149.

7 Matthews, John and Caitlin. *The Encyclopaedia of Celtic Wisdom* (Shaftsbury, Dorset: Element Books, 1994), p. 242.

8 Attributed to the sixth century Welsh bard Taliesin.

9 Matthews, John and Caitlin, 116–117.

10 Conway, *By Oak, Ash and Thorn*, 114.

11 Rees, Alwyn and Brinley Rees. *Celtic Heritage: Ancient Tradition in Ireland and Wales* (New York: Thames and Hudson, 1961), 315.

12 Matthews, John and Caitlin, 116.

13 Wolfe, Amber. *The Arthurian Quest: Living the Legends of Camelot* (St. Paul, Minn.: Llewellyn, 1996), 147.

14 Matthews, Caitlin. *The Celtic Book of the Dead* (New York: St. Martin's Press, 1992), 5–6.

15 Raftery, Joseph, ed. *The Celts* (Dublin: Mercier Press, 1964), 88.

16 Markale, Jean. *Women of the Celts* (Rochester, Vt.: Inner Traditions International, Ltd., 1972), 52.

IMMRAMA

Entering the Otherworld

CHAPTER FIFTEEN

Making an Otherworld journey is a relatively easy task, but locating what needs to be found in that world, perhaps fighting for it, then bringing back and implementing it in the physical world, is a lot harder.

The Irish language distinguishes between Otherworld "voyages," called *immrama,* and other adventures, called *echtrai.* This suggests that one is a deliberately planned excursion, and the other is fallen into as a result of chance or accident. By far you have the greatest chance of having your Otherworld adventures making a lasting impact on your life if you plan ahead somewhat. Granted, the Otherworld will always be full of surprises. That is its nature, and that is how it best teaches and initiates us into new levels of spiritual growth. But if we go in already having some idea of what we hope to achieve, we are more likely to find it. Compare it to starting a shopping trip when you have no idea what you need to buy. You are much more likely to waste too much time, spend too much money, and come home without that which you need most. Your Otherworld journeys are the same.

There is only one reason to enter the Otherworld—to grow. Along with your growth, other benefits will surely accrue. You will learn

163

to overcome unhealthy and inhibiting fears, you will connect more intimately with the divine, you will improve your divination skills, and you will build upon your warrior self.

Mythologist Joseph Campbell repeatedly wrote of the universal mythic theme of a human venturer who suddenly finds herself in an Otherworldly situation, triumphs over the obstacles placed on her path, and then returns to the physical existence with special gifts.[1] Each time you return from an Otherworld experience, you should bring back with you something of value. This can be something intangible, such as knowledge given, or an amulet or talisman that was given into your care. Though this object may not be visible to you once you are back in the physical world, it still exists, and will remain with you until the time you return it to the Otherworld, either by choice or request. Learn what you can from this gift while you have it, and share it as you are able.

The Blood Journey

It has been suggested by many people who practice a Celtic-based spirituality that men and women on shamanic journeys will find that their ultimate experiences are different based solely on their gender. Such a concept raises the hackles of feminists who do not want to believe that any gender-based disabilities exist in any realm, but precedents for this division exist in the Celtic traditions. Rest assured that, in the end, both men and women end up in the same place spiritually, it's just that their pathways for getting there must necessarily diverge at certain points.

According to one writer, a man's ultimate Otherworld journey takes him to a semen-colored world,[2] a "white" place of bliss and union with the God. For women it makes sense that the approach is one of a blood journey. Many times the imagery here is not just of a red world of blood, but one that features a horse, a sacred animal intimately linked to the feminine that men in Celtic myth often found hard to capture. The horse Goddess Rhiannon is one such example of a woman on horseback who could not be caught, no matter how hard her pursuers rode. Because the horse is linked to the darker reaches of the Otherworld and of the mother aspect of the Goddess, it is also linked with blood.

These journeys into semen and blood worlds are not aspects of the Otherworld journey that can be planned. They are a gift given in recognition of your efforts. The blood journey is likely to take a woman by surprise, suddenly catapulting her into an ecstatic realm of feminine mysteries where she finds herself at the source of all creation. When she emerges from this world, she will have been reborn in the spiritual sense. Being someone who is "twice born" is of importance to Celtic spirituality, in a way similar to how Christian fundamentalists today view their concept of being "born again." Both indicate an initiation into spiritual mysteries, of "knowing," and into a deeper connection with the divine.

In spite of the Celtic beliefs in rebirth, you are unique in the here and now. Your precise body, spirit, and mental self are in this exact configuration only once, and then you will never be this form again. You get only one chance at being the current you. The next time around you will be someone different. Being twice born is believed to prepare you to make your next-life transformations in a better way, with full awareness of the meaning of your death and the world(s) you choose to explore after this life ends.

Playing by the Otherworld's Rules

You should never make the mistake of thinking that your experiences in the Otherworld are not real, simply because they take place in your mind. Pagans, magickians, and other occultists have long recognized the legitimacy of these inner-world experiences, and have learned not to go into them in a poorly prepared frame of mind, or for sport. They have learned from centuries of experience that this attitude only leads to blockages, spiritual and physical setbacks. Ultimately, you find you are unwelcome in the places you most wish to visit, and the Terror of Threshold cannot be overcome so that you may pass through and complete your journey.

You should approach an Otherworld journey as you would any other ritual, with reverence and intent. Cleanse both your body and your spirit beforehand. Allow any anger, hatred, or other emotional upheavals to be set aside. Remember that on the great wheel of time what goes around comes around, and taking any negative emotion into the Otherworld will only rebound on you sooner or later.

When in the Otherworld, respect the privacy of others you meet there, whether they are spirits of the dead, deities, or other human travelers like yourself. If someone clearly is not interested in having a conversation or becoming your teacher or traveling companion, don't try to force a bond.

The Celtic Otherworld is governed by many of the same rules of hospitality that governed the Celtic physical world in times past. One of the strictest of these was the expectations of someone who had accepted the hospitality of a household at which they stopped to rest during a journey. This was called the "protection of bread and salt." Once food was offered—as it was required to be—and accepted, the guest was under obligation to live at peace while there, and the host could not ask the guest to leave for a least a year and a day. This was an important feature of Celtic life, when traveling warriors could create a quick crisis in someone's home. If you are offered food and drink in the Otherworld, choose to accept it with caution. Many times such a gift has been portrayed in folklore as a metaphor for trapping unsuspecting humans in certain areas of the Otherworld, particularly in the faery realms. If you do accept the offering, keep in mind the obligations you have just committed yourself to.

Be cautious about time in the Otherworld. Anyone who has ever practiced simple meditation knows about the phenomenon of time distortion. When you are in the Otherworld, you are outside the boundaries of time and space as we know it, and even scientists will tell you that time has no meaning outside the known universe. It is not unusual on an Otherworld journey to return only to find out that a great deal more or less time has passed than you expected. Many legends abound about people being stuck in the Otherworld, particularly in the faery realms, who are unable to get back, or who find it extremely difficult to do so. In most cases, the persons are not really stuck, merely unaware of the passage of time. Willing the self to move on or to return to your physical consciousness should always free you.

Another aspect of the Celtic Otherworld is that, since it is a place of rebirth, a deity or teacher there might place you under a *geis*. A geis is a taboo, a personal restriction usually placed upon someone at birth.[3] Sometimes this geis may apply to the non-physical you and have to be observed only in the Otherworld. At other times it will apply to your physical life as well. As seen many, many times in the Celtic myths, breaking the geis, knowingly or unknowingly, has severe repercussions. If you are going to make this commitment to spiritual advancement, be aware that you may have to accept its harsher side as well. It is all part of those Otherworld challenges whose intent is to help us grow.

One example of a geis laid upon someone while in the Otherworld, and of a severe case of time distortion, is seen in the myth of Niamh of the Golden Hair, who took the young hero Ossian to her Otherworld home for a visit. They were very happy there, and even had a son and a daughter together. More than nine hundred years passed, of which Ossian remained blissfully unaware. When he finally realized the great passage of time, he asked Niamh if he could go back and visit earth once before returning to stay with her and their children forever. She gave him her horse and told him he was free to go, but that he was under a geis not to dismount for any reason. Once back in Ireland Ossian quickly forgot the geis, and carelessly dismounted. He immediately aged, and turned to dust.

Methods of Entering the Otherworld

Today's Celtic Pagans have an entire arsenal of methods to crack open the Otherworld's doors. The four primary ways in which the Otherworld can be entered contain some overlap between them. These are:

> Dream incubation
>
> Through a symbolic portal
>
> Through guided meditation
>
> Through astral projection

Dream Incubation

It is an old doggerel that says our dreams are made of imagination, and your own power of creative imagination is one factor that will determine the ease with which you are able to enter the Otherworld.[4] Learning to trust what we imagine, or think we imagine, will allow us to follow its lead into other realms of reality.

Dream incubation, or creating conditions conducive to prophetic dreaming, is one of the oldest shamanic tricks. It uses the natural openness of the mind during the alpha and theta cycles of sleep to connect with Otherworld beings and receive messages or guidance from them. (See Appendix E for a chart of the four sleep stages and how they relate to meditation.) It is also a method for meeting with the ancestors or other spirits of the deceased. One old Celtic practice was for shamans to sleep atop burial cairns to receive messages form the Otherworld.[5]

Many ancient cultures set aside specific sleep temples to induce prophetic dreaming. The Greeks were especially noted for this practice, and both men and women priests slept in the *incubares,* or "sleep sanctuaries." Women were considered in many cultures to be the true masters of the art of prophetic dreaming due to the connection of the feminine with the night and the moon. The only thread we have of this among the Celts is the aforementioned practice of sleeping on burial cairns, sacred stones, in oak groves, and so on. Presumably, some sort of ritual preparation and prayer was a prerequisite to incubating these dreams so that the messages could be taken seriously by the dreamer or her clan.

The magickal repertoire of modern Paganism is full of tricks to help induce prophetic dreaming. These include the burning of jasmine incense in the sleeping room, or the consumption of jasmine tea just prior to falling asleep. Jasmine is also an herb linked to death rituals, and makes a good incense to use if obtaining messages from ancestors is of interest to you. Dream pillows are also popular devices. These are small cloth pouches stuffed with herbs such as jasmine, mugwort, lemon balm, or patchouly, hand-sewn by the dreamer, then placed under the "regular" pillow at night. The dream pillows are usually charged to their task with strict visualization, perhaps a chanted blessing, or by anointing them with a special oil. Each of the popular dream pillow herbs imparts its own unique character to the dreams. Patchouly is related to the earth and is most likely to take you into the underworld realms or connect with your underworld spirits. Mugwort is an herb used frequently in traveling spells or for assisting in astral projection, and is the one most likely to help you travel—via astral projection—in your dreams into the Otherworld. Lemon balm and jasmine are both related to the dream world and to prophecy, and will be likely to help your dreams include visions of the future. Lavender was considered a potent magickal aid to curing insomnia, and adding it to any pillow may help you fall asleep faster.

You are by no means limited to these old standards. Knowledgeable creativity will do more for your shamanic activities than following formulas. For example, if viewing the past is your interest, try using lilac. Past in this case does not refer only to past lives, but to unresolved present-life issues. If you seek dreams pertaining to your romantic situation, try rose.

Hot teas made with herbs that are known to magickally induce dreams can also help. Try jasmine, rosemary, eucalyptus, or sage. For banishing nightmares, use anise. Place about one teaspoon of the herb into a tea ball or cheese cloth for each single cup you wish to make, and steep it for about five minutes. Drink this just prior to falling asleep, while keeping your purpose firmly in mind.

After you have lit your incense, put your dream pillow in place, and consumed your dreaming tea, it is best to slip into bed (or wherever else you plan to sleep) as soon as possible. If you have any rituals you wish to do at this point to help bring on dreams, keep them brief. You do not want to jar yourself out of the receptive state you have lulled yourself into by having to think about complex rituals.

Though a lot of people balk at the idea of keeping a dream diary simply because of the time and effort it takes, they can be very useful, and are certainly entertaining to look back on over the years. When recording dreams, women of child-bearing age should make a note of their menstrual cycle, as well as recording any weather or astrological data you feel is important. The impact the cycle has on your psyche is not to be underestimated. Menopausal women may notice that they feel certain "womb rhythms" still at work in their bodies long after their periods cease, and if you are one of these, you should record these impressions as well. Over time, you will notice a clear pattern showing at the point in your cycle your dreams are most psychic, or when you are best able to enter the Otherworld, contact the dead, or achieve other goals. This can be useful information to have when you are looking for assistance in any of these areas later on.

Entering Through a Symbolic Portal

Understanding the meanings of Otherworld symbols is essential to ensuring that your journey follows the right path. Think of these symbols as the Otherworld's road signs. Symbols can also be used to condition the deep mind with your desire for the Otherworld journey, by setting up sympathetic connections between your deep mind and the energies of the Otherworld. The key to using them is in unlocking their mysteries, understanding their deepest meanings, and then using them on a regular basis. The two best symbols a Celtic shaman can use for the journey are the triskele and the labyrinth.

The triskele, or triple spiral (see Fig. A) is a very old Celtic symbol that represents the sacred number of the Celts and all its correlations:[6] the three stages of existence (birth, death, and rebirth); the Triple Goddess (virgin, mother, and crone); the three levels of the Otherworld (underworld, middleworld, and upperworld); and so on.

Several explanations have been put forth for the meanings of the individual spirals, based on the direction it spins and its placement against other ancient symbols on Celtic relics and sacred sites. One of the more interesting of these is that the two bottom spirals (see Fig. A) represent the equinoxes, the times of balance in the solar year,[7] one spiral heading into darkness and one into the light. Note that the spiral on the left moves counterclockwise. Both the direction of left and the anti-clockwise movement are related to the Otherworld. Note also that the spiral on the right moves clockwise, both directions associated with the upperworld or, sometimes, with the middleworld, which is viewed as an unseen realm parallel to and penetrating the physical world. The very design of this

Fig. A: The Triple Spiral

169

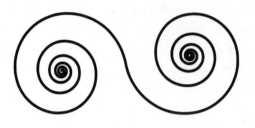

Fig. B: Otherworld Road Map Spiral

ancient symbol offers us a road map into the Otherworld. Though few think about its meaning, this "figure 8 on its side" design is present in many magickally symbolic situations. It often appears over the head of "The Magician" in tarot decks to represent the ability to take ideas in spirit and translate them into physical reality.

I have used this road map myself and find that it is nothing short of miraculous in the way it works. It makes all Otherworld journeys much easier to get into and out of. Before attempting any form of Otherworld journey, meditate on this symbol, scrying into it for insights. Then close your eyes and allow yourself to feel as if you are following this road map from the center point of its right spiral. Feel your inner self turning clockwise to reach the point where the two worlds meet, then feel your self moving counterclockwise as you follow the spiral into the very center of the left spiral. When you are ready to leave the Otherworld, you simply close your mental eyes and reverse the process (see the guided meditation in Chapter 16).

A similar device is the labyrinth. Though we tend to think of the classic labyrinthian pattern as being Greek in origin, it is a symbol of Otherworld and Goddess mysteries found throughout Europe. That the Celts recognized and used this symbol is obvious, since extant carvings of it can be found at many old sacred sites, including those near the sacred site now dedicated to St. Kevin at Glendalough, Ireland.[8] Other variations on the labyrinth are also found, and since a labyrinth differs from a maze in being a pattern where there are no dead ends to fool you, it can be argued that the spirals are also a type of labyrinth.

Traveling the labyrinth is a transformative experience. It is symbolic of spiritual initiation, death, and rebirth into a new life. Its center represents the womb of the Goddess

Classic Labyrinth Pattern

The Labrys

from which all things are born and reborn. I have been told that some English covens possessing enough land to create large labyrinths using hedgerows used the pattern to enclose their circle site, making it truly a space out of time, a place for creating change.

It is no accident that the feminist Pagan path known as the Dianic Tradition has adopted the labrys as its symbol. The labrys is a double-headed axe. Note that the classic labyrinth pattern is divided in the center and round on the edges, much like the double-headed axe.

Entering Through Guided Meditation or Astral Projection

Although these two methods of entering the Otherworld were mentioned separately, they are going to be treated together because they share much more in common than those who have not worked with them extensively might realize. The guided meditations presented in Chapters 3 and 16 offer prepared pathways into the inner worlds. Over time, and with your own experimentation, you can venture away from these paths and traverse the Otherworld on your own. In effect, you will be astral projecting.

The astral world, or astral plane as it is sometimes called, is conceptualized as an invisible realm that parallels and interpenetrates our physical world. It is around us and in us at all times, but remains unseen by us when we are in our normal state of consciousness. Astral projection is a means by which we deliberately expel our consciousness, or astral bodies, into the astral plane. In this fluid state we can travel anywhere. Time and space offer no barriers.[9]

Astral magick has been widely misunderstood, but was clearly popular among the Celts, or at least among their priestly classes. The Druids were reputed to have spells called *fith fath* that rendered them invisible. This was probably a metaphor for an astrally projected state, which enabled them to escape the bonds of linear time and work magick backwards and forwards in time to change present situations.

Whether you are astral projecting, or simply taking off on your own from a guided meditation, there are three ways to make your jump into the Otherworld easier:

> By shapeshifting
>
> By following a trusted guide
>
> By entering through a known place or time portal

I have heard lots of horror stories about Pagans who have allowed themselves to take on animal shapes during Otherworld journeys; most I have dismissed as scare tactics designed to prevent others from discovering these power techniques. It is true that you do not want to dwell overly long in another form. Doing so will eventually hinder rather than help you, because you will be relying on energies outside yourself rather than developing your own skills. But taking on the form of an animal known to be skilled at traveling the path between this world and the Otherworld is useful as a tool for learning, or for assistance when you have occasional difficulties.

Birds and horses are the two primary animals who possess this power. Horses are symbolic of the divine feminine, of death and transition,[10] and make an excellent choice for your shapeshifting efforts. Goddesses such as Rhiannon, Macha, Mare, and Epona all had a horse form. In Celtic mythology, it is common for both people and deities to take on bird shapes at the moment of death, such as when Blodeuwedd was turned into an owl when she was killed. Other well-known bird Goddesses are Ireland's Cliodna, who often took the form of a sea bird, and Scotland's Corra, a Goddess of prophecy who usually appeared in the form of a crane.

In the physical world, some intense ritual effort is needed to shapeshift into other forms, and the result will be a psychic rather than a physical transformation. You will see the change, and so will anyone with the ability to view you with psychic vision, but to the rest of the world you will appear to be only play-acting. In the astral world, all thought is action, and that which you will becomes real. This allows you to alter your form almost at will. Still, making these changes should have a purpose, and not be done just for sport. Abusing the power is a good way to either lose it or have it rebound to teach you a lesson.

To shapeshift in the astral world, simply allow your outer self to take on another shell, while recognizing your inner self as the real you, protected inside. Watch it happen slowly, allowing each individual part of you to make the complete change. If you find you are having trouble doing this, it may be because this animal's spirit is not willing to merge with you at this time, or because you have an inner fear of the process that is blocking your efforts. Once the change is complete, will yourself to travel in that form to the Otherworld.

When you reach your destination, take back your own outer form, changing it again for the return trip.

Do not worry about being "stuck," either in another form or in the Otherworld. Always keep in mind the "thought is action" principle and, if you do feel afraid, simply will yourself back to your physical self in the physical world.

You can also allow yourself to be met by a trusted guide and escorted in and then out again when you are ready to go. A guide can be a deity, the spirit of someone you know who has died, or an animal guide. Popular sacred animals in the Celtic world were dogs, traditional guardians of the gates of the Otherworld; salmon, who function like serpents in other cultures[11] as symbols of knowledge and transformation; boars, symbols of abundance and the warrior; bears, linked to strength and images of royalty; cattle and bulls, symbols of wealth; and sows, symbols of abundance, youth, Goddesses, and the Otherworld.

The old Celts believed there were numerous natural times and places at which the Otherworld became accessible. Any of the "times in between" are prime for beginning Otherworld journeys. These are times not easily distinguished as being in one time frame or another, such as midnight, noon, dusk, dawn, New Year's Eve, and so on. The most favored of these times was dusk, when day is not day and night is not night, but hovers somewhere in between while the world of dark mysteries encroaches.[12]

There were also places that were thought to be natural gateways to the Otherworld, all of which are easy to summon in guided meditations or astral projection. This is unlike the practice of other cultures, in which the shaman had to have some physical representation of her traveling powers nearby. The idea of the shaman possessing a pole or other symbol of the "world tree" is common worldwide.[13] This world tree represented a connection between the three levels of the Otherworld, all intersecting at the center of the universe, wherever the shaman had erected his pole. But the Celts saw space as being just as omnipresent as was time; therefore, they had numerous entry points to the Otherworld. Many mythic tales tell us of accidental ventures into the Otherworld when one of these places was approached wrongly.

Other natural entry points include sacred standing stones, cairns and other sacred sites,[14] shorelines, caves, hearths (especially those sacred to fire Goddesses like Brighid),[15] and the center points of structures such as labyrinths.

Beginning Your Otherworld Explorations

Understanding the Otherworld is so central to understanding Celtic spirituality, and to uncovering the deeper feminine mysteries, that its importance cannot be overstated. Certainly it is not a venture that should be rushed by those who do not yet feel ready for it. Nor should it be avoided indefinitely if you hope to grow on your chosen path.

Most people tend to feel most comfortable if their initial explorations are guided. The meditation in the next chapter will provide a beginning path for you to follow. Once you have gained experience, use it as a jumping-off point for venturing out on your own.

Notes

1 For instance, see his *The Mythic Image* (Princeton, NJ: Princeton University Press, 1974), or his *Transformation of Myth Through Time* (New York: Harper & Row, 1990).

2 Mann, Nicholas. *The Isle of Avalon: Sacred Mysteries of Arthur and Glastonbury Tor* (St. Paul, Minn.: Llewellyn, 1996), 186.

3 See John and Caitlin Matthews' *The Encyclopaedia of Celtic Wisdom* (Shaftsbury, Dorset: Element Books, 1994), p. 243, for further discussion.

4 Matthews, John and Caitlin, 221.

5 Ibid, 335.

6 Condren, Mary. *The Serpent and the Goddess: Women, Religion and Power in Celtic Ireland* (San Francisco: Harper and Row, 1989), 25.

7 Thomas, N. L. *Irish Symbols of 3500 B.C.* (Dublin: Mercier Press, 1988), 30.

8 Rodgers, Michael and Marcus Losack. *Glendalough: A Celtic Pilgrimage* (Blackrock, Co. Dublin: The Columba Press, 1996), 15.

9 There are several books on the market that teach astral projection using a variety of techniques. My three favorites are J. H. Brennan's *Astral Doorways* (Wellingborough, UK: Aquarian Press, 1986), D. J. Conway's *Flying Without A Broom* (St. Paul, Minn.: Llewellyn, 1995), and Melita Denning and Osborne Phillips' *The Llewellyn Practical Guide to Astral Projection* (St. Paul, Minn.: Llewellyn, 1979).

10 Walker, Barbara G. *The Crone: Woman of Age, Wisdom, and Power* (San Francisco: HarperCollins, 1985), 87.

11 Condren, 25.

12 Campbell, J. F. and George Henderson. *The Celtic Dragon Myth* (Wales: Llanerch Publishers, 1995), 129.

13 Conway, D. J. *By Oak, Ash and Thorn: Modern Celtic Shamanism* (St. Paul, Minn.: Llewellyn, 1995), 84.

14 Matthews, Caitlin. *The Celtic Book of the Dead* (New York: St. Martin's Press, 1992), 11.

15 Mynne, Hugh. *The Faerie Way* (St. Paul, Minn.: Llewellyn, 1996), 19.

VOYAGE TO TIR NA MBAN

Guided Meditation

This meditation will help open the doors of *Tir na mBan*, the Land of Women, to you. If you have already had experience in this area, please continue to use whatever method of entering and exiting the Otherworld that works best for you. Your deep mind is already conditioned to these cues; to try to make major changes now will only hinder your progress. If your experience in the Otherworld has not been specifically in *Tir na mBan*, you may want to incorporate archetypes from this guided meditation to help yourself into this particular Otherworld realm without altering your basic format.

Remember that the sections in the meditation marked off by brackets [ ] are either clarifications of terms and words used in the text, or are instructions to the one who is reading the meditation aloud: either with you reading into a recorder, or a partner reading to you. These sections are not to be read aloud to the journeyer, nor are they to be considered part of the body of the actual meditation. If you are unfamiliar with the practice of guided meditation, or are unsure of how to achieve the altered state of consciousness necessary for successful inner-world work, or how to ground yourself afterward, please refer to Appendix E for a full discussion, instructions, and tips.

Tir na mBan Meditation

Close your eyes and slow your thoughts; breathe rhythmically and deeply, center your spirit, relax, and let go. Focus inward and outward, drawing your consciousness away from the physical world.

Know that you are protected by your own inner powers and by the love of your Goddess. If you wish, at this time you may mentally call out to your Goddess and ask her for help and assistance, or you may wish to weave some other mental magick for the protection of your physical body as you start to become unaware of it. You may also ask her for protection and guidance in your spiritual travels. [A five-minute pause should suffice.]

Know that you are always in control and that you have the power to return to full, waking consciousness at any time you choose. If you wish to return at any point in your journey, you can do so by thinking the words "I AM HOME." Thought is action on the astral plane, and this simple act of will, constructed in a cohesive thoughtform, will trigger both your subconscious and conscious minds that you wish to return immediately to your normal consciousness, and it will immediately happen. You can then open your eyes and go about your daily life.

Knowing that you are protected and in control, you can fully relax. Take one more deep breath and release yourself to the experience that Tir na mBan has in store for you at this time.

Will yourself free of the confines of your normal consciousness and allow yourself to pass through the void that separates what we think of as "reality" from the Otherworld. [Pause for a moment to allow this visualization to take place.]

When your inner vision clears, you find that you are standing at the center point of the right half of a large double spiral. Cautiously you put one foot forward, and you begin to follow the spiral's path.

You are aware that the Otherworld is a limitless place with an almost infinite number of realms to explore. As you work your way out, you feel the need to take on a form, or find a guide that will specifically help you into Tir na mBan.

[At this point you must decide how to proceed. You can find a small silver boat waiting for you, or a white horse or black bird. Or, if you like, you can shapeshift yourself into the horse or bird form. If you choose the shapeshifting option (A), begin to feel the changes in your outer form now. If you wish to have a guide (B) or a boat (C), see it start to form for you now.]

As you wait at the point where the two spirals connect, you feel a change in the atmosphere. The world has become more fluid and light. Standing on either side of the path are two large dogs, one red and one white. These are the guardians of the gate of the Celtic Otherworld.[1] They are fearsome creatures, yet they regard you passively, as if they have been expecting you, and they make no move to stop your progress.

[A few times I have been stopped at this point, either by the dogs or by some other spirit being, and either ordered or advised not to continue. If you are unwell, angry, poorly motivated, or are carrying any other negative emotion that would make an Otherworld journey unadvisable at this time, you may also be stopped, or at least advised to turn back and try again later. This choice is usually left up to you, though these guardians can turn into true terrors of the threshold and make continuing on very difficult. At other times, you may be allowed to learn this lesson the hard way, permitted to forge ahead to your own detriment. I have had this happen as well. You must decide for yourself if, when stopped and asked to go back, you are receiving an Otherworld challenge or simply being ably guided by those who know more than you.]

[The Otherworld challenge, sometimes known in general Paganism as the "terror of the threshold," is a deeply recurring theme in Celtic practice, appearing in both ancient myth and modern ritual. Its purpose is twofold: 1) It forces the unprepared to either turn back or risk having to learn their lessons the hard way, and 2) It permits the worthy candidate who passes the test of the challenge to gain new knowledge and a renewed self-confidence as she passes on into the greater mysteries.]

[Now follow option A, B, or C, depending on which outer form you have chosen to gain access to *Tir na mBan*.]

A: Shapeshifting

Feel your outer self becoming as fluid as the world around you, changing to a very feminine form. Feel your arms becoming (insert the word *hooves* or *wings*), and sense their power as the real you is enfolded in this new shape. [Allow about three minutes for this to take place.]

You continue along the other spiral, moving clockwise through a counterclockwise world of water and mist. Inward you travel in an ever-tightening circle, until you come to a halt on the shores of *Tir na mBan*.

As you step out onto the beach, you feel your old form returning. The (insert the word *hooves* or *feathers*) melt into your skin, and you look out of your own eyes once more.

B: Horse or Bird Guide

From out of the mist in front of you comes a guide to take you the rest of the way to *Tir na mBan*. A beautiful (insert white mare or large black she-raven) comes to stand majestically in front of you, beckoning you to mount her. You climb willingly onto the creature's back.

You continue along the other spiral, moving clockwise through a counter-clockwise world of water and mist. Inward you travel in an ever-tightening circle until you come to a halt on the shores of *Tir na mBan*.

You step out onto the beach, and dismount your friend. You sense she will be waiting for you when you return to this spot again on your return trip.

C: Silver Boat

From out of the mist comes a small silver boat to take you the rest of way to *Tir na mBan*. You willingly climb into the boat, knowing it has been sent to you from the Otherworld.

You continue along the other spiral, moving clockwise through a counter-clockwise world of water and mist. Inward you travel in an ever-tightening circle until you come to a halt on the shores of *Tir na mBan*.

You step out onto the beach, and beach the boat. You know that it will be here waiting for you when you return to this spot again on your return trip.

From this place on the shore you see you are at the meeting point of two worlds. Behind you the world is misty and it is hard to see through the murky veil, but ahead of you in *Tir na mBan* it is summer, lush and green. A huge primeval forest spreads out endlessly before you. The only easy access to it seems to be a small pathway right in front of you. The sides of the path are marked by two small cauldrons. As you approach you see they contain a dark red liquid. The path itself is dark red, as if stained in blood from thousands of years of women's bleeding cycles. These are the cycles of the womb, of personal pain, of misogynism, and of joy at being female. They are the rivers of blood shed in agony, in violence, in happiness, and in unity. They are all here, all part of this Otherworld. You can feel the collective pulse of the universal feminine all around you. The whole area radiates a sacredness, and throbs with the potential of life, and you feel your own heart beat in sync with it.

You follow along this blood path deep into the forest until you come to a grotto. In the middle of the grotto is a silver and gold throne, and on it is seated a Goddess-like woman clothed in flowing green robes. Upon her blonde head is a crown of gold that radiates like the sun, and in the center of it sits the largest, clearest red ruby you have ever seen. She exudes serenity and quiet power, and she seems at one with her natural surroundings.

All around her are the astral forms of women like yourself who have come seeking the wisdom of *Tir na mBan*. At first it makes you sad to see how few women are lined up before her, waiting their turn to drink from the large, jewel-encrusted chalice this Goddess-queen offers them.[2] In comparison to all the women in the world, their numbers are few. [The cup is probably being offered by Scotland's Queen of Elphane, and is presented to women as an invitation to seek her wisdom. In the past few hundred years this Goddess has become a faery queen, a sovereign associated with Bealtaine. Thomas the Rhymer, a seventh-century visionary, claimed she appeared to him on a May eve all dressed in diaphanous green silks, riding a white mare with fifty-nine silver bells entwined in her mane.]

When it is your turn to drink, you approach the throne. The queen smiles at you with motherly pride, and you take the heavy chalice and drink deeply from it. The potion inside tastes a little like milk and honey, but it has a light, otherworldly texture and flavor that you have never experienced before.

You hand the heavy chalice back to the queen.

"Welcome to *Tir na mBan*," she says. "This realm belongs to you. Go and seek your wisdom, my sister."

With that command you are free to explore this world at will. You move into the forest again, noting as you travel along how rich the landscape is in feminine imagery. Chalices, cauldrons, hares, does, horses, ravens, and pools of sacred blood liberally enhance your surroundings.

[At this point you may explore any part of the Land of Women you like. You may visit your ancestor mothers, seek a personal vision in the cauldron of knowledge, seek out the Well of Segais (knowledge) that is traditionally guarded by a stag in the underworld, or seek your shadow self in the darker reaches of *Tir na mBan*.[3] Your shadow self will have all your same fears, loves, hopes, joys, strengths, and failings. It will be neither good nor evil, strong nor weak. It will just be you. This discovery can be the most daunting aspect of the Otherworld experience, but it is one that will ultimately make you whole and give you spiritual insights you are not able to get otherwise. As it has been taught to Pagans for centuries, you are your own best teacher. That which you cannot find within yourself, you will never find without.]

[This addendum to the guided meditation takes you through the process of dream retrieval, one of the most respected of shamanic arts. This optional section may be used if you have had a dream that you cannot remember and want to, or if you have one that was unfinished and you feel it is important to see it through to its conclusion.]

Knowing that you must find your missing or unconcluded dream, you allow your intuition to lead you to the cave of dreams. You are led through a misty land populated by fantastic creatures and images. In the center of a clear blue lake you see the mouth of the cave of dreams. The cave appears to be made of pure silver, and it glistens in the half-light of this dream world. Inside are all the dream images that have ever been made by women.

There is no boat nearby, or any apparently easy way to cross the lake to the cave. Then, knowing that in the dream world you can do anything, you step out onto the lake and find you are able to walk on the surface of the water. You walk toward the cave entrance and note that it has no guardian; its only protection seems to be the lake, an obstacle you discovered you could so easily overcome.

You step inside, and see that the cave of dreams is not dark inside, as you would expect a normal cave to be. Many pathways lead away from this central chamber. Because you have been contemplating retrieving this particular dream while in your waking state, you decide to follow your instinct and select a pathway.

You walk through the narrow chamber, which contains an infinite number of closed doorways. Most of the markings upon them do not look familiar, and you realize those rooms do not contain the dream you are seeking. Finally you come upon a doorway that you know without a doubt is yours. As you grasp the doorknob you vividly recall either the point at which your dream left off, or the feeling you had upon awakening from the dream you could not remember. You open the door, and step into the dream sequence.

[When you are satisfied that you have retrieved all of the dream information that is possible for now, you should begin walking back toward the mouth of the silver cave, following the same pathway you used to enter the dream. Then you may continue with the process of returning to your normal consciousness, which follows.]

When you are ready to leave *Tir na mBan*, you come back to the blood path and follow it back to the shoreline. [If it cannot be found, mentally will yourself to it.]

A: Shapeshifting

As you stand on the shore, you feel the animal form that you took on to come here reasserting itself, and you allow the transformation. Then you step off the shore and back onto the left-hand side of the spiral path, following it ever outward to where it connects with the right-hand spiral. At this point your form changes again to your own physical body.

B: Horse or Bird Guide

Waiting for you on the shore is the (horse or raven) that brought you here. You climb again on her back and she starts carrying you out onto the left-hand side of the spiral path, following it ever outward to where it connects with the right-hand spiral. At this point you dismount, thank the creature, and continue walking.

C: Silver Boat

Waiting for you on the shore is the silver boat that brought you here. You climb into it again and it easily slips back out onto the left-hand side of the spiral path, following it ever outward to where it connects with the right-hand spiral. At this point the boat stops, and you get out. The boat retreats back into the mist, where you know it will be waiting for you on your next trip to *Tir na mBan*.

You joyfully continue moving into the center of the right-hand spiral, feeling *Tir na mBan* growing farther away from you as the atmosphere loses its fluidity.

Feeling as if you have truly been born anew, and have received another level of initiation into the Celtic women's tradition, you reach the center of the right-hand spiral. You feel yourself suddenly fading away from the astral world as a gentle veil of space and time closes off your world from this one, and you say to yourself, "I am home."

Gently your consciousness transfers itself back to your physical body. Feel now the awareness of your physical self returning to your legs, arms, back, stomach, and neck. Flex them and relish the joy of being a living human being.

You are once again part of the waking physical world. You open your eyes and feel exhilarated, energized, and glad to be home with your new wisdom. Do not forget to ground yourself [see Appendix C if you are unfamiliar with this concept]. Touch the earth, eat, scream, or do anything else that firmly roots you in the present. Then be sure to record this experience in your Book of Shadows, or other magickal journal, for later reference.

Notes

1 Mynne, Hugh. *The Faerie Way* (St. Paul, Minn.: Llewellyn, 1996), 31.

2 Matthews, Caitlin. *The Celtic Book of Days: A Guide to Celtic Spirituality and Wisdom* (Rochester, Vt.: Destiny Books, 1995), 120.

3 A lengthy guided meditation specifically designed to unite you with your shadow self, and to extract a talisman of power from this union, can be found in my earlier work, *Celtic Myth and Magick* (St. Paul, Minn.: Llewellyn, 1995).

A CELTIC WOMAN'S WHEEL OF THE YEAR

The traditional Wiccan wheel of the year (see diagram) is very well known, and takes the majority of its festivals and symbolism from old Anglo-Celtic practices. These eight festivals, known as sabbats from the Greek *sabatu*, meaning "to rest," are divided into two categories: the Greater Sabbats and the Lesser Sabbats.[1] The Greater Sabbats are those thought to be Celtic originally: Samhain, Imbolg, Bealtaine, and Lughnasadh.

The Solar Year

The solar wheel of the year was the basic framework on which the Celts hung their eternal Goddess and the reborn/dying God. The Goddess moves through the year from the virgin who gives birth to the God in winter, to the time she mates with him in spring, to birthing him/his son at the harvest, to watching him die at Samhain.

Though the solar cycle dominates the modern Celtic wheel of the year, I have read many arguments about which of the solar sabbats were original to it and which were later additions. Later in this case is a relative term, with some sabbats being added to the calendar in Ireland rather than Gaul. Each time I think I have it all figured out, I read a new study that

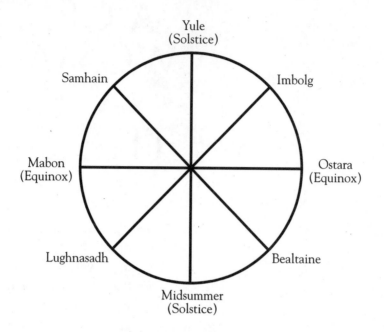

Yule
(Solstice)

Samhain

Imbolg

Mabon
(Equinox)

Ostara
(Equinox)

Lughnasadh

Bealtaine

Midsummer
(Solstice)

The Traditional Wheel of the Year

presents good evidence for another version, and feel compelled to change my mind. I have read that in Gaul only Imbolg, Bealtaine, and Lughnasadh were used. But since Lugh was a God of the Tuatha De Danaan, and not part of the Celtic pantheon until the Celts reached Ireland, this assertion seems suspect. It is also assumed by many scholars and Pagans that the solstices and equinoxes were not part of the Celtic wheel of the year until the invading Norse and Normans made it so. This too is suspect. The two solstices are easily the oldest solar festival dates known to humankind, recognized in some form by virtually every ancient culture and by many modern ones. The fact that we call these solstices by the names Midsummer and Midwinter tell us that these were placed at some point into the Celtic year, or these designations make no sense. On our modern calendars they serve as the starting point for the summer and winter seasons, not as "mid" points. Midsummer is halfway between Bealtaine and Lughnasadh, and Midwinter is halfway between Samhain and Imbolg. Only when placed in the context of the Celtic year do they become true halfway points in the seasons.

Today we have set firm—or fairly firm—dates for the Greater Sabbats. This too is a modern affectation. The original festival dates were based on agricultural times. For example, Samhain would have been celebrated when the last of the harvest was in, and Bealtaine would have been celebrated when the planting was done and the cattle were ready to be taken to summer pasture. Sometime in the early middle ages these dates were fixed according to astrological phenomena, criteria that would push forward the date of each Greater Sabbat by five to seven days if it were used today.

Having precise dates set aside for holidays seems to be important to our modern minds. We are so removed from agricultural cycles that we need these firm markers in place. We have conceptualized these festivals into what we call a wheel of the year, a paradigm of the eternal cycles of life, death, and rebirth. There are two basic schemes used by Celtic Pagans to symbolize the wheel of the year, one a perfect circle and the other a rough rendering of Brighid's Cross (see diagrams).

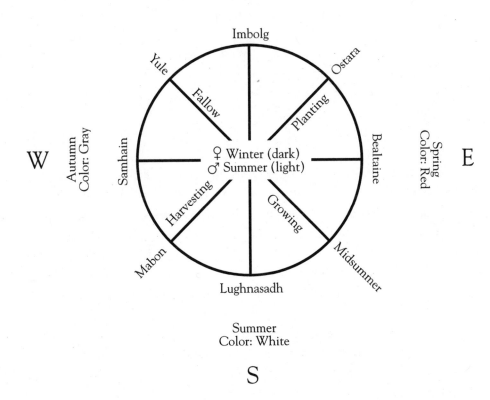

Celtic Wheel of the Year, Round

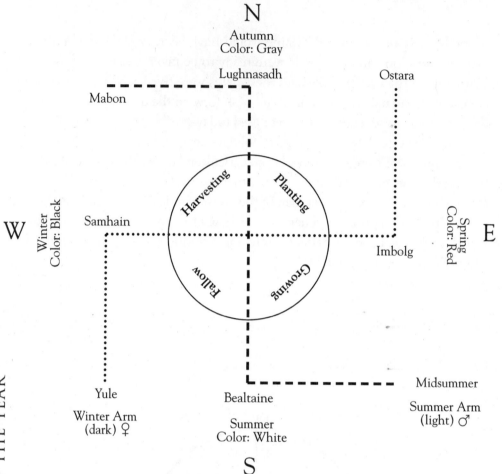

Celtic Wheel of the Year, Spoked

The Great Sabbats in Ireland were once linked to special sites and to Goddesses who were sovereign over those landscapes.[2] Samhain festivals were held on earth sacred to Tlachtga, an underworld Goddess; Imbolg was held at Tara, on earth sacred to Tea, a founder and guardian of this stronghold; Bealtaine rituals were held on ground sacred to Eire, the Goddess for whom Ireland is named; and Lughnasadh was held near Tara, on ground sacred to Taillte, a Goddess of competition, on whose land special games of skill were held each year.

The Celtic emphasis on the solar year has led some researchers to believe that this meant the male deities were more important to the meaning of the festivals. While this is true in several European cultures, it is not true of the

Celts, who did not neatly divide their divine archetypes neatly into male = sun, female = moon categories. There were numerous Celtic Goddesses associated with the sun or with fire, a solar attribute. In Ireland, several bear the name Grainne or Greine, which roughly means "sunny." One Grainne was the mother of nine daughters, who each lived in shelters called griannon, or "sun houses." She was probably a twin of Aine, a sun Goddess who represented the waning year, while Grainne was the deity of the waxing year, in much the same way we celebrate the Holly and Oak Kings today.[3] Even in modern Irish the word for sun, *grian*, is a feminine noun.

The Lunar Year

The machinations of the lunar year are not without their controversies. Today, many Pagans are aware of the Celtic Tree Calendar, based on lunar cycles, each cycle being given a tree name that represents its energies. Some say that this calendar was originated by the Druids, others say it was the invention of author Robert Graves for his book *The White Goddess*.[4] The truth probably lies somewhere between these two extreme viewpoints.

We have evidence of a lunar year being observed in Romano-Celtic Gaul. This is known today as the Coligny Calendar, because the bronze plate on which the calendar was engraved was unearthed near the present-day French town of Coligny in 1897.[5] The year was divided into twelve or thirteen units, which we assume to be lunar. The fact that one of the months, *Mid Samonios*, appears to be on standby in case it is needed[6] further underscores this since they are more than twelve, but less than thirteen, lunar cycles in the standard 365-day year. A solar year can have either twelve or thirteen lunations.

With or without *Mid Samonios*, the Coligny Calendar still does not break down into handy units when compared with solar time. Complex mathematical calculations bring it in at about 363 days, leaving the solar year about one and a quarter days short. Other scholars have tried to make a case for a 366-day Celtic year, to correspond with the Celtic year and day unit of magickal time, but none of these have matched our solar year any better than other lunar calendars have done.

The arguments may go on forever. All we are certain of now is that the Coligny Calendar began its year in October with a moon that bears the same root word, *sam*, of the festival of Samhain, the solar festival that begins the Celtic year. The Coligny months are:

Month Name	Translation
Samonios	Seed Time
Dumannios	Time of Darkness
Riuros	Cold Time
Anagantios	Unable to Get Out Time
Orgronios	Time of Ice
Cutios	Time of the Winds
Giamonios	Sprouting Time
Simivisonios	Time of Brightness
Equos	Horse Time
Elembios	Claiming Time
Edrinos	Time of Justice
Cantlos	Time of Song
Mid Samonios	Center of Seed Time

Modern Celtic Pagans enjoy their lunar tree calendar in spite of its controversy, which is as it should be. Many of the festivals that have been added to Pagan calendars are not ancient, though the concepts behind them are. The Tree Calendar has two forms, one that begins its year at Samhain, and the other at Midwinter. Midwinter became the new solar new year due to the influence of the Norse between 700–1100 CE. The order of the Tree Calendar also varies slightly due to different interpretations of the Ogham Alphabet, a system of lines and slashes that made up an old form of Celtic writing. That the oghams relate to trees and bear tree names is a given, but whether they were applied to months of the year before very recent times is likely an issue that will never cease to be debated.[7] The tree month names are included in the listing of Celtic festivals and holidays in this chapter for those of you who wish to begin using them this way.

A Celtic Woman's Calendar of Festivals

The model I suggest for a Celtic Woman's Wheel of the Year may not appeal to all women on the Celtic path. I can only suggest the festivals I feel have the greatest meaning for women, and offer my own ideas of creative ways to celebrate them. Some of these ways are ancient, others are based on ancient concepts, and some are modern interpretations.

Some of the festivals in this model are wholly modern in origin. I have seen them listed on Pagan calendars, often with conflicting dates. We can begin to work with these to create meaningful Celtic festivals for women, and we should always feel free to create our own festivals, either for our own use, or for that of our family or women's spirituality groups.

I can hear the traditionalists among you shudder in horror at the thought of us mere mortals creating new festivals. But the fact remains that someone, sometime, had to create the old ones. Trust that our deities did not hand them down to us on stone tablets, as the Gods of some other religions were wont to do. The Greater Sabbats we celebrate today do not follow the same format they did two thousand years ago. Spirituality just doesn't thrive in that sort of static environment. Spirituality and its expression has to evolve and grow with the people it serves, and who serve it, in order to keep it meaningful. True, many of the deeper aspects of these festivals have remained intact, and that has been their strength, but their outer forms have changed.

An Irish proverb says, "Neither make nor break a custom."[8] Yet in the course of only a century we can see changes in Irish celebrations. The old festivals, where everyone stopped working to join in the communal celebration, are on the wane. Some old customs are kept alive even though the original meaning is no longer clear to those who follow the customs; this is the perfect way to ensure their further demise or alteration. Only by making a concerted effort to embrace meaningful celebrations, old or new, will they continue to be an inherent part of Pagan spirituality.

My scheme for a Celtic woman's wheel of the year embraces nearly thirty solar and lunar festivals. For each of the major festivals discussed in this chapter, I offer some practical suggestions for its observance. But please don't let my concept inhibit you. That is not my intent. You should always feel free and able to try your own hand at creating special rituals and celebratory ideas, and you should never feel that you cannot add to or subtract from this wheel model as you see fit. Any idea given for group work can be adapted to solitary practice, and solitary ideas can be made workable for groups. If you are still unfamiliar with Pagan ritual forms, you can either look at the other rituals in this book for guidance, at Appendix C on circle casting and closing, or obtain one of the other books on the market that delve into this subject in more depth. While there are not too many ways you can go wrong, there are certain ritual markers that are inherently a part of Pagan practice, and their observance is important for helping impress the purpose of specific rituals on our psyches.[9]

As you will see by this listing, we can find women's mysteries in most any Celtic festival, old or modern. Feel free to adapt others or create your own as the spirit moves you. There are no limits other than those of your imagination and desire to stretch your potential as a woman and as a Goddess incarnate!

As it harms none, do what you will!

Samhain
October 31

So much has been written about this popular festival that it seems redundant, as well as daunting, to try to compress it all into a brief description emphasizing the women's aspect. This is primarily a celebration of the new year and a feast of the harvest's ending, and a reaffirmation of our beliefs in the eternal cycles of death and rebirth. On Samhain we celebrate the spirit world and honor our ancestors. This festival may even have roots far back into pre-history, to a time when unity through mother blood bound tribes together, and worship of female ancestors formed the basis of their spiritual orientation.[10]

There are two possible sources for the origin of the word *Samhain*. The most remote is that it is derived from the name of an Aryan death God called Samana; another is that it is from the Irish Gaelic word *samhraidhreadh*, which literally means "the summer's end." Still another is that the word may have originally meant "one together,"[11] which would accurately echo the meaning of this festival as a time when the veil separating the world of the living from that of the dead is parted, and our ancestors are permitted to walk among us.

The crone, as Goddess and ancestor, is the supreme deity of this festival. Samhain is the night when the old God, her son and lover, dies, and she goes into mourning for him until she can transform herself into the virgin who gives him rebirth. The image of her as the Halloween hag stirring her bubbling cauldron comes from the Celtic belief that all dead souls return, like the God, to her cauldron of life, death, and rebirth to await reincarnation.

To celebrate this sabbat you can follow an old Irish custom and place candles in your windows to illuminate the spirits' travels; host a Dumb Supper, a meal eaten in total silence, which the spirits of the dead are invited to; or make and give away Soul Cakes. These treats made to nourish the wandering spirits were handed out to Scottish and English children who came begging for them door to door, one of the origins of our modern trick-or-treat custom. You might also consider hosting a costume party to which women must come dressed as women of great strength and power from the past.

Because the doors to other times and places are wide open on this night, it is a good time to try some past-life work. This can be done alone or with a group. If you are not familiar with any of the methods for doing this, now is the season for discovery.[12]

Your Samhain rituals can feature Soul Cakes. They're not just for trick-or-treat anymore! Pass them out and have everyone make a wish on them for the new year. The communal breaking of bread was considered an act of good faith in many cultures, and can serve to help strengthen the bonds of your Celtic women's spirituality group.

You can also mourn the dead God with the traditional women's keening wail, and offer comfort to the grieving Goddess.

Bring photos or mementos of your female ancestors to your circle and honor their memories. Call upon the crone to assist the spirits of the newly dead to the Otherworld. Allow all present to share memories of passed-over women.[13] You might even want to host a memorial ceremony for all the women executed as Witches.

It is also a nice touch to allow part of the ritual to honor a crone within your group, a woman who is wise or who has recently entered menopause. Or take time to honor the crone within yourself.

The Day of the Banshees
November 1

This festival, which appears occasionally on Pagan calendars, is neither wholly modern nor wholly ancient. The banshee, or *beansidhe,* is a spirit from the Otherworld who is attached to a particular Celtic family. On the night before a death is to occur, her lamentations are heard over the countryside. Many do not find the wail of the banshee to be disturbing at all, but find it strangely comforting.

The banshee represents the Otherworld realm of women, known as *Tir na mBan,* or the Land of Women, a world where all dead souls must go in order to be reborn. The womb of the Goddess, as represented by the bottomless cauldron, is the essence of this realm.

The precise origins of the banshee have been lost in time, but it is reasonable to assume that she represents a mother-form from the Otherworld. She may also be derived from the keening of the Goddess Brighid, who was said to wail uncontrollably and fearfully about the death of her son, Ruadhan.

You can celebrate this festival by following an old Irish equinox custom, now practiced in some rural areas as Garland Sunday, and place apples on the graves of loved ones. Apples represent the Celtic Otherworld, rebirth, eternal life, and the crone Goddess. Alone or in a group you can meditate on the meaning of the word *banshee* (*ban* = woman, *sidhe* = faery). Though this word is Irish, the banshee is known in other Celtic countries as well, usually by names that roughly mean "one who keens."

Consider creating a ritual to honor the spirit guardians of your family, or host an all-women memorial ritual for passed over loved ones and engage in lots of banshee-like keening.

Birch Moon
November or December Full Moon

Called the Moon of Inception on the Celtic tree calendar, this is a lunar cycle in which to celebrate new beginnings and fresh starts. Think of this as a bonus New Year's Day.

The Feast of Potential
November 23

This festival is another that appears on modern Pagan calendars for which I can find no ancient roots, yet the concept is appealing. The holiday is sometimes referred to as the Secret of the Unhewn Stone, referring to the potential inherent in all that is yet unformed.

More specifically, to hew something means to strike it repeatedly with an axe, or other cutting or shaping tool, to make it take on a desired form. Another meaning of "hew" is to force something to conform, particularly in regard to abstractions such as ideas or principles.

This holiday is a solemn one for me, a time for the solitary to force herself to introspection and face what is not easy to face. It is a day for examining difficult ideas, mulling over changes, and eliminating the root causes of our resistance to them, a day to hack away, blow by blow, at our fears and insecurities. It is a day for facing those blockages to our spiritual progress that are spoken of and written about repeatedly, but for which few actually meet the challenge: the terror of the threshold, the shadow self, and the co-walker (see Chapters 13–15). Decide now to define as a blockage to spiritual progress anything that keeps you separated from fully knowing and connecting with the divine.

Prior to any feasting, force yourself to face up to something you do not want to think about. This can be a spiritual goal, a personal hurdle, or a current problem you must work through. Allow the feasting afterward to be your reward. Work a ritual, meditation, or guided journey that has always been difficult for you, perhaps one with imagery you have always found disturbing. Allow yourself to face this terror of the threshold and move past it. If you cannot face it, make an attempt to get closer than you have before. Call upon your warrior self for courage (see Chapters 4 and 5). Or take a guided meditation or astral project into a world where you must face the shadow self or co-walker.

Perhaps you might want to make a list of all the things you know in your heart you have the ability to do but have not done either out of fear or lack of confidence. Pick at least one and vow to accomplish it by the end of winter. If your women's spirituality group is having internal difficulties, take this time to retreat together to discuss the potential within the group as a whole and how each woman contributes to this. Consider using this untapped potential to take your group into new and more satisfying directions.

Consider creating a solitary ritual to honor and give thanks for your own will power and talents. Align yourself with a powerful Goddess and allow her strength and resolve to blend with yours. If you are in a group situation, go around the circle and allow everyone to tell each woman about her strengths. Sometimes we display them to others but are unaware of them ourselves. After this, you may want to chant each other's name out loud to make a verbal chain of power linking your group members to one another.

Rowan Moon
December Full Moon

Sometimes called the Moon of Vision in the Celtic tree calendar, this is a moon on which to travel inward to bring out inner strengths. This has also been called the Astral Moon, a good time to try your hand at the art of astral projection, or to try to contact the spirit world.

Midwinter
Winter Solstice

The winter solstice is the oldest of all the sabbats, perhaps as much as 12,000 to 20,000 years old. In the distant past, when winter was much more dangerous than it is now, this holiday marked the rebirth of the sun as it began to wax again, and it was greeted with joy and relief. Many legends abound of Celtic priestesses and Druids who arose early so as to be able to greet the sun as it rose. Most assuredly this reverence carried over into Midwinter, the day on which she again began to grow stronger and more powerful.

In most Pagan traditions, Midwinter is seen as the birthday of a male God/son/lover from the virgin Goddess. This is true within modern Celtic traditions as well, and there are many, many rituals to be found in print to give you ideas for celebrating from this perspective. Yet, with the preponderance of female Celtic sun deities, there is no reason that Celtic women should not mark this date as the return of the Goddess of sun and fire.

At this sabbat most Wiccans enact or pay tribute to the eternal battle between the waxing and waning forces of the year. Celtic mythology and folklore gives us many names for these archetypes: the Holly King and Oak King, the Red Dragon and the White Dragon, and others. All represent a reversal of universal energy patterns toward their polarities. The battling figures are usually portrayed as male, though occasionally they battle over a sovereign Goddess, like Wales' Creiddylad, who was fought over by the Gods Gwyn and Gwyrthur.

Though the idea of Goddesses battling for rulership of the year is not a common image, the idea that one would rule and the other vanish—or go to the underworld—for half the year is not unheard of. Aine, who has a festival occurring just after Midsummer, and Grian, whose name means "sunny," are likely the same Goddess showing a different face during different halves of the year. During the "dark half" of the year, Irish folk legends say that Grian lives under a hill called Pallas Green (underworld?) in County Tipperary. Therefore it can be said that Grian rules the light half of the year (Midwinter to Midsummer) and Aine rules the dark (Midsummer to Midwinter).

In your Midwinter rituals, consider enacting Grian's return from the underworld to rule over the waxing half of the year, rather than focusing on the battling of two male archetypes, or stage a birthing ritual to welcome back the newborn sun/son as a daughter.

To further celebrate this sabbat, consider rising before dawn and going outside to greet the rising sun on the day it starts to wax again. Or host a Midwinter party and bring into it Christmas customs, most all of which were borrowed from European Pagan traditions. Decorate your home with ivy, evergreens, holly, and mistletoe, as the old Celts once did. If you have children or pets you may want to consider artificial decorations, since many parts of these plants are highly toxic. Show your faith in the waxing year by making some tentative plans for summer.

Hogmanay
December 31

This Scottish New Year's Eve festival was once called *Hagmenai*, or Moon of the Hag, and honored the crone Goddess in the depth of her winter time mourning for her lost God. Though the modern festival is celebrated with divinations and sweet treats, much as in the past, the Goddess links have been forgotten.

Festival of the Threefold Goddess
January 6

I have seen this festival listed under several dates, including one in April and one in July. The January date corresponds to Twelfth Night on the common era calendar, a holiday taken from the Teutonic Pagan traditions that marked the end of the twelve-day Midwinter celebration that focuses on their mother Goddess. April and July have no other sabbats or major festivals within them, and moving this holiday could spice up an otherwise ritually dull period of time. The day is not as important as the intent.

Clearly the Festival of the Threefold Goddess is modern in origin, the brainchild of someone or some group who wanted a special day set aside to honor the Triple Goddess. Celtic women should be especially interested in celebrating this Goddess who is so intimately connected with us.[14]

Because there is no ancient precedent set for celebrating this holiday, there should be no conflicts—within yourself or a group—about observing it, and there is lots of room for experimentation. Enjoy!

The Feast of the Morrigan

January 7

A feast day to celebrate the power and majesty of the Triple Goddess of death and destruction. Remember that with death there is rebirth, and that what she destroys, she revives.

Ash Moon

January Full Moon

A lunar cycle for connecting with the flow of all life and crafting magickal tools. Ash wands are often used in healing magick.

Imbolg

February 2

Imbolg is one of the Greater Sabbats, a fire festival that celebrates the strengthening of the young sun and his waiting bride, the earth Goddess. It is also a festival that honors Brighid,[15] a Goddess with many attributes and correspondences, including fire. The fact that fire is linked to the heat of the sun makes Brighid a natural focus of this festival. Her festival was so deeply a part of Irish culture that the church could not banish it, and was forced to name it as St. Brighid's Day, in honor of an apocryphal saint who is in reality the old Goddess.[16]

Imbolg has also been referred to as a festival of women's mysteries, with many ritual practices having been reserved for women,[17] or at least for the leadership of women. This acceptance is probably modern in origin—modern here being a relative term—having to do with Brighid's female followers, who became the nuns who guarded her sacred flame at her shrine at Kildare for hundreds of years. The rites that took place within that cloister were a blend of Pagan and Christian ways whose precise forms remain a mystery.

As late as the early twentieth century, it was customary for young women in Irish villages to dress themselves as Brighid/St. Brighid in old clothing and carry her image with them through the streets. The girls would go from door to door begging alms for "poor Biddy," a nickname for Brighid. A good share of the money or food collected went into the community, either through the local parish church or directly from the girls or their families. Giving to Brighid was thought to bring good luck, particularly in matters of the coming harvest.

On Imbolg you can honor Brighid in the old way, by making a bed for her in a small doll's cradle, and dressing her as the waiting bride of the sun or as the young sun itself. You can follow another old Irish magickal custom by leaving a white cloth, called Brighid's cloak, out overnight to collect dew. When retrieved the next morning, it is believed to contain healing properties. Wear it during the coming year when you need healing, or when you are doing healing magick for others.[18]

This is also a traditional time for augury practices, or divining the future by reading naturally occurring signs. Birds, wolves, and snakes[19] have been used as February divination devices. The use of birds and wolves came to western Europe from Rome, where they are associated with the mating festival known as Lupercalia (February 14–15). Snakes are more in keeping with the Celtic world view, and represent a link between our world and the underworld, a symbol of the renewal of the earth in spring.

In your rituals you can honor Brighid or any other sun/fire Goddess you feel moved to honor. The Christianized name for this festival is Candlemas, a name taken from the old Pagan practice of lighting many candles on this festival to symbolize the growing power of the young sun.

The Feast of St. Blaize
February 2

In France, particularly in Celtic Brittany, the Goddess Brighid, or Brigindo, became a minor saint known as St. Blaize. She is a patron of healers and a source of protection through bad winters. The name Blaize is a cognate of our English word *blaze*, clearly underscoring her place as an old fire and sun Goddess.

Alder Moon
February or March Full Moon

A moon of action as spring nears. This lunar cycle quickens with the awakening earth.

Whuppity Scoorie
March 1–3

The festive rituals designed to awaken mother earth from her long winter's nap are a much cherished part of Pagan practice today as they were in the past. In Scotland this celebration was known as Whuppity Scoorie, the very name vaguely suggesting the sort of racket inherent in the holiday.[20] Both

Anglo-Saxon and Celtic custom teaches that we must go out and ritually tap the earth three times with a staff or wand, then call out to mother earth by name, telling her it is time to stir from her slumber.

Bonfires were lit at random sites around villages and farms, symbolizing the rewarming of the earth. As the communal procession of flame bearers passed from fire site to fire site, lots of drinking and rowdy merrymaking accompanied them. Noise was everywhere—pan banging, drum beating, chanting, and so on, all designed to stir mother earth awake again.

To celebrate this festival on your own turf, take your staff or other long stick and move from place to place, tapping mother earth while entreating her to awaken. Pay special attention to areas in need of rejuvenation: fields, gardens, or places where the earth has been ravaged.

The Feast of Rhiannon
March 4

Honors the Welsh horse, moon, and ancestor Goddess. Celebrate with horse imagery, lunar rites, and the honoring of your foremothers. The horse also symbolizes the ability to move at will between worlds, making this feast day a prime time to shamanically explore other worlds.

Rhiannon shares many similarities with two other horse Goddesses: Epona and Mare. Mare is the bringer of dreams and Epona a Goddess of transformative power. Libations offered to them may bring them into your dreams.

An old folk custom from western Ireland says that if you light fires just before dawn at each corner of a perfectly oriented crossroad (one that runs directly east, west and north, south), then sit down quietly at its side, you can see Epona ride by, fleeing west from the approaching sunrise.

Day of Sheila-na-Gig
March 18

This festival is another that occasionally appears on Pagan calendars, but for which no ancient source can be found. It honors the mysterious Goddess of thresholds and women's mysteries. This is a good day to scry into or meditate on her image, allowing her to open the portal to her secrets for you (see Chapters 2 and 3).

Eostre
Spring Equinox

This Teutonic festival is celebrated in modern Wicca and in many Celtic traditions as a day of balance and sexual awakening. Eostre is a Teutonic Goddess of spring and fertility who has been welcomed into the modern Celtic pantheon.

Tea and Tephi Day
Spring Equinox

The origins of this festival are hazy, and no clear case can be made for its antiquity. It is a celebration of the twin Goddesses of Tara, the old physical and spiritual stronghold of the Irish High Kings. Tea and Tephi were women of the Tuatha De Dannan who, as sovereigns, blessed Tara with protection and legitimized its king to rule over Ireland.

Lady Day
March 25

Lady Day, a festival from Cornwall and southern Wales, has been linked to several Pagan spring festivals and, occasionally, to Lughnasadh. Some sources date the festival to April 24, and others to mid-July, though the spring dates seem to dominate.

Like Whuppity Scoorie, Lady Day celebrates the return of the Goddess, "Our Lady," from her winter slumbers. Even in modern Cornwall many old Pagan practices are still observed on this day, including burying eggs to fertilize fields, decorating with spring flowers, and dancing and feasting. Any woman who gives birth on this day is thought to be blessed of the Goddess/Virgin Mary, and the afterbirth from this event was treated as a sacred object, often used as a sacrificial offering back to the Goddess.

For Cornish women who were having trouble conceiving, Lady Day provided a perfect opportunity to go to the famous standing stone formation known as the *Men-an-Tol*. This consists of a large, circular stone through which a natural hole had been formed (representative of the Goddess/woman) and one tall, upright, phallic stone (representative of the God/man). It was customary for the women to pass themselves nine times clockwise through the holed stone while weaving magick for their own fertility.

Modern Pagans often view Lady Day as a time of sexual awakening, when the virgin Goddess goes in search of her mate, the young God. This concept has roots in older Pagan beliefs about predestined matings, of the physical reunion of the two gender-halves of the divine in human form, which is why divination concerning romance is traditionally a part of this festival. Scrying for the face of one's future mate in pools of rainwater while drinking fresh milk is one popular exercise. As with most of the Celtic spring festivals, dairy products are a main feature of the ritual feast.

Like many Pagan holidays, Lady Day has been given its sinister aspects as well by the modern world. During the Middle Ages in southern England, Lady Day was moved to April 4 and renamed in honor of St. Mark, a saint who is often portrayed as shepherding souls to the Christian heaven. In southern England, there was once a folk custom that taught that if you sit inside the front door of a church at midnight on St. Mark's Eve, all the souls of those destined to die within the coming year will stroll past from east to west, towards the Otherworld.

Willow Moon
March Full Moon

Because willow is a feminine tree that thrives on the feminine element of water, and because its boughs were traditionally used to make magickal tools, this cycle of the Celtic tree calendar has been called the Witches' Moon.

Hawthorn Moon
April Full Moon

Blooming hawthorn is a faery flower, one said to have been gathered by sovereigns such as Guinevere on Bealtaine morning.

Bealtaine
May 1

The Bealtaine sabbat is one of the most popular festivals of the Wiccan year. In modern Celtic traditions, it has become the traditional time for handfastings (Pagan marriage rites). This comes from the sabbat's main purpose: the celebration of the sexual union or marriage of the Goddess and God. In truth, Bealtaine was the traditional time for divorce in old Ireland (known as handparting in modern Wicca), and marriages were made in November.[21] This makes sense in a herding culture. In November the cattle would all have been brought back to the village or tribal stronghold from their summer pasture, and the women who had gone with them to see to their care would be back with their clan.

As with Samhain, there is a great deal of controversy about how this sabbat got its name. One possibility is that it was named for an Irish death God called Beltene (probably a spurious addition to the pantheon). Another is that it came from the name of a Scottish God called Bel, or a Gaulish fire God called Belanos. The most likely etymology of the festival is that it simply derives from the word *balefire*, meaning a sacred bonfire. Even in modern times balefires are lit all over Britain and Ireland on May Eve. In Ireland, these fires were lit only after the one at Tara was ignited. In Scotland, each community lit its own from a source known as the *tein-eigin*, or "need-fire." This was a small fire kept burning out of necessity, either for home heat or for cooking. Because all winter fires had to be extinguished before this first official day of summer, relighting these fires was a sacred task, one often given to a highly ranking priestess or Druid. Within their own homes, it was women who had the honor of relighting the household fire, and it was women who would tend to it all year long.

To celebrate Bealtaine on your own, look into the many books on basic Wiccan/Pagan practice that provide either raw outlines or complete texts of rituals. The union of the male and female principles—an act known as the Great Rite—will be at the center of all of them. Light fires as you choose, setting aside a piece of burned wood as a talisman of protection against unwanted spirits.

You can also purify yourself before your rituals by anointing your body with morning dew from a hawthorn tree. Ritual purification was and is an important part of Pagan ritual practice, one that seems to have a healthy following in women's traditions. The Arthurian legends tell us that Queen Guinevere rode out early on Bealtaine morning with her handmaidens to gather white hawthorn, but if hawthorn is not available to you, any dewy tree whose energies you enjoy can work as well.

In a group setting, you can dance the May Pole, another old custom from Britain and Ireland whose roots are shrouded in mystery. (See Appendix G for dance tunes appropriate for the May Pole dance.) The May Pole has had three periods of popularity, a number modern Celts can appreciate. The first was in the years prior to the outbreak of the Black Plague in Europe (early fourteenth century), the second was after the plague and before England's Commonwealth period (1648–1660) when all Pagan practices were banned, and the last was in the post-Commonwealth period when the old customs were revived with joy.

White and red ribbons are attached to the pole's top. There are two interpretations of these traditional colors. One is that the white represents the virgin Goddess and red represents the God, the other is that the white stands for the virgin Goddess and the red is for the mother. The May Pole is a phallic symbol that symbolically impregnates the birth canal being woven around it by the dancers weaving in and out with their ribbons. Again, there are two interpretations of this symbolism. One is that the blending of white and red represents the union of Goddess and God, and the other is that it represents the virgin passing into the mother aspect by her union with the God.

Veneration of the Thorn
May 4

This is yet another festival for which no ancient origination can be pinpointed, though it was likely part of an older festival known as the Night of the Lunantisidhe (see later in this chapter), which honored the old faery guardians of the thorn trees.

Many Irish holy wells were once Pagan sacred sites, and thorn trees—usually whitethorn—are still found around them in larger numbers. Many modern Irish still believe that these trees are protected by faeries, and are not to be disturbed for any reason not in keeping with the holy traditions of the well site.[22] When near holy wells, we usually find small scraps of white cloth tied to the trees, to symbolize wishes made by pilgrims at the site.[23]

The blackthorn is another type of thorn tree, one that has two uses. In English traditions, it is a wood used to level curses. In Irish tradition, it is one of blessings, the same wood used to make *shillelaghs*, or walking sticks, by the Irish faeries known as the Leprechauns.

Night of the Lunantisidhe
May 16

Because the date of this celebration is so close to that of the Veneration of the Thorn, they were probably once the same holiday. Since thorn trees are used to make petitions to the deities in modern Irish pilgrimages to holy well sites, it can be surmised that the Veneration of the Thorn was the Christian version and the Night of the Lunantisidhe the older, Pagan one.

This is a night to pay homage to these fearful guardians of the Irish blackthorn tree. The Lunantisidhe have a wizened appearance, like stick figures, and possess long arms and fingers so they may easily climb through the blackthorn trees in which they live. Modern folklore says these faeries hate humans, but this may be a guilt projection for the way we have treated nature. One legend says that they leave the trees only on the nights of the full moon.

Oak Moon
May or June Full Moon

On the Celtic tree calendar this is a tree of strength associated with Midsummer rituals. It is also a masculine energy tree, but its symbol of strength and endurance is one women can share.

Midsummer
Summer Solstice

In Celtic Paganism we are usually taught that Midsummer marks the time of the sun at its peak, and that image is one of a male deity. As mentioned when discussing Midwinter, the Celts have many, many sun Goddesses, as well as Goddesses who have sun imagery within their archetypes. All of these can be used to create Midsummer rites meaningful to Celtic women.

Celebrate the full flower of woman-power at Midsummer: dedicate yourself as warrior, learn more about Celtic sun Goddesses, host a feast featuring hot foods, and revel in her warm face at its zenith.

The Feast of Aine
June 25

This fire festival was once a part of Midsummer rites. Aine is an Irish fire and cattle Goddess whose day has been taken over by St. John. Holy well pilgrimages are popular features of her festival. Aine's name has been linked to Midsummer Eve torchlight processions in her native Munster which took place well into the twentieth century. It was once an old Irish custom to wave her torches over growing fields of crops at Midsummer to bless and protect them.

Festival of Cerridwen
July 3

This is another festival with varying dates; July 3 is the one given by author Zsuzsanna Budapest.[24] Cerridwen is a sow Goddess of knowledge, wisdom, and plenty. Use her holiday to celebrate all you have learned.

Holly Moon
July Full Moon

A lunar cycle that emphasizes polarities, particularly that between male and female.

Rowena
July 15

Author Nigel Pennick[25] says this holiday was created in honor of Rowena, a Cornish Goddess of knowledge. In the Celtic traditions, the rowan tree has protective powers, and amulets of protection made from its bark and leaves were crafted on this day.

Amulets can be made in any number of ways. One simple method is to tie up some leaves and bark in a cloth of white or gold while visualizing the goal of the spell, then tying it off with red thread. White and gold are traditional colors of protection and red is a color of warning and defense. Carry it with you, or keep it in a prominent place in your home.

Lughnasadh
August 1

Lughnasadh is an old Irish word that now simply refers to the month of August in modern Ireland. The old Irish word may have meant "Lugh's wedding,"[26] which links Lugh, as a harvest lord, to the land or Goddess. This festival, which celebrates the first fruits of the harvest, is also known as Lammas ("loaf mass") in Wicca. The first harvest sets in motion the events that will lead to the sacrifice of the sacred king (see Chapter 12). This acceptance of the Goddess as his mate, her giving him the authority to be the harvest lord, makes him a sacred king.

In many Pagan traditions, this is the sabbat on which the king is slain, symbolically cut down with the harvest. In others it is the wedding of the sacred king only, and his sacrifice will come at Samhain, when the last of the grain harvest is taken in.

Celebrate Lughnasadh with a harvest or wedding feast. Focus your energies on the power of the feminine to bring forth the harvest from her womb (the land) and to grant sacred status to her harvest lord.

Taillte's Day
Early to Mid-August

The myths surrounding this Goddess of competition were the inspiration for Irish games of skill and endurance similar to the Greek Olympics. These were held annually in Ireland for several centuries, and had some successful revivals in the late nineteenth century. Celebrate Taillte's Day by hosting your own games, or by testing the limits of your own physical endurance.

Hazel Moon
August or September Full Moon

This is a lunar cycle to honor the crone and to celebrate wisdom.

Mabon
Autumn Equinox

Though many argue that the equinox was not celebrated by the Celts until the coming of the Saxons and Norse, today the sabbat bears the name of the Welsh God, Mabon, the "young son" of Modron, the "great mother."

The sabbat is the second of the three harvest festivals, Lughnasadh being the first and Samhain the last. It is primarily the harvest of berries and a time for making wines. Irish custom says that blackberries, sacred to Brighid, must be picked between now and Samhain, or left on the bushes for the pookas, the nasty cloven-hooved faeries who lay claim to unharvested foods after November 1.

Mabon is the time when the Goddess enters cronehood, and when it is proper to adorn graves with symbols of rebirth. It is also a time of balance, when light and darkness are equal, but after which the dark is dominant. Rituals that celebrate sacred burial space, the croning of the Goddess, and hopes for regeneration are appropriate.

Vine Moon
September Full Moon

A celebration of the harvest, particularly of products used to make alcoholic beverages.

The Feast of Brewing
September 28

Celebrates the making of alcoholic beverages for festivals and sacred purposes. This is a good time to honor the Breton Goddess of heather and heather wine, Uroica.

Garland Sunday
Late August or Early September

An old communal celebration in which people took garlands adorned with apples to local cemeteries. There they tossed the apples about and mourned the dead, then repaired to a communal gathering spot for dancing, drinking, and feasting. For the Celts, apples are symbols of the crone, and of both death and eternal life. One of the Welsh names for the Otherworld is Avalon, meaning "land of apples."

Ivy Moon
October Full Moon

Called the Moon of Resilience, which addresses our beliefs in rebirth, our triumph over death.

Reed Moon
October or November

A cycle of completeness, of home and hearth and looking inward.

Notes

1 The sabbats are explored in depth in several books, including Laurie Cabot's *Celebrate the Earth* (New York: Delta, 1994), Pauline and Dan Campanelli's *Ancient Ways* (St. Paul, Minn.: Llewellyn, 1991), Janet and Stewart Farrar's *Eight Sabbats For Witches* (Custer, WA: Phoenix, 1988), and my own *The Sabbats* (St. Paul, Minn.: Llewellyn, 1994).

2 Matthews, John and Caitlin. *The Encyclopaedia of Celtic Wisdom* (Shaftsbury, Dorset: Element Books, 1994), 198–199.

3 These figures represent the waning and waxing halves of the year respectively. They are conceptualized as two halves of the same being. At the two major turning points of the year they battle, with one emerging victorious.

4 New York: Farrar, Straus and Giroux, 1966.

5 Rees, Alwyn and Brinley Rees. *Celtic Heritage: Ancient Tradition in Ireland and Wales* (New York: Thames and Hudson, 1961), 84.

6 Matthews, Caitlin. *The Elements of the Celtic Tradition* (Longmeade, Shaftsbury, Dorset: Element Books, 1989), 92.

7 There have been numerous books exploring these connections. Three that can get you started in this study are Robert Graves' *The White Goddess* (New York: Farrar, Straus and Giroux, 1966); Pattalee Glass-Keontop's *Year of Moons, Season of Trees* (St. Paul, Minn.: Llewellyn, 1991); and Edred Thorsson's *The Book of Ogham* (St. Paul, Minn.: Llewellyn, 1992).

8 Delaney, Mary Murray. *Of Irish Ways* (New York: Harper and Row, 1973), 149.

9 For those unfamiliar with ritual format and purpose, I highly recommend Lady Sabrina's *Reclaiming the Power* (St. Paul, Minn.: Llewellyn, 1992) which explores Pagan ritual practices in depth.

10 Walker, Barbara G. *Women's Rituals: A Sourcebook* (San Francisco: HarperCollins, 1990), 116.

11 Raftery, Joseph, ed. *The Celts* (Dublin: Mercier Press, 1964), 89.

12 Try Raymond Buckland's *Doors to Other Worlds* (St. Paul, Minn.: Llewellyn, 1992), or any books published by the Spiritualist Churches for a beginner's overview of these arts.

13 The term "passed over" is synonymous with "deceased." In Wicca, it refers to our belief that the soul has passed on into the Otherworld.

14 This is not to imply that the Goddess is not connected with men, or that the God is not connected with women in any way. But no matter how much we feel connected, or how many invocation rituals we do, there will always be some barriers, some large and some small, to fully understanding someone/something of another gender while we are locked into a physical incarnation of a member of the opposite sex. Making the effort is important in Paganism, or any tradition, because it helps make us whole beings better able to contact the universal divine which is, ultimately, genderless.

15 Brighid is her Irish name. In England and Wales she was Brigantia or Brittania, and in Gaul she was Brigindo.

16 See Seamas O'Cathain's *The Festival of Brigit: Celtic Goddess and Holy Woman* (Dublin: DBA Publications, 1995).

17 Blamires, Steve. *Glamoury: Magic of the Celtic Green World* (St. Paul, Minn.: Llewellyn, 1995), 244.

18 Delaney, 150.

19 Blamires, 238.

20 In Cornwall, this festival was put on hold until after the passing of these "Blind Days," the first three days of March when it was considered unlucky to do any work. These are also called the "Borrowed Days," and their confusion probably comes from changes in the calendar made in the eighteenth century. In Cornwall, and in some parts of Scotland, this is celebrated on March 23.

21 Power, Patrick C. *Sex and Marriage in Ancient Ireland* (Dublin: Mercier Press, 1976), 27.

22 MacManus, Dermot. *The Middle Kingdom: The Faerie World of Ireland* (Gerrards Cross, Buckinghamshire: Smythe, 1973), 52–57.

23 Pennick, Nigel. *The Pagan Book of Days* (Rochester, Vt.: Destiny, 1992), 67.

24 Budapest, Zsuzsanna. *The Grandmother of Time* (San Francisco: Harper & Row, 1989), 141.

25 Pennick, 89.

26 Blamires, 277.

BECOMING PRIESTESS

Of all the roles women have played throughout history, none was so vigilantly and violently attacked as our position as priestesses among our people. As the patriarchy closed ranks with the church in Europe, the attack on all things feminine took a paranoid turn. Women who were spiritual leaders and teachers were feared as being too powerful to be safe. That some men still fear women's power today is evident by their continuing efforts to fight the Pagan revival. They have good reason to fear. When any disenfranchised group of people have their innermost expressions of the self routinely repressed, they find other ways to express themselves outside of the status quo, and they forge new paths to power that lie outside the boundaries of current law and custom.

When misogynists and other detractors of women's right to worship as they choose say that restoring women to their role as priestess would overturn life as we know it, they are right. Women who recognize that they have the power to contact and work with deity on their own, and who realize they are in control of themselves, cannot be controlled by others, especially by faceless authoritarian organizations like the church. The power of the divine is much stronger than that of any institution seeking to block people out. Pagan history has shown us over and over that the old ways find a way to survive no matter what is thrown against them.

That women have fought and died for their right to serve as spiritual leaders is well recorded in many parts of the world. In Celtic records it is sketchier, but still present. This is one of the hardest areas of Celtic studies to delve into, because the chroniclers of history were men. It is a fact that history is written by the winners, the conquerors; they place their view of events before us with no one to refute them or provide another point of view. Thus it should not be surprising that when priestesses are mentioned at all in Celtic literature, it is usually in a story about how they abused their powers and met their downfalls.[1] One such legend surrounds three hundred Irish women, presumably priestesses, who were slain at Tara by a king to whom they refused to swear their allegiance. Author Mary Condren[2] hypothesizes that these women may have been temple priestesses, similar to the Vestal Virgins of Rome, who refused to mate with the sacred king, thereby denying him the legitimacy of his kingship under the old Celtic laws. By killing them, the king severed his ties with the sacred spirit of the land personified by the Goddess of sovereignty, and the unbroken chain of sacred kingship that extended back thousands of years was severed for good. Kings no longer needed queens to be whole.

The expectations of a priestess within a religious setting have likely not altered drastically over many thousands of years. When her position is accepted by those she serves, we can surmise that her role remains the same simply because the basic functions of spiritual leadership have not changed much over time.

The Modern Pagan Priestess

Do you want to serve as priestess?

Think about the phrasing of that question. Whenever we refer to someone who functions as a religious leader, we almost always refer to their role as one of a servant. This semantic truth cuts across all religious lines, and remains true whether that leader is male or female.

Simply defined, a priestess is one who serves both her people and her deities. It is not a managerial position in which you get to give orders to others, and it is not an ego-enhancing office designed to allow you to feel set above the others in your circle. A priestess is a mediator, a facilitator, and a teacher. Pagan priestesshood is a life-long commitment to service, one that requires humility, good judgment, and self-responsibility to fulfill.

The concept of service is echoed in ancient mythology. That the cauldron or grail is symbolic of the divine feminine, especially in the Celtic traditions, is a given. They also symbolize the priestess as the Goddess incarnate. In the grail legends of the Arthurian myths, we have three questions being posed to those who seek the sacred grail. The first is, "Who does the grail serve?" The answer, of course, turns out to be, "It serves humanity."[3] Therefore, a priestess who has accepted the earthly mantle of the Goddess must serve humanity as she would the Goddess.

In Paganism, a priestess does not have exclusive rights to the divine, nor is she the only one who can successfully contact the deities, cast spells, or reach out to the Pagan community. Once anyone—male or female—is initiated into Pagan life, he or she is looked upon as a type of priest or priestess, able to connect with the divine and needing no intermediary.

A modern priestess is likely a woman of sound judgment, even temperament, good at working with others, and at home with the energies of the circle and of nature. She is someone who has put time and effort into her studies, and who realizes that this initiation into priestesshood is a new beginning, not an ending. Her learning will always continue. When she allows it to stop, the Goddess is likely to try to take back that honor that she bestowed—that of the priestess as her connection to nature rituals.

The precise route a modern woman takes to priestesshood, and the duties of this role, vary from tradition to tradition. There are two basic tradition structures: the hierarchical and the priestly. Which style a woman follows, or prefers, often determines her route to priestesshood and the title she is referred to by others.

Hierarchical traditions are those that have degree systems, or a hierarchy of initiations one must undergo in order to progress from one level to another. These types of groups, or covens as they are sometimes called, are popular among those who practice in Celtic traditions, though they are clearly less popular in women's spirituality settings. Usually priestesshood is granted with a second degree in a three-degree system; the title "high priestess" is usually granted upon completion of third degree studies. In hierarchical traditions, usually only those who have achieved a third-degree initiation or higher are permitted to lead rituals and teach newcomers. Those who achieve the high priestess rank are often referred to by others in their traditions by the courtesy title, Lady.

In a priestly tradition, there are no degrees to work through and no hierarchical ladders to climb. Everyone within the group is encouraged to achieve priestesshood for herself. No ritual is ever leaderless, but leadership roles are usually passed around or shared among members. A newcomer is generally initiated after at least a year and day of study. This is a term of magickal time mentioned frequently in Celtic myths and legends, and it has come into western Paganism as an accepted time frame in which a newcomer can study and prepare herself for dedication to the Pagan path. In my tradition, new initiates are encouraged to begin a study that leads them to initiation as priestess (or as priest, since this is not a women-only tradition) after a year and a day has passed. In this time the new initiate is expected to learn to deepen her connection with deity, hone her magickal and shamanic skills, and to take on leadership roles within the circle. I was initiated into an Irish-based priestly tradition in 1986, and as a priestess in 1987, a year and a day later.

Though a specific tradition might have other specific duties outlined for priestesses, they all share three common functions. Women's spirituality groups, no matter how eclectic, share these as well. The three functions are:

Facilitator

Mediator

Teacher

The Priestess as Facilitator

Even in the most egalitarian of circles, someone who knows something about what they are doing must lead. There must be a plan of action and a common purpose or the ritual disintegrates into a stage show—all image, but no substance. A priestess is the facilitator of ritual. In the hierarchical traditions she may work only with one or two others on these matters and then announce them to the others as a *fait accompli*, while in a priestly tradition she may work with the entire group, serving as a moderator and coordinator rather than making all the key decisions herself.

Once the circle has been cast, the priestess is the primary leader. Even though everyone else may have large parts to play—maybe even larger than the role of the priestess—it is she who cues participants to what is coming. She decides when raised magickal energy has reached its peak, she decides when the deities have come to the circle, and she watches carefully for breaks in the energy patterns of the circle and repairs them as needed.

If your coven is actively seeking to expand, it is likely the priestess who will be asked to meet first with the prospective new member to assess if her energies and interests match those of the group.

Priestesses were also facilitators who safely brought newcomers into the spiritual community of the Celts, both by adoption and by birth. Until well into the nineteenth century "knee-women," or midwives, routinely "baptized" newborn babies. Unlike the Christian baptisms that would take place at a later date, the women's baptisms offered a child protection from faeries and other ill-meaning spirits.[4] The power of three was evoked in as many ways as possible: three sprinklings of water, blessings of three elements, triple deity (of old or new religion), and so on. This type of birth blessing has ancient roots, and was once the function of Celtic priestesses.

Today, Celtic priestesses are still the ones most likely to offer newcomers a way into the Pagan spiritual community through their teaching and initiation rituals.

The Priestess as Mediator

Pagans have always rejected the idea that specifically ordained persons are the only ones who can contact the divine. We firmly believe that we all have the ability to pray and be heard, to call upon the divine, and even to bring the divine essence within ourselves. But we also recognize that doing so successfully takes study and practice. A link with the divine must be formed before ritual can succeed on the deeper level we all presumably aspire to, which is why we often ask an experienced woman to serve as priestess within a group. The whole purpose of religion is to link ourselves with the divine. A priestess who has learned to view the divine both inside and outside of herself ("as above, so below") can easily act as a channel for the Goddess within ritual, and can teach others to be one as well.

Our belief that the outer and inner world reflect each other was also a Celtic concept. The Celts saw no difference between inner and outer worlds. They believed each had its areas of separation, but that they also blended and overlapped. Where they met, great reservoirs of power waited to be tapped. Again, we see the acceptance of places "in between" as being sacred and powerful. In ritual, the priestess becomes that place in between as she provides a meeting point between deity and humanity, between the Otherworld and the physical realm.

The popular Wiccan ritual known as Drawing Down the Moon is one in which the full moon as mother Goddess is brought into the body of a priestess for the duration of a lunar-centered ritual. The priestess then becomes the Goddess incarnate. Less is heard about the ritual of Drawing Down the Sun, which is a similar ritual, except that it is solar-based and almost always involves pulling the sun as God into a priest. There has always been less emphasis placed on this solar ritual, perhaps because women have always been seen as the natural shapeshifters. This ability is almost exclusive to women in Celtic myths, including initiation themes, transmigration themes, and magickal and Otherworldly adventures. This is not to say that men cannot draw in the moon, and women the sun. It is merely that these are not yet widespread practices within our collective priesthood.

A priestess may also be a mediator among the larger community. She can apply to her government (state, provincial, or other) to be legally recognized as someone who can perform civil ceremonies like marriages, known among modern Pagans as handfasting.

The Priestess as Teacher

Many covens enjoy teaching Paganism/Wicca to newcomers. Some teach general Pagan/Wiccan ways and expect the student to strike out on her own afterwards. Others teach newcomers their own tradition, and may or may not expect the student to join their group when they have finished a specific course of study.

I was once part of a very good teaching coven, and know from experience how well organized this type of group must be. Someone has to coordinate the efforts, make sure every student is getting the attention she needs, and that no one who shows great skill in a particular area is left with a teacher who cannot help fully develop that talent. After all, we cannot all be talented in every Pagan art. It is usually the priestess who is expected to make sure the teaching group runs smoothly, and that each student is paired with the best possible teacher for her.

The priestess' role as teacher may also make the priestess a counselor, an arbitrator of disputes among members, and a contact person in community relations. More and more often, schools and law enforcement agencies are asking for accurate information about Paganism.

What a priestess is not is a know-it-all. If she is to be an effective teacher, she must understand her limitations and not be afraid to say, "I don't know," if the need arises. Unfortunately, those who look to you as their personal guru get very upset when you don't have all the answers; but it is best that they learn this now and not later, when they are the teachers struggling for answers they do not have. The best teachers are also students, who recognize that Paganism is a never-ending path of study, and that there is always something new to learn and to ponder.

The Solitary Priestess

Pagans don't expect others to carry their ritual burden for them. Part of what many of us found attractive about Paganism in the first place was the fact that we were all we needed to have a satisfying and personal relationship with the divine. This has been especially important for women, who have been kept on the outside of the mainstream religions, where our function has often been to serve as brood mares for creating more followers of the faith, rather than as thinking beings created in the image of the divine.

The solitary priestess may obtain her title through others or through self-initiation. In the Pagan world as a whole, either way is valid. Be aware that your self-initiation will not be accepted among all traditions. Many traditions require that you work within their framework, and take their initiations, in order to be considered a member of that particular tradition. Many of these traditionalists still recognize the validity of those on other paths, including the solitary one. Those who don't are not worth worrying over.

Always remember that any time someone argues about the validity of your solitary initiation as a Pagan/Wiccan or a priestess, they are likely operating with an ulterior motive. A few traditionalists balk at the idea that someone can be solitary at all, much less a priestess. Usually issues of ego are involved. These people fear an erosion of their power base in the same way the mainstream churches do. These are battles I have never understood. Certainly in the heart of the Goddess there is room for all of us who wish to serve her.

I have a friend who has been a self-initiated Wiccan priestess for nearly eight years. Her knowledge and skills are extensive, and she is often complimented on the excellence of the rituals in her small, eclectic circle. A few months ago she was called to question by a large Pagan group in another part of our state who wanted to know on whose authority she was priestess and if she had been "properly trained and ordained." They insisted they weren't trying to be ugly about it, they just wanted to "help" her. She had not asked for any help, and told them in no uncertain terms that the running of her circle was none of their business, and I applauded her stand.

Group work can be tiring for a priestess, especially if she is burdened with running the show month after month. Many times this happens when others shirk their duties or do not want to be leaders. This burden can make the solitary path look very attractive. A priestess will often choose a solitary path if she feels it will benefit her spiritual growth to do so. A solitary priestess can still petition her government for legal recognition to perform handfastings, she can still teach others, and she can still be a part of the larger Pagan community. She can serve both others and her Goddess without the pressures of operating a coven on a daily basis. For those of you who have done it, I don't have to tell you what a big job it is.

As a solitary priestess, you will feel an enhancement of your ritual, a connection with the Goddess that runs much deeper than before. You may even find yourself choosing or being chosen by a deity who will become your patron. This is a very common occurrence, especially among solitaries and in non-hierarchical traditions.

The Priestess as Shaman

Another function of the priestess is as shaman, and though shamanistic events are often thought of as being for the benefit of the community, they have their solitary aspects as well. Even when the results of the effort are for the community, the actual working is a solitary experience.

Shamanism is probably the oldest spiritual discipline on earth. It is not part of any one religion or culture, but was found at the heart of them all. A shaman is sometimes referred to as a medicine man or woman. This person was someone described as a "walker between the worlds," who could trance journey in an instant into other realms to heal, divine the future, correct the past, repatriate a shattered soul, retrieve dreams, or seek out information of importance to the tribe (see Chapter 13).

Celtic shamanism has become a popular area of study in recent years, and several good books devoted to the topic have been published.[5] Women have been attracted to the shamanic arts because, once mastered, they can increase feelings of personal power in situations where one can feel very impotent. They also directly connect the practitioner to the Otherworld, the realm of deity and the spirits. Shamanism can be practiced almost without anyone else knowing it is taking place, and requires no assistance from others. No wonder it was an art that the church viciously sought to stamp out.

Shamanism requires a priestess skilled in meditative arts, someone who is balanced and whole, whose intentions are not harmful (if they are, then the visions they seek out will eventually become tormenting), and who can read symbolic language with little trouble. These are skills and attributes most priestesses seek, but only the sincere fully succeed.

Choosing or Being Chosen by a Patron Goddess

In many traditions, a priestess is expected to dedicate herself as the priestess of a certain Goddess, who functions as her patron. This practice is ancient and, though it is not known if it was Celtic, it has a traceable history throughout other parts of the world. For example, in the Middle East priestesses lost their birth names and were called by the name of the patron to whom they were dedicated.[7]

A patron Goddess is one who actively becomes a part of you, who links you to the Otherworld and the other deities, and with whom you can align your energies for more successful magick and ritual. She is also someone who hears your prayerful petitions and can show you the way to achieve your desires.

There are some who argue that you cannot choose a Celtic deity as a patron, but that they must choose you. I once argued vociferously with this stance, but have since softened in my vehemence. In my tradition, a priest or priestess is always dedicated as the servant of his or her patron. When I began my study for the priesshood, I was convinced that I would have Maeve as my patron. I love that lady! She is fiery, resolute, arrogant, and wholly independent. In short, she was too much like the part of me that I had worked hard to overcome. I did not need a patron who embodied what I knew were the worst tendencies of a Leonine nature. Try as I might, the inner-clicking that would have told me she wanted to be my patron never happened.

In the meantime, I was being gently courted by another Goddess, though I tried hard to ignore the fact. This Goddess was Brighid, the primary Goddess of my tradition and the patron of the majority of those in my tradition. I wanted to be different, unique, so I fought her. I was lucky she didn't just smack me down and forget me.

During this time I found my skills and talents beginning to wane. These were not just my magickal talents, but mundane ones as well. I was having trouble studying, I was having trouble writing, my fingers faltered over the piano keys where before they had flown with confidence. Recognizing Brighid as a deity of wisdom and creative inspiration, I was forced to petition her for help. When I allowed myself to flow with her energies, everything was fine.

At this point I still did not recognize what she was saying to me, and I continued my quest for Maeve. I soon found I was being bombarded by symbols of Brighid, particularly her equal-armed cross. I also found that I was dreaming images of her and that I was most at ease with my life when in our coven's circle to which Brighid had been evoked. Our coven developed an elaborate set of ritual dramas using invocation, a process by which deity is brought into the self. I soon found that the role of Brighid was being assigned to me because everyone thought it felt right. When I insisted on being Maeve, or someone else, things did not work out as they were supposed to.

Dense as I was, it finally occurred to me that Brighid was reaching out and telling me that she wanted to be my patron. When I stopped fighting her I found a fulfilling relationship of patron and servant, one I have been delighted with for many years. I still use Maeve when I want to work with my warrior aspect, and for this she obliges me, but for day-to-day living, I serve Brighid and she patrons me.

When you are looking for your patron, whether as a priestess or an initiate of Celtic women's ways, allow yourself to be open to her overtures.

- Be aware of symbols that might give you clues as to the Goddess who is offering her patronage. These can come in sleep, while walking outdoors, in meditation, or through books or art you feel drawn to.

- Keep a dream diary in which you record unusual symbolism.
- Be aware of any entities who approach you while you are astral projecting or meditating. These may be your patron Goddess or her emissaries.
- Study as many Celtic myths as you can get hold of, and read not just with your mind, but with your heart. Who interests you most? Who calls out to you?
- Meditate on those Goddesses who seem to be reaching out to you. Make notes afterwards on those who seemed to be in sync with your own energy patterns.
- Make a list of your positive and negative qualities. If you find you cannot be objective about these, consult an astrology book that lists the negative and positive qualities of each sun sign, and work with those. You may discover, as I did, that the Goddesses who are most like you in terms of your solar-self are not the best ones with whom to find patronage.

When your patron has found you, you will know it pretty quickly. This is also one of the signs that you are being offered the mantle of priestesshood by a specific Goddess. Any ritual you do from this point on to confirm your acceptance of priestesshood is merely an outward affirmation of what the Goddess has already bestowed upon you. No human being can make you a priestess; only the Goddess can do this. Therefore, no human can ever take away your title.

Over time, other patrons may seek you out, and some of these may be Gods as well as Goddesses. If you are like me, you were taught that some pretty silly gender divisions exist in terms of the divine, and that women cannot have male patrons or successfully invoke a God. While it may be true that, while in a woman's body, you cannot fully comprehend maleness, you can connect with this part of your inner self and integrate it into your wholeness of being.

Accepting Priestesshood

If you have studied and worked and dedicated yourself to a Pagan path, it will probably only be a matter of time before you recognize your inner priestess. Once you become a part of any Pagan path, you are automatically accepted as someone who can commune with the deities, whether or not they or you are comfortable yet with your functioning in leadership roles. When you feel ready to make an official dedication of yourself as priestess, let no one sway you otherwise or attempt to invalidate your efforts by telling you that your self-initiation is not acceptable. It is every bit as right to initiate yourself as a priestess as it is to initiate yourself as a Pagan. Both are gifts from the Goddess, not something that can be conferred by humanity. An initiation ritual into priesthood, whether done by yourself or others, is no more than an outward statement of what has already taken place inside you. What the Goddess has bestowed upon you no human can take away.

If you were harshly tested by the deities upon your initiation into Paganism or into the Celtic women's tradition, think long and seriously about your commitment to your oath and your Goddess before committing yourself to her service as priestess. When you take on more responsibility, such as that of a priestess, you will get more challenges.

Questions for the Potential Celtic Priestess

The following questions address the priestesshood as it applies to you. As with the other questions that have been presented in this text, there are no right or wrong answers, only those that will help you see the issue more clearly and make the right choices as they apply to you. Answer them honestly, and any others that come to mind, before making your formal dedication as priestess.

How do I define the term *priestess*, and what do I see as her role in modern Paganism?

Why do I want to be a priestess?

Have many members of the clergy have I known well, both in and out of Paganism?

What do I know about the day-to-day life of clergy?

What do I see as the greatest benefit to me of being a priestess?

What do I see as the greatest benefit to others of my being a priestess?

What do I expect from the Pagan community in return for my service?

What can I give to the Pagan community in return?

Do I feel I can effectively minister to men, children, the elderly, gays, lesbians, polyamorous people, conservatives, liberals, and others, as well as to women like myself?

How long have I been Pagan? A Celtic Pagan? How long involved in women's spirituality? Is it long enough that my skills can be of value to others?

What things do I still feel I need to learn?

What things do I feel secure in teaching?

Do others look up to me?

Is my ego healthy? Is it inflated? Do I suffer from low self-esteem?

Do I feel I need others to look up to me in order to validate my chosen spiritual path?

How well do I know the women's mysteries? Do I feel I can effectively lead others to seek them?

How many times have I been challenged by the guardians of the threshold? What has happened each time? How can this experience help me as a priestess?

If I choose not to dedicate myself as a priestess at this time, how will this affect my spirituality?

If I do choose to dedicate myself at this time, how will it affect my spirituality?

Do I have a patron Goddess/God? How will this help/harm my ministry?

Do I wish to seek the status of legal minister in my state or province? Why or why not?

Do I plan to study other Pagan or Celtic Pagan paths and pursue priestesshood through them as well?

Notes

1 Condren, Mary. *The Serpent and the Goddess: Women, Religion and Power in Celtic Ireland* (San Francisco: Harper & Row, 1989), 70.

2 Ibid, 179.

3 Shuttle, Penelope and Peter Redgrove. *The Wise Wound: Myths, Realities, and Meanings of Menstruation* (New York: Bantam Books, 1990), 221.

4 Jones, Norah. *Power of Raven, Wisdom of Serpent: Celtic Women's Spirituality* (Edinburgh: Floris Books, 1994), 22.

5 An entire discussion of Celtic shamanism lies far beyond the scope of this work. Some of the concepts are touched upon in Chapters 14 and 15, but if you are interested in exploring this further I recommend starting with D. J. Conway's *By Oak, Ash and Thorn: Modern Celtic Shamanism* (St. Paul, Minn.: Llewellyn, 1995) or John Matthews' *The Celtic Shaman* (Longmeade, Dorset, UK: Element Books).

6 Conway, D. J., 239.

7 Conway, D. J. *Falcon Feather and Valkyrie Sword: Feminine Shamanism, Witchcraft and Magick* (St. Paul, Minn.: Llewellyn, 1995).

SELF-INITIATION OF THE CELTIC PRIESTESS

Solitary Ritual

The ritual in this chapter is not an initiation into a specific Pagan tradition or to Paganism/Wicca in general. Celtic women's spirituality is not a tradition per se, but a special or additional aspect of a woman's Pagan life. There probably are some Celtic-based traditions out there that appeal mostly to women, but if so, I have not yet been made aware of them. No doubt they will become more popular and public with the passage of time.

This initiation is for a woman who is already an initiated Pagan/Wiccan, and who feels ready to dedicate herself as a Celtic priestess in the service of a particular Celtic Goddess. As mentioned in the previous chapter, we are all priestesses in some sense after we have been initiated into Paganism, either by ourselves or by someone else, meaning that we need no intermediaries between ourselves and our deities. But this ritual takes that commitment a step further, by affirming it through ritual vows.

It is best to wait until you have been a part of Paganism for a least a year and day before trying to make yourself a priestess. A year and a day is the customary length of time a newcomer to the Craft/Paganism is expected to study in order to undergo initiation. Solitaries are usually cautioned to wait this amount of time as well before making a formal oath of commitment to their chosen path. A year and a day is a passage of magickal time in many Celtic myths and folk legends, and represents a cycle of completion and change.

If you have already been involved in spiritual studies for more than a year and a day, or have already been initiated into the Craft/Paganism through a self-initiation or by someone else, then you will still have to decide if the role of priestess is one you want to fulfill. As previously mentioned, it is not a position of ease, but one of service to others and to one's Goddess. If you have thought long and carefully about this role and feel chosen by the Goddess and ready to accept her challenges, then this ritual will no more than formalize something the Goddess has already given you.

The Meaning and Challenge of Initiation

Your real initiation is not a physical act or event—it is what comes after. The word *initiation* means "to begin," and speaks of the new life that awaits you once the vows have been taken and the circle closed. When you begin this new phase in your life, you accept with it new challenges and responsibilities, and you will find yourself tested by the Goddess to whom you have dedicated your spiritual self. If this was not something you were told when you were first initiated, it was likely something you learned for yourself rather soon after. This is why no one else can tell you which initiation is valid and which isn't; only your inner self and your deities know what is "real" and what is a game, and they will at some point make the pretender aware of her transgressions.

Those who argue against the validity of self-initiation are usually those who fear losing some power-base they have built for themselves. It is true that there are many self-styled "gurus" in modern Paganism, vastly so in Celtic traditions. Many of them just decided that being a priestess sounded like fun, a good way to get a leg up on others. They abuse their office simply because they do not know any better. However, this does not mean that we must look down upon all self-initiates as pretenders. The majority are good-hearted, sincere people trying to do the best they can on their chosen path. The Goddess makes a Witch, and the Goddess makes a priestess; it is not done by the blessings of another person, no matter how long she has been Pagan. The two questions we have to ask of those who insist that someone be initiated by another initiated person are:

By what right do you claim the power to tell me what I am?

Who do you think initiated the first Witch to begin with?

An initiation ritual is an outward expression of something you already possess, a gift of the Goddess that no one else can bestow by mere words and gestures. The event is designed to open yourself to the true initiation when it comes to you. This serves two purposes: it humbles you, and it shows you areas in which you need more study. Being a priestess does not mark the end of your study, but "initiates" a new phase of it. Shortly after my initiation into the Craft, I found myself in a magickal battle with someone on a negative path. I immediately went running for help, only to find that the power to deal with the problem was within me all the time. But the challenges do not stop. After I was initiated as a Priestess of Brighid, my creative side was challenged until I recognized and acted upon what the Goddess was trying to tell me.

There is an old metaphysical adage that says, "When you change, everything around you changes." Initiation awakens aspects of the inner self once left sleeping, and alerts the outer world to interact with you in new ways. This is why you are challenged upon any spiritual initiation, whether a first, second, priestess, elder, or any other. The energy patterns attracted to the new you are naturally going to be different, and you will need time to adapt to them.

Expect these trials and challenges to continue throughout your spiritual life. They are not a one-time event, but an ongoing process of learning and growing, the very thing you declared you wanted when you dedicated your life to a deity. All are a part of the ongoing initiation process, which will take you further and further into the mysteries of the Goddess. The purpose is always for your benefit, even though it may not always seem that way at the time. The deeper you go, the more you learn, the more you will be expected to prove yourself, and the more you will be expected to give back. The universe seeks balance, and reciprocity for things given and taken is part of that balance. So be very sure that you are doing the right thing for you, for once the ritual of initiation is complete and you have aligned your energies with those of the Otherworld, there is no turning back. To resist later on will only make the challenges quite dreadful.

Occasionally one runs across someone who claims they have never been challenged in their spiritual life. Nothing ever appeared to test them, and nothing that had to be overcome challenged them. In these cases I am forced to believe that they are either lying, or simply did not recognize the challenge for what it was. A friend of mine, a priestess who operates a small study circle, questions if those people made a sincere commitment to Paganism, or if their initiation was just a lot of words and ceremony with no substance. In any case, if more than a year passes without any circumstances or forces coming upon you that cause you to grow spiritually, you need to rethink what you did and where you are going.

Preparing for the Ritual

As with the warrior dedication ritual in Chapter 5, you should prepare for this ritual with a spiritual and physical cleansing. For an initiation into priestess-hood, some women choose to add fasting and long periods of meditation to this prerequisite.

Both fasting and feasting have been important to women's spirituality. These two opposing approaches towards our food have been called by some feminists the only area of their lives that women have always had under their complete control. They could choose what they put into their stomachs. Women were the hunter-gatherers and the food preparers. Food availability was under their jurisdiction. Sometimes her cook fire or kitchen was the only place where a woman could make a decision on her own. Little wonder food became a preoccupation. This obsession with food, and our association of it with personal control, is still evident by the frightening fact that nearly ninety-nine percent of people with eating disorders are women. If you choose a pre-ritual fast, do it for spiritual reasons, not appearance-related ones. It is not a diet aid.

This ritual will follow this format:

> Blessing of the self
>
> Vows of service
>
> Vows to the Goddess
>
> Announcement of your priestess name
>
> Anointing by oil and "blood"
>
> The bestowing of the symbol of office
>
> The sacrifice
>
> The libation

The items that will be required are:

> Two chalices or small cauldrons
>
> Water
>
> Salt
>
> Soot
>
> Olive oil
>
> A symbol of office
>
> A token of sacrifice
>
> Optional: Celtic mood music and/or incense

The chalice or cauldron has already been discussed at length as a symbol of the womb of the Goddess. You should place some water in the bottom of it before the ritual begins. The olive oil will be used to anoint your skin later on, and should be placed in the other chalice or cauldron. Olive oil has been used as a substance for anointing royalty and priestesses for several millennia. It is non-irritating to the skin, which is not the case with some oils, and serves well as a base for other oil or herbal blends. It is best to avoid adding other essential oils to the olive oil, unless you know for certain how they will react on your skin. If there is a special herb you like or one you often work with, and you would like to include this in your olive oil, powder it well and add some to the oil before the ritual begins. Be sure as you do this to visualize the purpose for which you are using it: to seal your dedication as a priestess of a Goddess.

Soot is made up of carbon deposits, and these can be obtained from a fireplace, a lamp globe, or by holding a heat-resistant glass or plate over a candle's flame until you have enough soot to scrape into a small pile suitable for anointing yourself and for representing your blood.

Blood initiations were once an accepted part of spiritual initiations in many cultures. The shedding of blood was often prerequisite to "joining a secret society" such as the priestesshood.[1] The magical nature of soot, its appearance during a time of transformation (when fire consumes or changes) links it to the archetypal function of blood. Some feminist researchers also believe that the inclusion of soot in many old flying ointments[2] and magickal formulas was no more than a metaphor for a woman's blood.[3]

The most common symbol of investiture is a necklace or garter. Having a necklace holding a pendant symbolizing some aspect of spirituality is common enough in Pagan circles. The necklace represents the unbroken circle in which we work, that place that is at the center of the universe. By wearing it, a priestess makes the statement that she is in command of the circle, able to direct the energies that join at this sacred juncture. The pendant may be a pentagram, Brighid's Cross, triskele, moon symbol, astrological glyph, or other representation, but it will have meaning to you as a Pagan, and to the tradition you have chosen to follow.

The garter has a noble history among priestesses in the Anglo-Celtic traditions and in what is known as British Traditional Witchcraft. It is a descendant of the hip belt or girdle worn by priestesses in ancient times. With the coming of the new religion in Europe, such obvious outward expressions of involvement with Witchcraft were dangerous, and priestesses began to wear garters that could be discreetly tucked up under their clothing. Modern custom in the British traditions says that whenever a new coven "hives off" from the primary one run by a priestess, she is to add a new buckle to her garter to mark that distinction. In some traditions, having more than three buckles makes you a "queen Witch."

The garter as a Pagan symbol was immortalized in the mid-fourteenth century, during the creation of England's prestigious Order of the Garter. At a court ball in 1349, King Edward III was dancing vigorously with the Countess of Salisbury when her garter slipped off. The wearing of garters was so deeply associated with Witchcraft that the fair countess was at risk of arrest, but the King picked it up and declared aloud that evil should be visited on those who would think evil of the garter. The King may have been well aware of the role of his sacred kingship, and he felt compelled to protect the Witches. From this incident formed the elite Order of the Garter, a fraternity still intact today. These knights—thirteen in number!—are the only ones permitted to observe certain parts of the coronation ceremonies (the hallowing?) of English monarchs.

You can make or buy a garter almost anywhere, though if you want one with a buckle you may have to purchase a nice dog collar. Fortunately, these come in many styles from simple to "jeweled." I chose a necklace for my priestess symbol, and the garter I keep in my magickal cabinet was a gag gift from a coven member. He was browsing in one of those mall outlet stores that specializes in sexy women's lingerie—he never did tell us why—when he saw a tabletop covered with black satin garters, decorated with little red satin roses, on sale for only fifty cents each. He couldn't resist buying one for everyone in the coven—the four men included! We actually wore them from time to time, and they came to symbolize our unity and friendship.

Another symbol of power that you might want to adopt is the mantle. These cloaks were worn regularly by the Celts. Their color, fabric, and condition were an outward sign of the wearer's rank in society. It was also a vestment of personal significance that denoted a clan chieftain or king, hence the expression, "inheriting the mantle," used to refer to the passing of authority from one person to another.

If neither the necklace, garter, nor mantle appeals to you as a symbol of office, feel free to be creative. Choose a ring, a crown, a sash, a bracelet or any other item that, to you, symbolizes your office and your duty to your Goddess.

You will also need to have on hand a token of sacrifice to show that you are willing to accept the challenges of the Goddess as you take on this new life and leave a great part of the old behind. This should be some symbol of your past: an icon from your old religion, a page of notes from your initial lessons in Paganism, or a similarly significant object.

As you discard this item you will also take on yet another name, your priestess name. Some women like to simply add the title "Lady" to the front of their old Craft name. Lady is a designation by which priestesses in many traditions are known ("Lord" is used for priests). Or you may simply add a second name or word to your current Craft name. Because I see the role of priestess as being a lamp lighting the path for others, I simply added the Irish word *solus* to the front of my Craft name, the way some women would add "Lady." Solus means "light."

Long before this ritual begins, you will need to spend time meditating on the Goddesses to whom you feel closest, to see which one you wish to serve as her priestess. If you have made a choice the Goddess agrees with, you will know it. If not, that inner connection you want to feel will be missing and you will realize it fairly soon. In some cases you will feel that your Goddess has chosen you. This was certainly true in my case. I wanted very much to be a priestess of Maeve, and I set out on my year and a day study of priestesshood with that goal in mind. But nothing in that direction seemed to go right for me. Instead it was Brighid whose image, archetype, and correspondences kept asserting themselves. I fought Brighid's offering mostly out of a need to be different. Brighid and Lugh are the principal deities of my tradition, and the majority of people within it have one of them as a patron.

I am not the first Pagan to find that when we do not want what is best for us, we are made uncomfortable until we do realize the right path and start taking steps to walk it. While I was resisting her, all the aspects of my life under Brighid's jurisdiction—creativity, inspiration, mental prowess, transformational abilities—waned until I was forced to petition her help. Somewhere during this process I realized what I had been fighting, and accepted Brighid as my patron. I have never regretted it.

The Self-Initiation Ritual

Open your circle and call your quarters as usual. As you call upon the deities to come to the circle, be sure to call upon the particular Goddess whom you have chosen to serve.

When the circle is cast, take the chalice/cauldron of water and bless it, saying:

> Blessed Be the water, the blood of the Goddess from which all
> life emerges, from which I was created and to which I shall
> someday return.

Then take the salt and bless it saying:

> Blessed Be the salt, symbol of the earth, the body of the
> Goddess, the earth mother who nourishes and sustains me.

Put the salt into the water and stir it three times counterclockwise. Bless this mixture by saying:

> Water and salt. Blood and earth. By these she blesses those
> who serve her.

Using the ritual found in Chapter 7, offer yourself the Threefold Blessing on behalf of the Goddess.

The next step is to make your first vows. These should be vows of service, not to the Goddess but to others and, if appropriate, to your chosen tradition. In the Celtic tradition, this is your *adbertos,* an old Gaulish word that literally means "a sacrifice." *Adbertos* was a positive part of the Celtic religious and community world view, in spite of its negative English translation. It refers to giving to others, to the tribe and clan—sacrificing your needs to put them first. The Celts saw the giving or receiving of personal sacrifice as being an inherent part of every living moment, as a symbol of the interplay and oneness of all things.

If you intend to teach others in your role as priestess, you should declare that you will do this ethically and with only the highest of intentions. Since the Irish word for "teach" also means "to sing over," you may wish to chant-sing this portion of your vows. All the words should come from your heart and be written by you. No one can make promises on your behalf.

Next you will stand and face the direction where you perceive your patron Goddess-to-be, and you will make your vows to her. These should also come from your own heart and should include the following elements:

- Address your Goddess by name
- Vow to serve her
- Vow to be receptive to the gifts she will bring you
- Vow to be ready to accept her challenges
- Vow to grow and learn
- Vow to live a life she will be proud of
- An oath that if these vows are not kept that your tools will turn against you and your powers desert you

You will end your vows by declaring them holy in your new priestess name. Say something like:

> From now on I am known as (insert priestess name here),
> Priestess of (insert name of your patron Goddess here). We
> have chosen one another, we shall serve one another; in honor,
> in truth, for all positive ends, until she takes me to Tir na mBan
> to be with her again. By being spoken in the sacred space my
> words are holy, and by my name I seal these vows. So mote
> they be.

When you have made your promises, you will seal them with an anointing. Take the soot and mix it in the oil with words such as:

> By the blood of the womb all things of the earth are made holy.

Place one finger in the olive oil[4] and say:

> Oil of the earth, of the tree of Life,—Blood of the womb, sacred
> and holy—seal the vows I make in this sacred place. From me
> to the Goddess, from this world to the Otherworld, the link is
> forged, ever to stay. So mote it be.

Place the oil on your forehead and say:

> My vows are sealed, never to be revoked. My mind will ever
> turn to my Goddess.

Place the oil on your lips and say:

> My vows are sealed, never to be revoked. My mouth will know
> when to speak and when to keep silent.

Place the oil on your heart area and say:

> My vows are sealed, never to be revoked. I will love under will.

Place the oil on your womb area and say:

> My vows are sealed, never to be revoked. I will create in beauty.

Place the oil on your knees and say:

> My vows are sealed, never to be revoked. I will kneel to no one,
> yet I honor my Goddess, and like the willow I can bend.

Place the oil on your feet and say:

> My vows are sealed, never to be revoked. In beauty I will walk
> all the days of my life.

Next take your symbol of office and anoint it with the oil blend saying:

> By the donning of this (insert name of object) I declare myself a
> Priestess of (insert name of Goddess). If I ever shame the office
> I seek, or cause my Goddess embarrassment, may this symbol
> leave me and my powers be gone.

Put the item on and say:

> So mote it be.

Next make your sacrifice. Explain to the Goddess why this item represents a part of your old life that you are now leaving behind. You may either bury it or burn it (if it is safe to do so), or set it aside to be buried or burned later. Cast the ashes onto the bare earth.

Close your circle whenever you are ready.

After you have closed the circle, make a food and/or drink offering to the Goddess and her creatures that can safely be left outdoors.

Notes

1 Shuttle, Penelope and Peter Redgrove. *The Wise Wound: Myths, Realities, and Meanings of Menstruation* (New York: Bantam Books, 1990), 72–73.

2 These are ointments rubbed on the body to help facilitate astral experiences. They are still in use today, usually without the baneful ingredients listed in the old formulas.

3 Shuttle and Redgrove, 248.

4 The olive tree was seen as a tree of life in the Middle East, and was sacred to several Middle Eastern Goddesses. Adding the crushed bark from a more "Celtic" tree, such as the oak, willow, elder, alder, hazel, apple, or birch is appropriate for this ritual.

THE BONDING
OF SOULFRIENDS

Ritual for Two

The Celtic concept of the *anamchara*, or soulfriend, is both a spiritual and an emotional obligation. Unlike the usual hierarchical relationships that characterized Celtic society, the soulfriends were partners, equals. She was your teacher and student, your dependent and your solace, your confessor and your leader, a person with whom you shared wisdom and spiritual teachings.[1] This was someone you trusted with your life and with your soul, and who trusted you in return. So ingrained and special was this practice that it was adopted as an integral part of monastic life in the early Celtic church in Ireland.[2] Though this practice is not very widely known, it is still very much a part of the living tradition of Celtic Paganism, and is growing in popularity, especially among women.

The soulfriend is a concept foreign to the mindset of most modern religious leaders, who are used to thinking only in terms of leader/follower. While in many ways the soulfriend functions like a godparent in modern Christianity, it is primarily a bonding of two equals on the same spiritual journey. Soulfriends balance out each other's strengths and weaknesses. They want what you want for yourself, they give without jealousy, and they take as they give.

It is not hard to see why such a concept is finding favor with modern Pagan women. Women are the ones most likely to eschew hierarchies and seek co-leaders on equal terms.[3] It is no accident that the majority of covens (at least those that I know of) that operate in an egalitarian manner are made up either of all women, mostly women, or are operated primarily by women. Women seek to bond and, as the popular books that discuss the language differences between men and women have pointed out, we are inclined to use interaction to find parity and common ground, not to seek rank.

Women enjoy the "best friend" status, a relationship that many men have a great deal of trouble fully understanding. Best friends are admitted into the court of the true inner self. A woman's best friend is often closer to her in many ways than is her mate, and is privy to thoughts and feelings, hopes and dreams, that are frequently withheld from the mate. It is a relationship of give and take. Sometimes one woman is the stronger; sometimes the roles are reversed. We are not ashamed to bare our souls to our best friends. We are not lessened by our tears and anxieties, nor is our pride or sense of our inherent femininity impaired by displaying weak moments. In the Celtic spiritual tradition, this makes two women on the same spiritual path naturals for the role of soulfriends.

By ritualizing this soulfriend commitment, we acknowledge to each other and to our Goddesses that we understand this dual role of mentor/follower, teacher/student, godparent/child, strong/weak, and so on. We outwardly make the commitment to what we have been committed inwardly all along. We are now conscious of our obligation to, and our dependence on, one another. When this commitment is ritually made, it grows deeper as the meaning of the ritual becomes impressed on our psyches and we become consciously aware of the depth of our bonding. This takes the soul of two friends into the realm of wholeness and of the divine, as the unity of two souls has been seen in many cultures as symbolic of the union of Goddess and God—a totality of being.

What a soulfriend is not is a crutch. She is not someone who bears all your burdens, but who shares them so that your load is lightened. She does not have the answers to all your problems, but will lend a sympathetic ear and a shoulder to cry on, and will help you seek out the best answers for yourself.

Soulfriends are, above all, equals. This cannot be stressed enough. The ritual is not an excuse for divvying up the workload caused by newcomers to your coven so that you can pair them off with your more experienced people. The soulfriend relationship is a *consensual union of equals* who are on the same spiritual path, at about the same level of experience, who choose to help each other and to ritually make a commitment to deepen their already tight bonds.

Preparing for the Ritual

The ritual in this chapter may be used or adapted as you like. Your bonding ritual can be joyous or solemn, or contain elements of both. It should symbolize your unity and your commitment, but should also have personal meaning based on the common ground you already share. If you wish to include a private joke or a symbol that doesn't mean anything to anyone but the two of you, go ahead. This will make your ritual more meaningful.

Do not be tempted to use binding spells in your ritual that will literally tie your souls together. Though this union should be thought of as a relationship that will endure throughout this lifetime, more permanent and stable than most marriages, you are each there of your own free will, and nothing should interfere with that. In the same way that you might ask yourself how much satisfaction there is in having a lover who is with you because she came to you and stayed with you under the influence of binding magick, ask yourself how satisfying a soulfriend would be who was coerced in the same way. The Celts cherished their freedom, and so should you.

Prior to the ritual, you both should spend lots of time in meditation, apart and together, considering the implications of formalizing your bonds of friendship. If, at this point, either party wishes to cancel or postpone this ritual, that decision should be respected. Many people get nervous about ritual commitments at the last minute. This only shows that your potential soulfriend is taking her obligation seriously, and her hesitation should not alter your close friendship in any way.

For the ritual in this chapter you will need the following items:

- Three taper candles; one to represent each of you, and one to represent your union. You may choose any colors you like, but it is nice if the colors have a theme of unity. For instance, if your individual candles are blue and red, you might want to make the unity candle violet. Mixing blue and red make violet, a color related to the soul in magickal spells.

- Three candleholders that fit your chosen candles and that are wide enough at the base to keep wax drippings off the floor.

- A chalice to represent your unity, and two other smaller chalices, cups, or drinking glasses to represent each of you as individuals. The two smaller cups should be filled about one-third full with water or some other liquid (which you will be drinking) before the ritual begins.

- Acrylic paints in assorted colors.

- Paint brushes in assorted sizes.

- Two three-foot dowel rods (unfinished) about 1 to 1½ inches wide. These are inexpensive and very easy to find in craft or hardware stores. Prepare them for the ritual by sanding the ends until they are gently rounded. As you do this, you should be visualizing the wand as a channel of power for future rituals done in your unity.

- A gift or spiritual token for your soulfriend. It should remain your secret until it is presented during the ritual.

- An altar cloth or floor covering (optional).

- A box of tissues. This ritual can be very emotional!

The Anamchara Bonding Ritual

Gather all your needed items and go, at the appropriate time, to the place you have chosen for your ritual.

Do not plan to use a traditional altar for this, but instead place all the items on the ground or floor in the center of the circle (in a manner similar to the drawing shown in this chapter). If you are of the belief that your magickal implements will be lessened or their power grounded by this contact, you may use some type of floor covering or altar cloth.

Cast your circle together, sharing all duties equally (see Appendix C for guidance if you are unfamiliar with this practice). When the circle is cast, sit down near the middle facing one another, orienting yourselves in any directions you feel comfortable with. This face-to-face posture has been traditionally used in Wicca for passing information and teachings, and is believed to promote the efficient flow of power of teacher to student and back again.

At this point you should both pick up the cups that represent you as individuals. Starting with whichever one of you that you chose (this will be you in this example), take a sip of the liquid and make this or a similar statement:

> I drink deep from the cup of the Goddess. Her blood is mine and I am
> hers. She who knows every secret of my heart blesses you who shares
> this knowledge. Drink deep of my spirit.

The concept that drink-sharing can bond people and seal vows is an ancient one still seen used in the marriage ceremonies of east Asia and the Middle East. The often-heard phrase, "Let's have a drink on it," has its origins in these beliefs.

Pass the cup across the circle to the other woman and allow her to drink from the cup. When she is done, she should set it down at her side and lift her

Anamchara Bonding Altar Set-up

own cup. The ritual of drinking, speaking, and passing the cup should be repeated by her. When you are both finished drinking, take your cups and slowly pour their contents—in unison—into the larger center chalice, which represents your unity. As you pour the liquid together, make a prepared statement in unison such as:

> Two bodies sharing one soul. Two hearts beating in unison. Two lives
> striving to know, to teach, to learn, to take, and to give. In you I have
> found my soulfriend.

The other woman should lift the chalice and hold it to your lips for you to drink and say:

> By this I acknowledge before our Goddess what I have given you all
> along—myself. I am your friend. I am your teacher. I am your student. I
> am your dependent. I am your solace and comfort. I am your shield and
> your rock, your child and your mother, your sister and your mentor.

After you have taken a drink, hold the cup for your soulfriend and make the same pledge to her. Then allow her to drink from the chalice.

Starting with the one who was not the first to speak over the cups (the other woman in this example), that woman should take a match and light the individual candle sitting at her right hand. As she does this she should make a statement about it representing her spiritual self. After she is done you should do the same.

The unlit candle that sits in between you and your soulfriend represents not only your unity, but the greater potential of two spirits on the same journey, each encouraging and helping the other. As you move to join your flames over the wick of the center candle, make a prepared unison statement such as:

> By this ritual I am bound to you as your friend of the soul—your
> *anamchara*. See our flames shine brightly, burning hotter and stronger
> together than they can separately. As we continue on the Celtic path,
> on the way of the Goddess, I vow by earth and air, by fire and water,
> by moon and sun, to be your teacher and student. I am your shoulder
> for crying upon, and I am the lamp that lights the path of your feet. I
> am the one whose eyes eagerly seek you out in a crowded world. I am
> your child, to be nurtured and taught, to be cared for and cherished. I
> am your shield and your sword, your book and your circle—part of
> your center of being, as you are mine. All my wisdom and all my se-
> crets I share with you for as long as this life endures. Until we meet in
> *Tir na mBan*, so mote it be.

At this point you may each have a chance to speak about other feelings you have. Trust that at this moment your emotions will be running very high, which is why you have that box of tissues nearby!

You may at this time present to each other the gift or token you have brought to seal the soulfriend ritual. I suggest that you select something that can be used in a ritual setting. A piece of Celtic-style jewelry such as a torque (neckpiece) or a *niam-linn* (headband) is very appropriate. So are other pieces of ritual jewelry, special stones, divination devices, or magickal tools.

When you have exchanged gifts, set all your other materials aside leaving only the unity candle burning between you and your soulfriend. Take the dowels and paints and begin making a soulfriend wand for the other woman. This will be a tool that represents your spiritual unity, and is to be used in situations where the two of you are working together or doing magick or healing for one another. Don't feel these have to be made seriously. You may add touches of merriment or symbols of private jokes to the wand. A sense of humor is a cherished thing in a friend, and laughter can be as bonding as any formal ritual. Feel free to keep talking as you work, basking in your bond, your memories, and your newfound soul-status with each other.

When you are both done, pass the wand to your new soulfriend and explain anything painted on it that has not already been explained during the course of its creation. Allow the time for both of you to add your own touches to your new wands.

When you feel ready, extinguish the unity candle and close the circle.

Lastly, take the liquid from your unity chalice outside and, together, pour it onto mother earth as a libation to her. As you do this, visualize your commingled spirits becoming a part of the great mother from whom you came.

Notes

1   Matthews, Caitlin. *The Elements of the Celtic Tradition* (Longmeade, Shaftsbury, Dorset: Element Books, 1989), 104.

2   Rodgers, Michael and Marcus Losack. *Glendalough: A Celtic Pilgrimage* (Blackrock, Co. Dublin: The Columba Press, 1996), 97.

3   Actual "traditions" (as opposed to eclectic groups) that are egalitarian in nature are also called "priestly traditions" because they encourage everyone to seek out the priest or priestess within. In a priestly coven everyone can be, and sometimes is, a leader and a priest or priestess.

LIVING AS A CELTIC WOMAN

The modern Celtic woman has many roles, shows many faces, has many interests, and is involved in a wide variety of activities. But in her heart she is invincible; she wears her warrior-self like a second skin. The power she has is one of power-with, not power-over. She recognizes her spiritual links to all living things, and seeks to wield her power harmoniously, not to hold it above others like a weapon. Her true weapons are her wisdom and self-confidence. Her strength is in her willingness to learn and grow. Her inner peace comes from her sense of place in creation, and her recognition that she carries a spark of the Goddess within her at all times.

This warrior woman knows when to fight like a lion and when to flee like a rabbit; when to speak, and when to be silent. The courage of her convictions is her shield, her soul is her spear, and her will is her cauldron—the limitless womb from which she can birth anything she desires.

The Celtic woman is a mother and a crone but, most importantly, she is a virgin, one who is complete unto herself, and who needs no one else to satisfactorily practice her spirituality. When she gathers with other women or with mixed gender groups to worship her Goddess, she does so to enhance those rituals and expand her spiritual horizons, not because she needs anyone else to make her rituals meaningful or to help her connect with the divine.

Making Connections

It is hard for modern people to fully appreciate the importance of community to the Celts. Today we are so focused on the strength of the individual that we often overlook the fact that strong individuals make for strong communities. It was for the sake of communal strength that the Celts fostered their young in a way that would bring out their talents—talents that could be used for the good of all.

Group or coven workings fulfill this same need in modern Celtic Paganism.

No one ever said making satisfying connections within the Pagan community was easy, but it can be done. If and when you do seek contact with other women who share your spiritual interests, you will find several books on the market that can help guide your steps. They can also provide glimpses into what a good working group—coven, study circle, discussion group, network, and so on—is like. Some books I recommend are:

The Witches' Circle by Maria Kay Simms (Llewellyn, 1996) looks at a network of hierarchical covens, their rituals, and their organization. Very interesting and entertaining book.

Creating Circles of Magic and Power by Caitlin Libera (Crossing Press, 1994) describes how one women's study group evolved into a working coven. This book follows their group's evolution, from first meeting to networking with other women's groups and the community.

Inside A Witches' Coven by Edain McCoy (Llewellyn, 1997) looks at the way one coven works, and gives extensive tips and instructions for finding, organizing, and running a coven. Also goes into networking with other groups.

Circle Guide to Pagan Groups by Circle Sanctuary. First published in 1970, this guide had been updated every few years ever since. It is far from complete, but each issue has more listings than the one before. If you have a Pagan gathering place, occult store, open circle, or similar organization, please consider being listed in their next edition. See Appendix F for the address.

Circle Network News, Summer 1986: "Group Dynamics." As of this writing, back issues of this periodical are still available. Please see

Appendix F for the address, or check out a current copy of the paper for information on ordering this back issue.

The Phoenix From the Flame by Vivianne Crowley (Aquarian, 1994) contains a whole chapter of good networking tips, and an appendix called "Pagan Resources Guide."

Positive Magic by Marion Weinstein (Phoenix, 1981) has a chapter on group dynamics called "Widening the Circle." This book also provides an excellent introduction to natural magick.

To Ride a Silver Broomstick by Silver RavenWolf (Llewellyn, 1993) has a chapter called "Webweaving" that focuses on ideas for making safe Pagan/Wiccan contacts. This is also an excellent introduction to eclectic Wicca.

Wiccan Resources: A Guide to the Witchcraft Community by Michael Thorn (self-published, 1992) seeks to be a guide to the entire North American Pagan/Wiccan community. Write for current price with self-addressed, stamped envelope (SASE) to Michael Thorn, P. O. Box 408, Shirley, NY 11967–0408.

Women's Rituals by Barbara G. Walker (HarperCollins, 1990) is a collection of rituals and group celebration ideas from an eclectic women's spirituality viewpoint. This is a great book for generating fresh ideas for any Pagan group.

Casting the Circle: A Women's Book of Ritual by Diane Stein (Crossing Press, 1990) is a collection of rituals for eclectic women's spirituality groups. It also contains rituals for women's rites of passage.

Also be sure to check out other Celtic, Pagan/Wiccan, and women's spirituality journals for ads about contacts (see Appendix F). If you run your own ad, be as specific as possible about what you're looking for while still sounding flexible. If someone perceives you as too rigid, or thinks that you might be difficult to work with, they will ignore your ad and look elsewhere.

Above all, use common sense about when, where, and how you meet people for the first time. Don't put yourself in danger. Don't rush, and don't push. Trust that, with effort, the right women will make themselves known to you. Then enjoy whatever relationship develops.

The eight women with whom I explored facets of Celtic women's spirituality all came together almost by accident. No one ever expected that we would really meet again after our first contact. My friend Avi and I had placed an ad in an alternative publication seeking women interested in exploring women's spirituality in an eclectic setting. We got one response from a woman named Pam; we met her for the first time at a well-lit coffee shop. Though she was then practicing as an eclectic solitary, Pam had once been part of a Celtic coven and had taught herself to read Irish Gaelic. This fit in nicely with both my Irish focus and with Avi's Scottish one. Needless to say, the three of us got along great, and agreed to meet again.

Pam was so enthused about our second meeting, at which the three of us talked until nearly dawn, that she asked if we wanted to meet some other women she knew—not with the idea of starting a coven, but just to have a women's network for the benefit of us all. Avi and I agreed and, three weeks later, the other five women met with us on a sunny Sunday afternoon in a northeast San Antonio park.

Like Avi and myself, three of the other women were already involved in another coven. To our delight it turned out to be the very large, active coven that had grown out of the one in which Avi and I had been initiated seven years before, and we found we knew several people in common. The other two women had previously worked only with one another and weren't really interested in changing that pattern. They had lots of experience in Paganism, but had been hesitant about meeting with others, and came to Pam's impromptu gathering very reluctantly.

As we all began to talk about our spiritual backgrounds and current interests, a decidedly Celtic theme began to emerge. The two hesitant women, Cheryl and Karen, had been defining themselves as general Goddess worshippers who had once focused on Middle Eastern and Polynesian Goddesses, but had recently been looking into the spiritual traditions of their Celtic heritage. The other three, a mother and daughter and the mother's best friend, were part of an eclectic coven, but were centered on the Celtic in their personal practices. The mother, Donna, was a Priestess of Cerridwen. Her daughter, Tracey, was only seventeen, but was impressively knowledgeable about the Arthurian traditions. Donna's best friend, Joanne, had Rhiannon as her patron Goddess.

Though we never developed into a fully working coven, we got along great and enjoyed exploring women's spirituality with a Celtic focus. We had no fights or ego wars, we respected each other's traditions, and we always remained free to work within our own covens.

Those seven women represented some of the best attributes of the modern Celtic woman. They were self-possessed and giving, curious and wise.

Questions About Groups for the Celtic Woman

The following questions are among the many you should ask of yourself before seriously looking for a group or coven to work with. After a group is contacted you will think of many more questions to ask yourself—questions that should be dictated by common sense rather than your deep-felt desire to be a part of a group. Being part of the wrong group can be a hellish experience, even when there is nothing inherently wrong with the women you have connected with, or with their spiritual philosophy. Sometimes energies just don't blend well; this is no one's fault. Paganism differs from most religions in that one person is not asked to carry the ritual load. Everyone must do her part, and this requires a consensus from all concerned, a commonality of belief and a similar view of the purpose and meaning of what is being undertaken. Think carefully before taking this step.

Do I classify myself as a Celtic eclectic, or is there one special Celtic tradition in which I am most interested?

Is there a special cultural focus I lean toward? Irish? Scottish? Welsh?

How would I feel if the women in my group or coven decided they wanted to open the group to men?

How many women, at most, would I feel comfortable working with in a group?

Do I want a group that is egalitarian, or do I prefer a hierarchical structure?

What do I want to contribute to a group?

What do I expect a group to give to me? What do I expect to get out of our efforts?

How often do I want to meet with these women? Do I want coven-mates I see once a month, or do I want deeper connections with them?

How would I feel if a woman in the group was a lesbian? Straight? Polyamorous? A mother? A grandmother? A teenager? A transsexual?

What do I know about covens? Have I been in one or known someone who has?

What are the basic ingredients I feel I must have in a group in order to be happy with it? On what issues do I feel I can compromise?

Would I feel the need to start a new group if I cannot find one in which I can be content? Do I know how to go about doing this safely, effectively, and for the good of all concerned?

The Celtic woman walks in peace, but unobtrusively carries her battle weapons; she sees herself as part of the web of all creation, but also as a unique individual of great worth. She loves and respects her family, friends, and community, but also finds inspiration in her solitude. She is a leader, but knows when it is time to let others show the way. She strives to learn and to teach, to share and to keep secrets, to change and yet to remain herself, to be human and be Goddess.

The planet needs more Celtic women, whose bottomless cauldron of inner strength serves as a womb from which a new and better world may be born.

Celtic Goddesses and Women of Power

In this appendix are listed many—but by no means all—Celtic Goddesses and heroic figures, along with the Celtic sub-culture in which they were known or worshiped. The body of extant myths about some of them is quite large and a complete discussion of them cannot hope to be covered here. If any of these Goddesses/women appeal strongly to you, it is recommended that you seek out the myths and legends surrounding them. The Bibliography in the back of this book will provide references for beginning this study.

Achall. (Irish) The sister of a young warrior who was killed in battle. When he died, she grieved so intensely that she died as well. The Hill of Achall near Tara is named for her.

Achtland. (Pan-Celtic) A Goddess/queen whom no mortal man could sexually satisfy, so she took a giant from the faery realm as her mate.

Adsullata. (Continental) A Goddess of hot springs, possibly the prototype of the Anglo-Celtic sun/hot springs Goddess, Sul. Possibly once a sun Goddess.

Aerten. (Cornish, Anglo-Celtic, Welsh) A Goddess of fate who presided over the outcome of a series of wars fought between rival clans.

Aeval. (Irish) A Munster queen who, according to legend, held a midnight court to hear a debate on whether the men of her province were keeping their women sexually satisfied or not. After hearing the evidence, she proclaimed the men of Munster to be prudish and lazy, and commanded that they keep their women satisfied.

Aibheaog. (Irish) A fire Goddess from County Donegal. Her sacred well contained great healing power, especially for toothaches.

Aife. (Irish, Scottish) A Goddess/queen/warrior who commanded a legion of fierce and expert horsewomen on the Isle of Shadow (sometimes said to be in the Hebrides). She and her sister, Scathach, ran a school in which they trained male warriors in battle skills.

Ailbhe. (Irish) A daughter of King Cormac MacArt, famous for her brilliance and clever wit.

Ailinn. (Irish) A Leinster princess and Irish Juliet. She and her lover, Baile of the Honeyed Speech, were wrongly informed of the other's death. They both died of grief, and were buried in adjoining graves where two trees, an apple and a yew, grew and entwined.

Aille. (Irish) Succeeded her husband, Meargach of the Green Spear, as clan chief after he was killed in battle.

Aimend. (Irish, Scottish) A sun Goddess.

Ain and **Iaine.** (Irish) Princesses who married their brothers so that no other family would be able to rule their island. They are also credited with inventing war in order to lay claim to the rest of Ireland for their clan.

Aine. (Irish) A waning year, fertility, cattle, sun, and fire Goddess, still very popular in her native Munster. A torchlight procession was held in her honor at Midsummer until well into the twentieth century in both Munster and Donegal.

Aine. (Irish) A Goddess of love, who may or may not be one and the same as the more famous cattle Goddess.

Airmid. (Irish) A daughter of the God of medicine, Diancecht, who was a skilled healer in her own right. She cultivated all the herbs of the world on the grave of her brother, the healer Miach, who was killed by their jealous father. The father scattered the herbs and lost for humankind the knowledge of many kinds of healing. Airmid was also a silversmith and helped forge the famed silver hand of King Nuad.

Amerach. (Irish) An Ulster Druid who was able to cast spells of agelessness (probably a metaphor for time manipulation).

Andraste. (Anglo-Celtic, Continental) A Goddess whose presence was evoked on the eve of battle to curry favor. Queen Boudicca of the Iceni offered sacrifices to her in her sacred grove before going to battle against the invading Romans.

Anu. (Irish) The virgin aspect of one of the many Triple Goddesses of Ireland, linked to the functions of prosperity and abundance. Her mother aspect is

Dana/Danu, and her crone aspect is often cited as Badb (one of the Morrigan). In modern Celtic practice she is sometimes invoked as a moon deity.

Ardwinna. (Breton, Continental) A woodland Goddess who wandered the forests of the Ardennes riding a wild boar.

Argante. (Welsh, Cornish, Breton) A healer from Avalon, probably a Druid.

Arianrhod. (Welsh) A Goddess of reincarnation, the Wheel of the Year, the full moon, sex, weaving (possibly a link to a lost Celtic creation myth), fertility, and the stars (particularly the Corona Borealis); a primal figure of female power.

Arnamentia. (Anglo-Celtic) A Goddess of spring waters, healing, and purification.

Artio. (Continental) A bear Goddess of abundance, strength, and the harvest.

Badb. (Irish, Continental) A war Goddess, part of the Morrigan, a Triple Goddess (usually of three crones, but not always) associated with death, destruction, and battle who helped drive the Formorians from Ireland. She appeared over battlefields as a hooded crow, or ran alongside warriors disguised as a wolf. She is also a deity of rebirth who watches over the Otherworld cauldron of regeneration.

Ban-Chuideachaidh Moire. (Irish) A Goddess of childbirth.

Banbha. (Irish) A musician, warrior, Goddess, and sovereign who protected Ireland from invaders. She is part of a Triple Goddess with her sisters Eire and Fodhla.

Bean Naomha. (Irish) A sun and well Goddess, seen in the form of a trout swimming in its shining waters. In Celtic lore, the salmon is a fish of great knowledge and prophecy. The Salmon of Knowledge, usually perceived as being a male deity, may have at one time been linked to her as consort.

Becuma. (Irish) A Goddess of boats.

Belisama. (Anglo-Celtic) The Goddess of the Mersey River.

Bellah Postil. (Breton) A woman who traveled to aid her fiance by riding a staff, probably a metaphor for astral projection.

Bellona. (Scottish) A Goddess of battlefields.

Birog. (Irish) A Druid who helped the warrior Cian defeat Balor.

Blathnat. (Irish) A daughter of the faery King Midhir, she helped Cuchulain steal her father's magick cauldron. She traveled with three white and red cows, and demanded that warriors she met perform battle feats for her entertainment.

Blodeuwedd. (Welsh) A woman who was created from the flowers of oak, broom, and meadowsweet by Gwyddion and Math to be a wife for Gwyddion's nephew Llew. Blodeuwedd failed to be the biddable little woman they intended her to be, and succeeded in helping her lover slay Llew.

Bo Find. (Irish) This ancient Goddess' name means "white cow." One of Ireland's earliest legends says she appeared on its barren face with her sisters Bo Ruadh ("red cow") and Bo Dhu ("black cow") and created the trees, animals, and grass. This Triple Goddess is the earliest known example using the three colors of the Celtic Triple Goddess, which are still used in many modern Celtic Pagan traditions.

Boann. (Irish) Goddess for whom the River Boyne was named after she was drowned in a flood surge.

Boudicca of the Inceni. (Anglo-Celtic) A warrior queen of the first century who led a successful rebellion against the occupying forces of Rome. The war Goddess Andraste was her patron deity; Boudicca offered sacrifices to her. Her totem animal was the hare, which she released from her cloak to alert her followers to rebellion and to help divine the outcome of the conflict.

Branwyn. (Welsh) Married to Mathowch, an Irish king who fought a battle with her brother Bran after a wedding feast insult.

Brighid. (Irish, Continental) One of the most pervasive divine images in the west. Her Gaulish name is Brigindo and her Anglo-Saxon name Brittania. All versions come from a root word meaning "power." She probably derived from Dana/Danu, the principal mother Goddess of the Celts. She is a deity of fire, fertility, smithing, childbirth, protection, livestock (particularly sheep), healing, and creativity. Her sacred site at Kildare, where a perpetual flame was tended by her priestesses, was overtaken by the new tradition, and the fire tended by nuns. In patriarchal times she became St. Brighid.

Caer Ibormeith. (Irish) A Goddess of sleep, dreams, and love. She frequently took the form of a swan adorned in necklaces of silver and gold.

Cailleach, The. (Scottish, Irish, Manx) Cailleach is a label, not a name; it means "old woman" or "hag." It is one of the many ways in which the crone Goddess of the Gaelic-speaking Celts is identified. In modern folklore she has become the old blue faery woman of winter who can turn into a beautiful young virgin with the coming of spring.

Caireen. (Irish) A protector of children, probably a protective mother Goddess in now-forgotten myths.

Campestres. (Continental) The Roman name of a Celtic Gaulish Goddess of fields, fertility, and the harvest.

Canola. (Irish) This very ancient Goddess is credited with being the inventor of Ireland's enduring symbol, the harp. While dreaming at seaside she heard beautiful music, and awakened to discover that its source was the wind playing across the sinews of a gutted whale. She re-created the music in the harp.

Caolainn. (Irish) A queen who became the guardian of a magickal well in County Roscommon where wishes are granted. These wishes teach the wisher what she really does and does not want.

Carravogue. (Irish, Continental) A crone Goddess once popular in County Meath.

Cartimandua. (Anglo-Celtic) A warrior queen of the Brigantes tribe who fought against the Roman invaders. Her name is sometimes translated as "silken pony," which links her to the archetype of the horse Goddesses.

Cebhfhionn. (Irish) A Goddess of inspiration who was seen at the Well of Knowledge, from which she filled an endless vessel. To taste these waters was to be bestowed with great knowledge, wisdom, and divine inspiration, but Cebhfhionn kept this water from humans because she felt they could not handle its gifts.

Cerridwen. (Welsh) A sow, dark moon, grain, and crone/mother Goddess. She possessed a great cauldron of knowledge, and a knowledge potion that had to simmer for a year and a day; when her servant spilled and tasted some, he accidentally acquired all the world's knowledge. He fled, and she chased him down by shapeshifting into forms best suited to capture the shapeshifted forms he assumed. When she consumed him, he was reborn to her as the bard Taliesin.

Cessair. (Irish) An ancestor deity, considered to be the first ruler of Ireland.

Cliodna. (Irish) A sea and Otherworld Goddess who frequently took the form of a sea bird (an image of transition to the Otherworld). She was the "ruler of the waves," personified in the "ninth wave," the traditional distance of exile from Ireland.

Clota. (Scottish) A healer and Goddess of the River Clyde.

Condwiramur. (Welsh, Cornish) The guardian of the feminine mysteries, and Goddess of sovereignty.

Corchen. (Irish, Manx) A serpent Goddess.

Corra. (Scottish) A Goddess of prophecy who can appear in the form of a crane.

Coventina. (Anglo-Celtic, Scottish) Goddess to whom shrines were erected and offerings left along Hadrian's Wall, the Roman fortification that separated ancient Scotland from England.

Creiddylad. (Welsh) A Goddess of sovereignty.

Cymidei Cymeinfoll. (Welsh) A war Goddess who, with her mate, owned a magickal cauldron into which they could cast and regenerate their warriors killed in battle.

Dahud-Ahes. (Breton) Her undersea island off the coast of Brittany was built for her by her father, King Gradion of Cornwall, so that she could escape the persecution of the monks who declared her to be a witch. Her crime? Opposition to their bringing Christianity to her kingdom.

Damara. (Anglo-Celtic) A fertility Goddess celebrated at Bealtaine.

Damona. (Continental) A cow and fertility Goddess.

Dana/Danu/Don. (Pan-Celtic) Dana was the first great mother Goddess of Ireland, the namesake of the Irish deities known as the Tuatha De Dannan. In modern Celtic Paganism, she often fulfills the role of tribal ancestor and the sovereign. Many European rivers that flow through lands once occupied by the Celts, such as the Danube, bear traces of her name. The *Mabinogion* lists her famous children, one of whom is the popular and powerful Goddess Arianrhod.

Deae Matres. (Continental) A triple mother Goddess whose name survived only through numerous inscriptions and sculptures. The Goddesses are usually depicted holding flowers, grains, and fruit, which show them as fertility, harvest, and seasonal deities; flowers in spring, grain in summer, and fruit in autumn.

Dechtere. (Irish) In her myths, Dechtere plays a triple role of virgin, mother, and crone. She is the mother of Ulster hero Cuchulain. Described as a "large" woman, she was likely once a fertility or ancestor Goddess. Dechtere possessed the interesting gift of transforming herself and her haidmaidens into a flock of birds.

Deirdre of the Sorrows. (Irish) The heroine of a popular folktale known as "Deirdre of the Sorrows." Several versions of her legend still exist, most of them written to condemn her for being born beautiful and causing men to war with each other over her.

Domnu. (Irish) A mother Goddess of the sea.

Drem. (Welsh) A prophetess employed at the Welsh court, she had the power to foresee any aggression plotted against her homeland.

Druantia. (Breton) A fir tree Goddess and patron of tree faeries.

Dwyvach. (Welsh) An ancestor Goddess who built an "ark" to survive the great floods with her husband, Dwyvan.

Eadon. (Irish) Likely a bard who became a Goddess of poetry.

Early, Biddy. (Irish) A "wise woman" of nineteenth century Ireland whose legends continue to grow and be retold. She was able to find cures and foretell the future by looking into a blue bottle supposedly given to her by the faeries. Before she died, it is believed she tossed it into a lake near her home, where it remains to this day.

Ebha Ruadh Ni Murchu. (Irish) A warrior queen.

Ebhlinne. (Irish) A Goddess of midsummer and fire native to Munster.

Edain/Etain. (Irish) Edain's triple form is a personification of reincarnation. She lived as a mortal and as a faery queen.

Eire/Eriu. (Irish) The Goddess for whom the land of Ireland is named. She serves today as a deity of protection, sovereignty, and the land itself.

Elphane, Queen of. (Anglo-Celtic, Scottish) A faery Goddess whose name is likely a corruption of the world 'elfland." Also a Goddess of death and disease in patriarchal times. In sixteenth-century Scotland, it was a capital offense, under charges of Witchcraft, to be accused of consorting with her. Her association with Bealtaine and with death carry her image through the "wheel of the year," making her a Triple Goddess.

Emer. (Irish) A beautiful, intelligent, and multi-talented woman, transformed by myth into a mere consort for the hero Cuchulain. She was an excellent harpist and a seer who accurately predicted her husband's death.

Epona/The Eponae. (Pan-Celtic) This horse Goddess was so powerful an image that she was adopted by the invading Roman forces in Celtic Gaul. She is seen as an intermediary between this world and the Otherworld, as a bringer of nightmares, and as a potent feminine archetype. Epona is also a Goddess of fertility, sex, and wealth.

Ernmas. (Irish) The sometimes-mother of many famous Goddesses, including Anu, Badb, Macha, and Erie. Her name is translated as both "murderer" and "she-farmer," and she was once likely a strong ancestor deity whose myths have been forgotten.

Ethne. (Irish) To retaliate for her near-rape at the hands of love God Aengus — whom she escaped by turning herself into pure light — she took from her people the famous Veil of Invisibility which had once protected Ireland from the invading Milesians (the first Celts in Ireland).

Fachea. (Irish) A Goddess of poetry, probably once a patron deity of bards.

Fand. (Irish, Manx) A faery queen once married to the sea God Manann. She is also a Goddess of the sea in her own right, and a deity of earthly pleasures.

Fedelma. (Irish) A faery queen of Connacht, she accurately prophesied Queen Maeve's victory over Ulster and the death of their hero Cuchulain.

Finchoem. (Irish) She swallowed a worm she found crawling on the rim of a magickal well and conceived the hero Conall of the Victories. A Goddess of wells and fertility.

Fionnuala. (Irish) The tragic heroine in the folklore "The Sorrows of the Children of Lir." She and her three brothers were turned into swans by her jealous step-mother. While swimming, they made beautiful singing together; when changed back to human form nine hundred years later, they turned to dust.

Flaithius. (Irish) A prophet and "old hag" (crone) who would transform herself into a young and beautiful woman if she could persuade a heroic young man to kiss her. In this form she is a Goddess of sovereignty, who bestows the right to rule on the man she kisses.

Fleachta of Meath. (Irish) A moon Goddess associated with the Irish stronghold at Tara, possibly a fertility deity of the High Kings and Goddess of divination for the Druids.

Flidais. (Irish) A chariot-riding, shapeshifting Goddess of the woodlands and animals.

Franconian-Die-Drud. (Irish) A Druid whose name is sometimes linked with that of the horse Goddess Mare, the bringer of dreams, making her a possible Goddess of prophetic dreams.

Garbh Ogh. (Irish) A giant who was a Goddess of the hunt. She drove a chariot pulled by elks. She lived on deer milk and eagle meat and, when ready to die, built herself a triple cairn.

Genovefa. (Welsh, Cornish, Breton) A sovereign Goddess who rode her white deer in a land competition with her brother Edern. When she saw she was losing, she caused a cock to crow to halt the contest.

Gillagriene. (Irish, Scottish) The daughter of a sunbeam and a human man. When she learned of her unorthodox parentage, she threw herself into Lough Griene (The Lake of the Sun). She drifted along until she beached near an oak grove, where she died.

Godiva, Lady. (Anglo-Celtic) A sovereign deity whose legends became attached to those of a human woman who rode naked through the streets of Coventry until her corrupt husband agreed to lower taxes.

Goewin. (Welsh) A Goddess of sovereignty who held the feet of Math while he reigned as king. She was only exempt from doing so when he went to war.

Goleuddydd. (Welsh) A sow, mother, and woodlands Goddess who made a mad dash into the forest to give birth to her son.

Grainne. (Irish) Once a sun Goddess, her myths now center on her betrothal to Fionn McCumhal and her jilting of him for Diarmuid of the Love Spot. Grainne also has sovereign aspects.

Grainne Ni Malley. (Irish) A pirate who preyed on English ships during the Elizabethan age. Legends say that Queen Elizabeth I invited Grainne to her court and offered her expensive bribes to secure a promise that she would cease to prey on English vessels. Grainne refused the offer and returned to Ireland where she captured an English noblewoman and held her hostage until the British admiralty acknowledged her sovereignty over the Irish seas.

Grian. (Irish) A faery Goddess from County Tipperary, probably once a solar deity. She had nine daughters who lived in homes called *griannon*, or sun houses.

Guinevere, Queen. (Welsh, Cornish) The sovereign power behind the throne of King Arthur. The oldest Welsh legends list three different queens for Arthur, all of them named Guinevere.

Gwendydd. (Welsh, Cornish) The sister of Merlin, magician of Arthurian legends, she was the only person who could approach him after he had gone to live in the woods. He supposedly taught her the art of divination.

Gwennolaik. (Breton) A heroine who shapeshifted into a bird to fly to the rescue of her beloved foster brother, Nola.

Gwyar. (Welsh) Her name translates as both "shedding blood" and "gore," perhaps an indication of her former role as a Goddess of regeneration.

Henwen. (Anglo-Celtic) A sow Goddess who brought abundance to the land by giving birth to litters of different animals at various locations.

Igraine. (Welsh, Cornish) King Arthur's mother.

Inghean Bhuidhe. (Irish) One of a Triple Goddess with her two sisters, Lassair and Latiaran. She was a deity of Bealtaine, the personification of the start of summer.

Isolde. (Pan-Celtic) Famous Irish heroine who functions as a sovereign Goddess between King Mark of Cornwall and his nephew Tristan.

Kele-De. (Irish) Ancient Goddess steeped in mystery, she was at the center of an all-female spiritual order known as the *Kelles*. Among other practices, her high priestesses reserved the right to take any and all lovers they chose. The Catholic order known as the Culdees probably has its origin in the worship of this Goddess.

Kyteler, Dame Alice. (Irish) A fourteenth-century Irishwoman who was tried and condemned as a Witch. A neighbor had caught her outside at night, sweeping towards her door while chanting a spell to bring in prosperity.

Lady of the Lake, The. (Welsh, Cornish, Breton) A sovereign Goddess who is also a deity of life, death, and regeneration. It was she who bestowed the famous sword Excalibur upon King Arthur, and to whom it was returned at his death.

Lassair. (Irish) A Goddess of fire and Midsummer, part of a Triple Goddess with her sisters Latiaran and Inghean Bhuidhe.

Latiaran. (Irish) The youngest of three sisters who made up a Triple Goddess. Latiaran was the Goddess of the harvest festival Lughnasadh. Also a Goddess of the forge.

Latis. (Anglo-Celtic) A lake Goddess who became a Goddess of ale and meade.

Lavercam. (Irish) Born a slave, she became a poet and bard at the court of King Conor MacNessa. She was a famous runner, and the assigned guardian of Deirdre of the Sorrows.

LeFay. (Welsh, Cornish) A Goddess of healing, the sea, and the Isle of Avalon.

Liban. (Irish, Manx) She and her sister Fand were the twin Goddesses of health and earthly pleasures.

Liban. (Irish, Manx) A faery queen/Goddess who was the guardian spirit of Ireland's holy wells. One day she forgot to guard the well, and the ensuing flood formed Lough Neath. She was able to take the form of a salmon, a fish symbolizing great knowledge.

Luaths Lurgann. (Irish) A warrior Goddess known as Ireland's fastest runner.

Luned. (Welsh) An "enchantress" (Witch? Druid?) from Arthurian legend who frees Sir Owain from the Black Knight by granting him the power of invisibility. Later he rescued her from being burned at the stake.

Macha. (Irish) One of the Morrigan, a Triple Goddess of death, battle, and destruction. Also a horse deity who cursed the male Red Branch warriors to suffer nine days of birth pangs when Ulster needed them the most. The famous Ulster fortress, Emain Macha, is named for her.

Maer. (Irish) A Druid who attempted to entrap Fionn McCumhal with a love spell.

Maeve, Queen. (Irish) A warrior queen of Connacht who was certainly once a powerful Goddess. She is a deity of sovereignty who embodies the highest attainment of feminine power.

Magog. (Anglo-Celtic) The female half of a divine team of mountain deities, depicted as a four-breasted woman astride a horse. Probably once an earth, fertility, and/or mother Goddess. In patriarchal times she became England's St. Margaret.

Maire Ni Ciaragain. (Irish) A warrior queen.

Mamionn, Biddy. (Irish) This Innishshark midwife was a healer of great repute who was once said to have been taken into the faery world to cure their children. For her assistance she was granted access to their healing knowledge.

Marcassa, Princess. (Breton) She possessed the power to cure an old king of a deadly disease if only she would sleep with him. The Princess refused to help him and went into "hibernation" until he died. When she woke up she married a younger man of her own choice.

Mare. (Irish) A horse Goddess; the bringer of dreams, especially nightmares.

Meg the Healer. (Scottish) A healer so famous that the faery folk came to her for assistance. One of the few humans allowed to walk freely in and out of the world of faery, she helped trapped mortals escape the faery ream and, upon her death, was taken there to be with the faery folk.

Melusine. (Breton, Scottish) A serpent Goddess banished from her father's kingdom (with her two sisters) when her father, the king, discovered she was a faery. They staged a mock sacrifice of him for revenge. Their mother retaliated by turning her into a serpent from the waist down on Saturdays.

Modron. (Welsh) Means "great Mother." Likely an ancestor Goddess. Also a deity of fertility, childbirth, sex, and the harvest.

Moingfhion. (Irish) A Goddess of death and regeneration honored at Samhain.

Momu. (Scottish) A Highland Goddess of wells and hillsides.

Morgan LeFay. (Welsh, Cornish, Breton) A half-sister of King Arthur, possibly once a Goddess of Glastonbury Tor, the sacred Pagan site associated with the Arthurian myths which functions as a gateway to the Otherworld. Also a sea Goddess.

Morrigan, The. (Pan-Celtic) A Triple Goddess composed of the three Goddesses of war, battle, death, and destruction: Badb, Macha, and Neman. At battlefields the Morrigan took the form of a crow or raven and flew shrieking overhead, often calling upon the spirits of slain warriors. Celtic war trophies (severed heads) were offered to her and were "the Morrigan's acorn crop."

Muireartach. (Irish, Scottish) A battle Goddess who was the personification of the storm-tossed seas between Ireland and Scotland.

Nair. (Irish) A sovereign who personified the concept of regicide, the king-killing rites of the Anglo-Celts. Legends foretold that all kings who slept with her would die. (See Chapter 12.)

Nantosuelta. (Continental) A river Goddess from Celtic Gaul, sometimes depicted cradling a cornucopia in her lap. Probably a fertility/prosperity Goddess, and a personification of the great waters of the cauldron of rebirth.

Nehalennia. (Anglo-Celtic, Continental) A dog Goddess who was a patron of sea traders. Many statues and reliefs still exist which bear her inscription. These show her as a Goddess of harvest, fertility, sun, water, and prosperity.

Neman. (Irish) One of the Morrigan.

Nemetona. (Anglo-Celtic, Continental) Her name contains the Gaulish word *nemeton*, meaning "sacred space." A deity of all sacred places.

Nessa. (Irish) A scholar and warrior who arranged to make her son, Conor, the High King of Ireland.

Niamh of the Golden Hair. (Irish) A Goddess who leads warriors to the Otherworld when they die.

Olwen. (Welsh) A sovereign Goddess fought over by her father and her lover.

Plur Na mBan. (Irish) A flower Goddess.

Princess of the Sun, The. (Breton) Cursed by some evil faeries to appear as a swan except for a short time at sundown, she got a warrior to help her escape her enchantment, then carried him away in a fiery chariot.

Ratis. (Anglo-Celtic) Goddess of protective fortifications and boundaries.

Rhiannon. (Welsh, Cornish) A Goddess of death, the Otherworld, magick, music, and the moon; a bringer of dreams who is symbolized by a white horse. She was accused of killing her child by devouring him and, as punishment, forced to carry travelers on her back through the gates of her kingdom. Her horse form also shows her to be a mediator between the earth plane and the Otherworld.

Rosmerta. (Anglo-Celtic, Continental) A Goddess of healing and hot springs, worshiped by both the Celts and Romans in Gaul.

Saba. (Irish) She was lured into the forest while pregnant and became lost. Faeries turned her into a deer, and it was in this form that she gave birth to her son, Ossian. She became a Goddess of the deer and the woodlands.

Sabrina. (Anglo-Celtic) She became Goddess of the River Severn when she was drowned there.

Scathach. (Irish, Scottish) Famous warrior Goddess who ran a battle school that trained some of the greatest Celtic warriors. She was famous for her magickal battle leap and war cry. She passed along an invincible sword to the Ulster hero, Cuchulain, making her a Lady of the Lake of Irish lore.

Sequana. (Anglo-Celtic, Continental) Earth Goddess who lived beneath the rivers. She was sometimes depicted as a duck, and at her festival offerings was tossed into the rivers.

Sheila-Na-Gig. (Irish) Called a Goddess, though her origins are shadowy. She is a pervasive image found carved on Irish doorways and stones, a squatting feminine figure who invitingly holds open her vulva in a triangular pattern.

Sin. (Irish) Goddess of war and wine.

Sionann. (Irish) Namesake of the River Shannon. She approached the sacred Well of Knowledge (Well of *Segais*) in an irreverent manner and was washed away as punishment for her disrespect.

Sirona. (Breton, Continental) A Goddess of the hot springs whose name means "star."

Stine Bheag O' Tarbat. (Scottish) A beautiful Witch with a talent for weather magick. Patriarchal legend reduced her to a hag or baneful faery who uses her powers for evil.

Sul. (Continental) A Goddess of hot springs and healing. The root of her name means "eye," which archetypally also links to the sun.

Taillte. (Irish) A Goddess of fertility and first grains of the harvest. She was also an earth Goddess, a patron deity of games competition, and the deity in whose name trial marriages (handfastings) were consecrated. The famous Telltown games were held in her honor until the twelfth century.

Tamara. (Cornish) Goddess of the River Tamar, which divides the Duchy of Cornwall from the rest of England.

Tanit. (Cornish) A Phoenician moon and fertility Goddess. Many scholars and mythologists believe she came into the Celtic pantheon as Dana or Don, both mother Goddesses. Tanit was worshiped as Tanat in Cornwall on Bealtaine.

Taranis. (Continental) A death Goddess to whom human sacrifices were once offered.

Tea and **Tephi.** (Irish) Co-founders and protectors of the sacred site at Tara.

Tlachtga. (Irish) A magician (Druid?) of Meath who died giving birth to triplets who each had different fathers. Also a Goddess of sacrifice, honored at Samhain.

Triduana. (Scottish) A Goddess who chose to pluck out her eyes and destroy her beauty rather than submit to marriage with Nechtan, a king of the Picts.

Triple Goddess, The. (Pan-Celtic) The three-in-one archetype of the feminine divine which is part of not only Celtic culture, but many others as well. She is an exceptionally strong image in Celtic lore. She is symbolized by the three faces of the moon, and the colors white, red, and black.

Turrean. (Irish) A beautiful dog Goddess.

Uairebhuidhe. (Irish) A bird Goddess.

Uathach. (Irish, Scottish) A daughter of battle teacher Scathach. She is also a warrior/Goddess who taught male warriors magickal battle skills. Her name means "specter," which may link her to sovereignty archetypes.

Uroica. (Breton) A Goddess of heather and heather wine.

Veleda. (Continental) A warrior queen of a continental Celtic people called the Bructeri.

Vennolandua. (Cornish) A High Queen of Cornwall who killed her husband and drowned his mistress. She then held the throne until her son came of age and she could turn it over to him.

Vivianne/Nimue. (Welsh, Cornish, Breton) The lover of Merlin of Arthurian myth, sometimes associated with the Lady of the Lake who gave Arthur his famous sword, Excalibur. A potent magickian and shapeshifter whose powerful image has been reduced to one of pettiness in patriarchal times.

Vivionn. (Welsh) A giantess who dwelt in the Otherworld realm known as the Land of Women.

Celtic Goddess Symbolism, Functions, and Correspondences

The Celts did not divide their deities into clear spheres of predominance, as mentioned earlier. For instance, a Goddess of fire could also be a Goddess of childbirth. For this reason, the listings in this appendix contain much overlap. As much as possible, I have tried to include all aspects of the Celtic feminine figures covered within this book: their areas of control, their symbols, and other correspondences.

Abundance, Prosperity, Harvest

Anu

Artio

Bo Find

Campestres

Deae Matres

Godiva, Lady

Henwen

Latiaran

Nantosuelta

Taillte

Ancestor Goddesses of Celts

Arianrhod

Cessair

Dana

Dwyvach

Ernmas

Modron

Animals, general

Ardwinna

Flidais

Henwen

Apples

Ailinn

Badb

Cailleach, the

Astral Projection/Invisibility

Bellah Postil

Ethne

Luned

Battlefields

Bellona

Morrigan, the

Bears

Artio

Beauty/Physical Fitness

Aife

Deirdre

Luaths Lurgann

Scathach

Taillte

Triduana

Bees

Derbforgaille

Birds

Aife

Brighid (lark)

Caer Ibermeith (swan)

Cliodna (sea bird)

Corra (crane)

Dechtere

Derbforgaille

Edain (swan)

Fionnuala (swan)

Garbh Ogh (eagle)

Gwennolaik

Gwenddoleu

Princess of the Sun (swan)

Rhiannon

Sequana (duck)

Uairebhuidhe

Blackberries

Brighid

Boars

Ardwinna

Boats/Ships/Shipping

Becuma

Grainne ni Malley

Boundaries

Coventina

Ratis

Tamara

Butterflies

Edain

Cattle

Aine

Blathnat

Bo Find

Damona

Cauldron

Badb

Blathnat

Cerridwen

Cymidei Cymeinfoll

Morrigan, the

Chalice/Grail

Condwiramur

Chariots

Flidais

Garbh Ogh

Princess of the Sun

Children/Childbirth

Ban-Chuideachaidh Moire

Brighid

Caireen

Modron

Courage and Strength

Artio

Lavercam

Taillte

Craftsmanship/Smithing

Airmid

Brighid

Creativity/Inspiration

Brighid

Canola

Cebhfhionn

Crones

Badb

Cailleach, the

Carravogue

Cerridwen

Gwyar

Morrigan, the

Macha

Neman

Crows

Badb

Cailleach, the

Dawn

Genovefa

Death/Otherworld/Regeneration

Badb

Cliodna

Cymidei Cymeinfoll

Dahud-Ahes

Elphane, Queen of

Gwyar

Lady of the Lake

LeFay

Macha

Moingfhion

Morgan LeFay

Morrigan, the

Nantosuelta

Neman

Niamh

Rhiannon

Taranis

Vivionn

Deer

    Garbh Ogh

    Genovefa

    Saba

Divination/Prophecy

    Andraste

    Corra

    Drem

    Emer

    Fedelma

    Fleachta of Meath

    Franconian-die-Drud

    Gwendydd

Destructive Magick/Banishing

    Badb

    Elphane, Queen of

    Macha

    Morrigan, the

    Neman

Disease (giving and curing)

    Airmid

    Elphane, Queen of

Dogs

    Nehalennia

    Turrean

Dreams

    Caer Ibermeith

    Canola

    Franconian-die-Drud

    Mare

    Rhiannon

Druids

    Amerach

    Argante

    Birog

    Drem

    Eadon

    Franconian-die-Drud

    Luned

    Maer

    Tlachtga

Ducks

    Sequana

Earth

    Achall

    Bo Find

    Campestres

    Eire

    Magog

    Sequana

    Taillte

Eels

    Morrigan, the

Equal Armed Cross

    Brighid

Faery World

    Achtland

    Beansidhe, the

    Biddy Early

    Biddy Mamionn

    Blathnat

    Caer Ibermeith

    Cailleach, the

    Cliodna

    Cred

Faery World (continued)

Druantia

Edain

Elphane, Queen of

Fand

Fedelma

Feithline

Grian

Lady of the Lake, the

Liban

Meg the Healer

Feminine Mysteries

Kele-De

Sheila-Na-Gig

Fertility

Aine

Anu

Arianrhod

Bo Find

Brighid

Campestres

Damara

Damona

Deae Matres

Epona

Finchoem

Fleachta of Meath

Magog

Modron

Nantosuelta

Tanit

Taillte

Fire

Adsullata

Aine

Brighid

Ebhlinne

Inghean Bhuidhe

Lassair

Princess of the Sun

Rosemerta

Sul

Fish

Bean Naomha (trout)

Liban (salmon)

Flowers

Aine (meadowsweet)

Blodeuwedd

Deae Matres

Guinevere (hawthorne)

Plur na mBan

Fortifications

Macha

Ratis

Tea and Tephi

Giants

Garbh Ogh

Vivionn

Harp

Canola

Eire

Hawthorne

Guinevere

Healing/Herbalism

Airmid
Aibheaog
Airmid
Argante
Arnamentia
Biddy Early
Biddy Mamionn
Brighid
Clota
Iefay
Liban
Marcassa, Princess
Meg the Healer
Rosemerta
Sul

Heather

Uroica

Hens

Cerridwen

Horses

Aife
Caer Ibormeith
Cartimandua
Edain
Epona
Franconian-die-Drud
Godiva, Lady
Macha
Mare
Rhiannon

Hot Springs

Adsullata
Rosemerta
Sirona
Sul

Hunting

Flidais
Garbh Ogh

Justice

Aerten

Love

Ailinn
Aine
Deirdre

Magick (general)

Biddy Early
Caolainn
Gwendydd
Luned
Morgan LeFay
Rhiannon
Tlachtga
Vivianne

Milk

Brighid

Moon

Anu
Arianrhod
Fleachta of Meath
Rhiannon
Tanit

Moon, dark

Cerridwen

Moon, waning

Cailleach, the
Badb

Mother Goddesses
Brighid
Caireen
Cerridwen
Cessair
Dana
Deae Matres
Dechtere
Domnu
Dwyvach
Latiaran
Macha
Magog
Modron
Taillte

Mountains or Hillsides
Aine
Magog
Momu

Music
Banbha
Canola
Eire
Emer
Fionnuala
Rhiannon

Otters
Liban

**Pleasure/Diversion/
Games/Competition**
Fand
Liban
Taillte

Poetry
Brighid
Eadon
Fachea
Lavercam

Precious Gems
Fand

Protection/Guardianship
Aine
Badb
Brighid
Caolainn
Eire
Ethne
Ratis
Tea and Tephi

Purification
Arnamentia

Queens/Clan Chiefs
Aeval
Aife
Aille
Ain and Iaine
Boudicca
Caolainn
Cartimandua
Ebha Ruagh ni Murchu
Maeve, Queen
Maire ni Ciaragain
Veleda
Vennolandua

Ravens
Cailleach, the
Morrigan, the

Regicide
Nair

Reincarnation
Arianrhod
Edain

Sacred Sites
Nemetona
Tea and Tephi

Salmon
Liban

Seasonal Rites
Aine
Arianrhod
Damara
Ebhlinne
Inghean Bhuidhe
Lassair
Latiaran
Moingfhion
Tlachtga
Tanit

Serpents
Corchen
Melusine

Severed Heads
Morrigan, the

Sex
Achtland
Aeval
Arianrhod
Epona
Fand
Maeve, Queen
Modron

Shapeshifters
Badb
Cerridwen
Dechtere
Edain
Flidaid
Flaithius
Liban
Melusine
Morrigan, the
Gwennolaik

Sheep
Brighid

Shields
Badb
Brighid
Derbforgaille
Maeve, Queen
Scathach

Sleep
Caer Ibermeith
Fionnuala

Staff
Arianrhod
Cailleach, the

Stars
>Arianrhod
>Sirona

Storms
>Cailleach, the
>Muireartach

Sovereignty
>Achall
>Ain and Iaine
>Condwiramur
>Creiddylad
>Deirdre
>Eire
>Flaithius
>Genovefa
>Godiva, Lady
>Goewin
>Grainne
>Guinevere
>Isolde
>Lady of the Lake
>Maeve, Queen
>Nair
>Olwen
>Scathach
>Vivianne

Sows
>Cerridwen
>Goleuddydd
>Henwen

Sun
>Adsullata
>Aimend
>Aine
>Bean Naomha
>Gillagriene
>Grainne
>Grian
>Princess of the Sun
>Sul

Swans
>Caer Ibermeith
>Edain
>Fionnuala
>Princess of the Sun

Teachers
>Aife
>Scathach
>Uathach

Trees
>Druantia
>Gillagriene

Trefoil/Shamrocks
>Brighid
>Olwen

Time Manipulation
>Amerach

Triple Goddesses

Anu/Dana/Badb
Badb/Macha/Neman
Bo Find/Bo Dhu/Bo Ruadh
Brighid
Deae Matres
Dechtere
Edain
Eire/Fodhla/Banbha
Elphane, Queen of
Epona
Fiongalla
Flaithius
Garbh Ogh
Guinevere
Latiaran/Inghean Bhuidhe/Lesair
Melusine/Melior/Palatina
Morrigan, the
Olwen

Triskele

All Triple Goddesses

Turnips

Cailleach, the

Victory

Andraste

Virgin Goddesses

Anu
Isolde
Nemain
Triduana

Warriors/Warfare

Aerten
Aife
Ain and Iaine
Andraste
Badb
Banbha
Boudicca
Cartimandua
Cymidei Cymeinfoll
Ebha Ruagh ni Murchu
Grainne ni Malley
Luaths Lurgann
Macha
Maeve, Queen
Maire ni Ciaragain
Muireartach
Nessa
Scathach
Sin
Uathach
Veleda

Water/Seas/Lakes/Rivers

Adsullata
Arnamentia
Boann
Cebhfhionn
Cliodna
Clota
Dahud-Ahes
Domnu
Fand
Lady of the Lake

Water/Seas/Lakes/Rivers
(continued)

Lefay

Latis

Liban

Melusine

Morgan LeFay

Muireartach

Nantosuelta

Nehalennia

Sabrina

Sequana

Sionnan

Tamara

Waves

Cliodna

Weather Magick

Stine Bheag

Weaving

Arianrhod

Wells

Aibheaog

Brighid

Bean Naomha

Caolainn

Cebhfhionn

Finchoem

Liban

Momu

Wine/Ale/Meade

Latis

Sin

Uroica

Winter

the Cailleach

Wisdom, Intellect, Knowledge, and Wit

Ailbhe

Bean Naomha

Cebhfhionn

Nessa

Wolves

Badb

the Morrigan

Woodlands

Ardwinna

Flidais

Garbh Ogh

Saba

Opening and Closing the Ritual Circle as a Celtic Solitary

For those unfamiliar with the art of opening and closing a ritual circle, this appendix provides a detailed outline for a solitary woman to follow for beginning and ending her Celtic women's spirituality rites. This formula follows the basic format found in many Wiccan/Pagan traditions, but you should be aware that this is not the only correct way to open (or "cast") and close (or "ground") a circle. Experienced practitioners often devise their own unique and meaningful methods, especially when they are working alone or with a long-established group. If you are experienced at the process, or have yet to find a method you like, this will offer a starting point for exploration.

The circle has three functions:

1. To protect the person(s) inside from uninvited outside forces that may be attracted to the energies raised

2. To contain raised energy until it is needed and can be properly and deliberately directed towards its magickal/ritual goal

3. To open a space between the worlds of form (the earth plane) and spirit (the Otherworld), at which they meet and blend

Circles are cast with the power of the mind and the projection of personal energy. They usually remain unseen, except to the psychic "eye," but they are very real, and their boundaries should always be respected. Some traditions permit doorways to be cut in the "wall" of the circle should someone find it necessary to pass in and out, but such comings and goings are wisely kept to a minimum. Before you cast a circle, you should have everything you will need for your ritual inside the working area. This does not mean that you need lavish accouterments. Many rituals work just as well without them, and in most cases their use is a personal choice and not a requirement. The same holds true if you wish to use an altar as a place to arrange your tools and equipment, and as a focus for your devotions. Although an altar is not required, it can make for a smoother ritual and can help you keep your directional alignments straight. No matter what Pagan tradition one works in, each of the four cardinal directions is designated as the realm of a particular element and has its own elemental beings and rulers. In most of the Wiccan traditions these directional attributes are:

Water to the west

Earth to the north

Air to the east

Fire to the south

The example in this book had to adopt some standard in order to be understandable, and so it uses the common Wiccan attributes, but you should always feel free to change these to suit your personal world view or that of your own Celtic tradition. If you have a ritual tool for each of the directions and you are using an altar, it is customary to place the tools at the four edges of the altar that correspond to those directions. The following is a list of common Celtic tools, and the element with which they are thought to share an affinity. You will note some overlap among the elements. This is because traditions occasionally assign their tool correspondences differently. It should be remembered that each system serves its followers very well, and that none is inherently right or wrong.

Earth
Shield, stones, clay, wood, soil, salt, sand, wheel, club, drum, bronze, bow

Water
Chalice, cauldron, hollow horn, bowl, trident, any cool liquid, silver, convex shield, sea shells, sickle

Fire

Candle, athame and sword (and all blades forged in fire), wand, iron (not usually used in Celtic paths that refer to themselves as "faery" traditions, due to a belief that faeries cannot come into contact with iron), claymore, flint, torch, solar disk (equilateral cross within a circle), broom or besom, gold, spear

Air

Staff, trident, athame and sword, wand, feather, incense, claymore, broom or besom, dirk, spear, broach, horn, smoking pipe, arrow, flint

You will need to open your circle in a private, uncluttered place at least four feet in diameter (for freedom of movement), in a location where you are not likely to be disturbed. You may choose to use a ritual tool, such as an athame or wand, to help project the energy that will create the circle, but the energy from your own hand will work just as well. Pinpoint the cardinal directions — west, north, south, and east — and mark them so that they will be easy for you to recognize. Candles and stones are commonly used for this, but as a solitary woman, you might consider chalices or bowls, which are feminine symbols. These could all be different colors, or be filled with various colored waters (using food coloring or juices) to differentiate between directions. For example, you might use blue water for west, green for north, yellow for east, and red for south. You should take some time to purify the circle area first, driving away any negative energies that are lingering there, and raising the vibrational rate of the area to higher spiritual levels incompatible with those of any lower level entities who may be attracted to your working. Salt water and incense are commonly used for this, and should be accompanied by clear visualization as well. Taking your broom, or besom, and sweeping the unwanted entities away is another common practice, especially with women. Remember Dame Alice Kyteler! (See Chapter 13.)

Stand in the center of what will be your circle, close your eyes, and center your energies. Then, when you are ready, raise your chosen tool or your arms skyward and feel yourself filling with energy—either drawn down from the Otherworld, or drawn up from inside mother earth. Fill yourself and the area where you are working with this positive force. Next, walk to the edge of your circle in the direction that you or the Celtic tradition you follow has deemed to be the proper place to begin casting the circle. Sometimes these are fixed points; at other times they change with the turning of the wheel of the year. This example uses the western quarter as a starting point because that is the one my tradition uses. West is the direction of the Otherworld, the home of the Celtic deities. Point your finger or tool at the ground—it does not actually have to touch the ground—and begin visualizing energy coming from the end of your fingertip or tool, creating a wall of intense protective energy. You may choose to see your circle either as a wall, a dome, or a sphere, but its power will remain the same. Walk slowly sunwise around the circle, the traditional direction associated with growth, increase, construction, and so on, until you have reached your starting point again. Project as much energy into the creation of your circle as possible. Make it real and respect its reality. Most circles are cast in the sunwise direction and then closed by moving anti-sunwise. But keep in mind that, in some cases, the opposite is true. Some rituals are best cast anti-sunwise and closed sunwise. An example of this would be any type of ritual in which you want to cultivate the energies of decrease, destruction, or loss, in order for the circle to be more compatible with the ultimate goal of the rite. This does not mean that the ritual to take place will be negative. Negative rituals can just as easily take place in a circle cast clockwise. The intent of the ritual, not its outer form, determines whether it is negative or positive.

You may wish to walk the perimeters two more times to invoke the magickal power of the Celtic sacred number three. This is not an uncommon practice among Celtic Pagans, and is a standard if you will be working with Triple Goddess energies. (See Chapter 6.)

After the circle is cast, the elemental powers of each direction are called upon to witness and lend support to the ritual. This practice is known by a variety of terms, including calling the quarters, summoning the elementals, invoking the watchtowers, evoking the elements, calling the elemental rulers, or summoning the guardians. Custom also dictates that the elemental rulers must heed your call, at least in their most basic forms. If they feel insulted by your invitation, or if you are a beginner and your powers of evocation are still weak, you may not get the full benefit of elemental presences. Begin calling your quarters at your original starting point (in this example in the west). If you have a tool designed to correspond to each element, it is customary to carry it from the altar to the quarter as you make the call. This helps strengthen your connection to the element, and forges a stronger sympathetic link between your tool and the element it represents in order to make it a better working tool for you. This sample ritual is written without the use of tools, so that it can be immediately usable by a greater number of women, but feel free to incorporate them if you have them present.

Facing the west, prepare to summon that quarter. Visualize your voice reaching out to the farthest reaches of that direction, covering the vastness of time and space, and connecting you with the powers of the west and the element of water. Making a verbal statement solidifies your purpose in your mind, and helps you to begin to connect with the energies and beings who want to help you succeed. Thinking things through carefully may work as well in some cases, but only if you have fully thought out all elements of your ritual first. If for any reason you cannot speak aloud (privacy issues, illness, or other concerns), you may wish to write out your words at this point. You can burn the paper later to reinforce the idea that your words have power and that they have been taken into the Otherworld to manifest. But, please, work out each word carefully in advance, just to make sure any ritual is exactly what you want it to be. We have all had the experience of announcing that we have just gotten a great idea and then someone asks us to tell them about it; it is then, as we put it into words, that we suddenly see all its faults.

Since your rites in this case are those of Celtic women's spirituality, as you call out to the western quarter think of the spirits you are calling upon as being feminine in character, even when that element is a masculine one (air and fire are the masculine elements). Everything in creation has both a masculine and a feminine side, regardless of which one is physically dominant. Though the elemental rulers of the directions are often characterized as masculine, there are many elemental and faery beings who reside in these worlds and can fill these roles just as well. Many of these are feminine in character.

To call the west, say the following:

> Powers of the west—undines, guardians, spirits, elementals,
> and feminine spirits of the watery realms—hear and heed my
> invitation to you. Fertile powers of the west and of water, I call
> you from the Otherworld and ask your presence at this circle
> this eve ["eve" is used here for its poetic sound only, and you
> may use the words *day, night, afternoon, full moon, equinox,* and
> so on, as fits the occasion]. Join me in this place which is out of
> places, at this time which is outside of time, the sacred circle
> wherein (state purpose of your ritual). Lend balance to this
> sacred space as you protect, witness, and worship with me this
> eve, adding your powers and blessings to this rite. By the power
> of three, and in the name of Virgin, Mother, and Crone, I
> welcome the powers of water. Blessed Be.

You may opt to use a ritual gesture to reinforce your intent when calling the quarters, such as an invoking pentagram. This is a five-pointed star designed to symbolize the drawing in or drawing down of certain energies. The choice to use it or not is yours to make.

Remain facing the west for a minute or two and allow yourself to feel the presence and power of water and her attendant spirits.

When you feel ready, walk to the north and begin the process of evoking that quarter. (If you are using tools to represent each element, do not forget to return to the altar each time to get the corresponding tool!)

> Powers of the north, elemental home of the mother who sus-
> tains us—gnomes, guardians, spirits, elementals, and feminine
> spirits of the earth realm—hear and heed my invitation to you.
> Stabilizing powers of the north and earth, I call you from the
> Otherworld and ask your presence at this circle this eve ["eve"
> is used here for its poetic sound only, and you may use the words
> *day, night, afternoon, full moon, equinox,* or other word that fits
> the occasion]. Join me in this place which is out of place, at this
> time which is outside of time, the sacred circle wherein (state
> purpose of your ritual). Lend balance to this sacred space as you

Invoking Pentagram

protect, witness, and worship with me this eve, adding your powers and blessings to this rite. By the power of three, and in the name of Virgin, Mother, and Crone, I welcome the powers of earth. Blessed Be.

Remain facing the north for a minute or two and allow yourself to feel the presence and power of earth and her attendant spirits.

Walk next to the eastern quarter.

Powers of the east—sylphs, guardians, spirits, elementals, and feminine spirits of the airy realms—hear and heed my invitation to you. Thinking powers of the east and of air, I call you from the Otherworld and ask your presence at this circle this eve [or other word that fits the occasion]. Join me in this place which is out of place, at this time which is outside of time, the sacred circle wherein (state purpose of your ritual). Lend balance to this sacred space as you protect, witness, and worship with me this eve, adding your powers and blessings to this rite. By the power of three, and in the name of Virgin, Mother, and Crone, I welcome the powers of air. Blessed Be.

Remain facing the east for a minute or two and allow yourself to feel the presence and power of air and its attendant spirits.

Finally, walk to the south quarter.

Powers of the south—salamander, guardians, spirits, elementals, and feminine spirits of the fiery realms—hear and heed my invitation to you. Passionate powers of the south and of fire, I call you from the Otherworld and ask your presence at this circle this eve [or other word that fits the occasion]. Join me in this place which is out of place, at this time which is outside of time, the sacred circle wherein (state purpose of your ritual). Lend balance to this sacred space as you protect, witness, and worship with me this eve, adding your powers and blessings to this rite. By the power of three, and in the name of Virgin, Mother, and Crone, I welcome the powers of fire. Blessed Be.

Remain facing the south for a minute or two and allow yourself to feel the presence and power of fire and its attendant spirits.

Before you continue on with the invitation to the Goddess(es), you should walk to the west quarter again, the one in which you began your quarter calls, to symbolically complete the cycle. Remember that symbolism is the essence of ritual—every gesture and word you use should be intended to affect your inner self in positive ways in conformity to the overall goal of the ritual. Take advantage of every chance you get to strengthen these symbolic links.

It is customary at this point to invite both the God and Goddess into your circle. The two together represent balance. However, in women's spirituality, more often than not, only a Goddess, or several Goddesses, are asked to witness and bless the proceedings. You may either call on the universal spirit of the feminine creator by her titles Goddess, Lady, Mother, and so on, or use the name of Goddess who is your patron, or who is important to the ritual at hand. You can offer this invitation at your altar, or by facing whatever direction you perceive to be her home.

The invitations should be just that—invitations—and the words should come from your heart, sincerely felt and expressed. They can be spoken with a Goddess symbol in hand, such as a chalice or shield, or with your arms open to symbolize your welcoming and embracing of the Goddess. The following example uses the mother/ancestor Goddess Danu:

> Blessed Danu, mother of our tribe, originator of all creation,
> giver of life, of death, and rebirth, I, your warrior and child, ask
> your presence at this circle this eve (or whatever time of day or
> whatever event best expresses the moment). Witness my ritual
> of (insert purpose of ritual here). Lend your creative energies
> and bless my efforts to your glory. Welcome to you from whom
> all blessings flow.

If you wish you may light a candle to honor the Goddess and allow it to burn as tangible evidence of her presence within your circle. This is another common practice in many Pagan traditions. It symbolizes the light that is the Goddess being present within your circle.

In many Celtic traditions, it is considered a must to "feed" any being who has been called from the Otherworld with a ritual portion known as a libation. Usually bread or some other grain product, and wine or juice is offered. However, you may offer whatever you feel is right and appropriate for the ritual you are doing. Place the items either on a plate on your altar or near the west quarter. You may want to verbalize your offering, or choose not to; what is important is making the offer in the first place. After the ritual, this libation

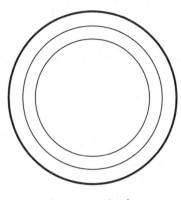

Concentric Circles

should be burned, drowned, or left out for animals where practical.

For some Celtic Pagan rites you may need or want to cast other inner circles within your primary circle. The three most common styles of Celtic inner circles are:

The Concentric Circles

This is easily the most commonly used inner-circle pattern. It involves the casting of two more circles inside your primary one for a total of three, the Celtic sacred number.

The Figure Eight

This pattern casts two inner circles, one above the other, in a rough figure eight pattern. The lower one may represent the physical plane and the upper one represents the Otherworld or underworld, or one may represent the divine realm and the other the human realm.

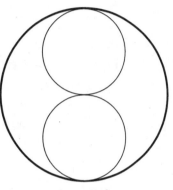

Figure Eight

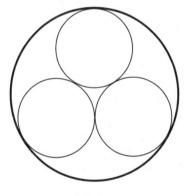

Triskele Pattern

The Triskele Pattern

This pattern uses three inner circles in a triangular pattern in a rough representation of the triskele. The three circles can represent the three faces of the Triple Goddess; or the underworld or faery realm, the middleworld or physical plane, and the upperworld or Otherworld.

After all your circles are cast, you may start to work the body of your ritual. This means doing whatever it is you created the sacred space to do. This may include magickal efforts, honoring of the Goddess, rites of passage, seasonal celebrations, or many other activities. When your ritual purpose has been completed, the circle(s) must be closed and grounded. The reasons for this are fourfold:

APPENDIX C

275

1. To allow you to thank and say farewell to the spirits who have come to assist you

2. To follow a long-standing custom of exiting a deliberate change in consciousness by the same route you took to enter, creating a sense of order that keeps your conscious mind happy and cooperative

3. To keep the sense of ritual, which is important to the success of your effort

4. To prevent unstructured energies from running wild and causing you to feel frazzled or "haunted."

Close any inner circles first, doing so in the opposite manner from which they were cast. Then prepare to close the primary circle by reversing all the processes used to open it.

Some women prefer to say thank you and good-bye to the Goddess(es) first, and then do the quarter dismissals; others prefer the opposite format. For the Goddess, saying a simple thank you with added blessings is sufficient. You can do this standing at your altar, or facing whatever direction you perceive to be her home. If you have a lit a candle in her honor, extinguish it as you finish your farewell, to symbolize the light of the Goddess leaving the circle area.

Banishing Pentagram

You will formally close the circle by the same method you cast it, doing everything in reverse order. Begin by walking to the last quarter you called (the south in this example) to begin dismissing them. The word *dismiss* is traditionally used to refer to the practice of releasing the quarters, but its implication of command can sometimes be confusing. You are really thanking and saying goodbye to the energies that have so graciously come to assist you. The word *release* would probably be a better term. As before, if you have a tool that corresponds to each quarter, you may return to the altar each time to get it before going to the quarter of your circle.

> Thank you, powers of the south and fire for your presence here
> this eve [or other appropriate time], for lending your passionate
> energies to this ritual, and for blessing me with your presence.
> Thank you and farewell.

You may wish to incorporate a ritual gesture of dismissal, such as a banishing pentagram, as you release each of the quarters. The choice is yours.

Continue walking anti-sunwise (counterclockwise) around the circle to the eastern quarter. Counterclockwise does not mean that the gesture is negative in any way, only that the intent of the ritual or spell requires the symbolism of decrease or banishment. In modern Irish covens, this is sometimes referred to as moving *tuathail*. This term contains in it a word that means "of the country or backwoods," and is construed as being a slur by some. They feel it is like saying country people are backwards, and that it puts of value judgment on the counterclockwise movement. Another etymology says that this word only means "going left." In the circle, where time and space have no meaning, remember that there is really no backwards or forward, any more than there is good or evil if no evil intent is present. There is just power to be manipulated as a means to an end.

> Thank you, powers of the east and air for your presence here
> this eve (or other appropriate time), for lending your thinking
> energies to this ritual, and for blessing me with your presence.
> Thank you and farewell.

Then go to the north.

> Thank you, powers of the north and earth for your presence
> here this eve (or other appropriate time), for lending your
> stabilizing energies to this ritual, and for blessing me with your
> presence. Thank you and farewell.

Go finally to the west, the place where you first began.

> Thank you, powers of the west and water for your presence here this eve (or other appropriate time), for lending your purifying energies to this ritual, and for blessing me with your presence. Thank you and farewell.

Starting in the south again, take your tool or forefinger and begin walking the perimeter of the circle anti-sunwise. By this action you ground or close the circle. As you walk, visualize the energy you raised to create the circle either being sent deep into the lap of mother earth or being reabsorbed into your hand or tool. You may walk the perimeter of the circle only once, or you may walk the circle three times as you did to cast it.

Once the circle is closed, you may wish to make a statement acknowledging this. This helps all levels of your mind, body, and spirit to know that the open portal between the worlds is now closed, and that you are once again ready to function on the earth plane. To just walk away can leave some people feeling "spacy" or ungrounded, and it can be a very frustrating experience until you recognize the source of the problem and discover how easy it is to overcome. To help root yourself in the physical world, try making a loud noise or uttering a simple phrase such as, "The rite is done, the circle is closed," or the traditional Wiccan closing: "Merry meet, merry part, and merry meet again." If you still feel spaced out and unable to concentrate, try eating. This very physical action is a sure remedy to those residual feelings that can occasionally follow you home from a ritual. Foods heavy in salt are especially useful for this.

Basic Ritual Format

The following outline can be used to help create your own rituals. It is a framework only, which combines the accepted general practices of both eclectic Wiccan and Celtic traditions. Within this framework there is always room for individual interpretation, alteration, deletion, and augmentation.

1. Know the purpose of your ritual. It need not be a lofty goal, but you must know why you want to do a ritual in order for it to be meaningful and successful.

2. Have all items you will need for the ritual, or for any spells you wish to do, with you before the circle is cast. This includes ambiance items such as music and decorations. Make notes beforehand if you need to, and check them over. If you do forget something, decide now whether you want to improvise without it, or stop the proceedings, cut a doorway in the circle, and go searching.

3. Ground and center your energies, both mentally and physically preparing yourself to be inside sacred space. Personal meditation, purification rites, and so on are encouraged.

4. Cast your circle. (See Appendix C.)

5. Call your quarters. (See Appendix C.)

6. Invite, but never command, any friendly spirits, faeries or other elementals you wish to have join you. In Celtic traditions it is common practice to invite ancestor spirits to join you as well, especially during the dark days from Samhain to Imbolg when it is believed that the portal between our dimensions is at its thinnest.

7. Invite any deities you wish to have present. Many traditions light a candle to honor the presence of each one invited.

8. It is customary in Celtic traditions to feed beings you call from the Otherworld. Feed them with energy, offerings, food, or drink. At the end of the ritual, these items should be buried or left for animals, if the items are safe for them to eat and will not draw unwanted critters to your home. They generally are not eaten by those who performed the ritual.

9. If you wish to cast an inner circle—a figure eight, a triskele, or other variation—for a special working, do so now. (See Appendix C.)

10. State out loud, or write out, the purpose of your ritual to help your energies align with your goal.

11. If you are working with invoked energies—those that you draw into yourself—invoke them now.

12. Begin the body of your ritual work. You can improvise here as much as you like. The words, gestures, tools, drumming, dances, drama, messages from the invoked deity, rites of passage, sabbat/esbat enactments, and so on can be uniquely yours, or those of your group. Celtic ritual dramas are nice to do with groups.

13. If you are planning on working magick during your ritual, do so now.

14. Raise and send magickal/healing energy.

15. Release any invoked energy.

16. Close any inner circles that have been cast.

17. Thank and bid farewell to any deities you invited, and extinguish their candles.

18. When you are ready to close the circle, thank the elementals and spirits who have joined you and release them in the opposite order in which they were called.

19. Close the circle. (See Appendix C.)

20. Ground your energy and record your experience.

The Art of
Guided Meditation

Guided meditation is the art of going into an altered or meditative state of consciousness, then mentally following along a prepared (written, read, or orally planned-out) inner-world journey with the purpose of gaining knowledge, personal insights, or transformation. The process is also known as pathworking, a name derived from Ceremonial Magick, and guided journeying. The term "altered" in this case is not a synonym for something dangerous or aberrant, it simply refers to a deliberately slowed level of brain activity unlike that associated with routine waking consciousness.

All types of meditation have their practical occult applications, and guided meditation is no exception. Having detailed prepared imagery available can help the mind stay in its altered state focused on the meditation. This is an excellent way for beginners to the meditative arts to help train the mind to achieve and stay in an altered state. In any altered state, the mind is more receptive to ideas and symbols, and you are much more likely to discover interesting insights than you would be with straight meditation alone. You will also find that as you reach inward you can more easily reach outward. In other words, what takes place in guided meditation is in the mind, but that does not make it unreal. Remember that in magickal faiths such as Paganism, we recognize that our thoughts have tremendous power. As you journey, you will truly be creating a new reality for yourself, and the beings you meet in this inner world can help or hinder you in ways they would be unable to in the physical world.

Guided meditation allows you to try on other personalities, meet with deities, and visit environments and magickal sites that are usually unavailable to you in physical form. It is also a great way to discipline your mind.

The combination of structure and free thought, which is the nature of guided meditation, allows you to place your right and left brain hemispheres in sync so that they can better work together, both during the meditation and after it has ended. The right brain is the seat of intuition and creativity, the left brain is the seat of reason and analytical thought. When they work in tandem, they both function at peak efficiency. This increases the strength of the *corpus collosum*, the tissue that connects the two hemispheres—a connection that is already stronger in women than in men. Therefore, the monadic experience your brain gains from guided meditation can be carried over into all aspects of your life in which you need and want to be thinking and intuiting at optimum levels.

Achieving an Altered State

Achieving an altered state of consciousness is not a mysterious or difficult process. It happens naturally to everyone, every day. You may not always recognize it for what is is, but you cannot stop it from happening. When you sleep, read, watch television, or daydream, your brain waves slow and the space between their cycles increases. This can be measured on an EEG (electroencephalograph), a machine that monitors brain activity. The only difference between these natural altered states and those induced in spiritual disciplines is that your are bringing the process under conscious control.

A rough chart of brain wave levels and their corresponding physical conditions appears on page 283.

Attaining at least the upper levels of alpha is necessary for successful inner world/astral world work, including guided meditation. If you already have a method for inducing an altered state you like and that works for you, it is suggested that you keep it. Part of learning to alter one's consciousness with ease is to have a routine practice that alerts the mind that a change is about to take place.

State	Cycles per Second	Condition
Beta	15–18	Normal Wakefulness, Alertness, Study, Conversational Level (Person is aware of all physical sensations and bodily needs)
Alpha	8–12	Light to Medium Meditation, Daydreaming, Focused Concentration, Drowsiness, Cat-Napping, Some Astral Projection, Easy Guided Meditations, Very Light Sleep, Drowsiness (Person finds waking from this level mildly annoying, but not difficult)
Theta	4–6	Deep Meditation, Medium to Deep Sleep, Complex Astral Projection, Complex Guided Meditation, Light Unconsciousness (Person finds waking from this level moderately to very difficult)
Delta	0.5–2.5	Very Deep Sleep, Coma or Deep Unconsciousness (Person has little or no consciousness of physical sensations or bodily needs)

If you are not familiar with altered state work, there are some simple exercises you can try to help gently take you into the alpha levels. Continued practice will allow you to alter your consciousness almost at will.

For all altered state work, you will need to be in a quiet, private place, wearing comfortable, loose clothing. You may either sit or lie down, but if you choose the latter make sure you will not fall asleep, or your effort will be negated. You should not cross arms or legs; these postures set up stresses that will become apparent after twenty or thirty minutes of motionlessness. Such stress will become uncomfortable, possibly even bringing you out of your meditative state. You may want to gently play some New Age or environmental music in the background to mask outside noises. Incense can also help.

Begin your altered state practicing with any of the following methods. Each practice session should run twenty to thirty minutes.

Counting Your Breaths

As you lie/sit still, count each breath starting from number one. There is no limit to how high you can count. Each breath you exhale is one count. Focus on this to the exclusion of all else. When you tire of this, you can modify the exercise by altering your breathing patterns. For instance, breathe in deeply for four counts, hold for two, and exhale for four. Many mystery schools teach special patterns and what they can do for you, but no such Celtic pattern seems to have been used; or, if it was, the method was not preserved.

Counting Down

Starting at any number you like, begin counting slowly and rhythmically backward. You can coordinate this with your breathing pattern, or not. Start with 100, 500, or 1,000, depending on how long you wish to practice. When you reach zero you can start to bring yourself up again.

Using a Mantra

Using one word, sound, or phrase as a focus for your mind is called using a "mantra," a Sanskrit word derived from the hymns of praise found in the Hindu sacred writings known as the *Rig Vedas*. Repeat the mantra over and over in a steady, rhythmic pattern, with or without coordinating it to your breathing pattern.

Focusing on a Symbol

You can use a symbol the same way you use a mantra. This often works better for those who are more visually oriented. Select something basic to start with, like a simple geometric form. Or you can go for a Celtic symbol like a triskele. Hold its image in your mind to the exclusion of all else for as long as you can.

Daydreaming with a Focus

This type of meditation is the closest to guided meditation, and can have the added benefit of leading to a state of mind known as divided consciousness, where you are literally in two places at once. Select an adventure you wish to explore, then relax and jump into it. Pay close attention to homing in on every detail, making each sharp and precise. At this point, try not to allow the inner-world adventure to take on a life of its own. That will come eventually, and can signal that you have achieved immersion in the inner world, but for now you want to improve the mental discipline that comes with complete control.

If at any time in your meditation practice you find your mind wandering, simply bring it back where you want it, and keep working. Even the most experienced meditator will have off days, so don't be too hard on yourself for not being perfect.

Once you are in a relaxed state of mind you can begin your guided meditation. You can either plan to work with a partner and have that person read the meditation aloud to you, or you can read it yourself into a tape recorder and play it back whenever you wish. Allow your inner self to follow along with all the events, seeing and feeling them from the point of view of your inner self.

Unless there is an emergency to deal with, or you accidentally fall asleep, always finish a path once you have begun. It is very important to both your subconscious and conscious minds to make clear the point of separation between the inner and outer worlds. Failing to do this can make both halves of your mind feel out of whack. You consciousness will be sluggish, and given to slight disorientation, and your subconscious will remain wide open to the inner worlds and become an open portal for anything in the inner or astral world to come through and confound your physical reality with its presence.

Sealing this portal is easy and takes no time at all. As soon as you become cognizant of the physical world again do one or more of the following:

1. Make noise. Shout, sing, clap your hands, or make any other sound that strikes you as being an expression of your physical manifestation.

2. Make a statement that tells you the inner world journey has ended and "regular" life is now resuming. Try something such as, "The rite is done," or "I am home again," or "The worlds of form and spirit are separate once more. So mote it be."

3. Eat. Eating is a very physical action, one highly recommended for ending any ritual. Because it serves to ground us in the physical world, this is one of the reasons that feasts in group rituals come at the end of all the other rites.

4. Engage in physical action. Stomp your feet, dance, work out, run, shower, have sex (safe sex!), or do anything else that celebrates your corporealness.

When you are grounded once again, be sure to write down your impressions in your magickal journal or Book of Shadows so you will have a record for later study or comparison. If you want to discuss your pathworking experience with a friend, either one who did or did not do the working with you, it is best to do it only after you have had time to contemplate all its meanings for yourself, so that your judgment will not be clouded by comparison to someone else's experience.

Resources for Women's Spirituality and Celtic Magickal Living

This listing is intended to get you started with networking, or in seeking out your own resources; it is not, by any means, a complete listing of all the Celtic or women's spirituality resources available. Having access to Pagan organizations and to the major Pagan, Celtic, and women's spirituality periodicals can provide you with the information you need on women's gatherings, products, and festivals, many of which are seasonal and cannot be adequately listed here. Remember that when requesting information from any publisher, retailer, or promoter, it is wise—and polite—to send along an SASE (self-addressed stamped envelope), or an IRC (international reply coupon) with a self-addressed envelope when soliciting replies outside your own country.

If you are reading this book two years or more from the date of initial publication, it would be wise to query contacts with return postage to check on prices and the availability of goods and services.

Women's Spirituality Periodicals

The Beltane Papers
P.O. Box 29694-SW
Bellingham, WA 98228-1694

Quarterly "journal of women's mysteries." Sample issue $8.50 U.S., $9.50 elsewhere. Subscription $21 in U.S., $35 elsewhere.

Crone Chronicles
P.O. Box 81-I
Kelly, WY 83011

A quarterly "journal of conscious aging." Sample issue $6.50. U.S. subscriptions $18.

Daughters of Nyx
P.O. Box 1100
Stevenson, WA 98648

Quarterly of "Goddess stories, myth-making, and fairy tales." Sample issue $5.

New Moon
P.O. Box 3587
Duluth, MN 55803

Bimonthly written and edited by and for girls ages 8–14. In U.S., $25. A companion guide for parents and teachers is also available. Both subscriptions for $45 in U.S.

Of A Like Mind
Box 6677
Madison, WI 53716

A "newspaper and network for Goddess." Sample issue $4. $15–$35 subscription, sliding scale in U.S., bulk mail; $20–$40 first class. Outside U.S. $25–$45.

Thesmorphia
"Women's Spirituality Forum"
P.O. Box 11363
Oakland, CA 94611

Small newsletter published by feminist Pagan author and lecturer Zsuzsanna Budapest. Eight issues, $15.

Sage Woman
P.O. Box 641
Point Arena, CA 95468

An award-winning journal of feminist/Goddess spirituality, "Celebrating the Goddess in every woman." In U.S., $18; $24 elsewhere. You may charge your subscription to a major credit card by calling 1-707-882-2052.

Woman's Way
P.O. Box 19614
Boulder, CO 80308
(303) 530-7617

A quarterly encouraging spirituality, creativity, and self-discovery. Sample issue $3.50. Annual subscription in U.S., $14,

Celtic and General Pagan Periodicals

Bealoideas
Department of Irish Folklore
University College
Dublin, 1
Ireland

The quarterly journal of the Department of Folklore of Trinity University. Write with IRC for subscription information.

Celtic History Review
216 Falls Road
Belfast 12 6AH
Ireland

Published quarterly. Current subscriptions to the U.S. are $15 as of this writing, but it is best to query first.

Emania
Department of Archaeology
Queen's University
Belfast
Northern Ireland BT7 1NN

This is the journal of the Navan Fort Research Group, which studies Celtic prehistory. Write for information.

The Cauldron
Caemorgan Cottage
Caemorgan Rd.
Cardigan, Dyfed
SA43 1QU, Wales

Send one IRC for updated subscription information on this quarterly which covers many nature spirituality paths.

Celtic History Review
216 Falls Road
Belfast 12 6AH
Ireland

Published quarterly. Current subscriptions to the U.S. are $15, but it is best to query first.

Celtic Renewal
P.O. Box 30
Greens Farms, CT 06436-0030

Newsletter for those interested in all Celtic spiritualities. Write with SASE for more information.

Circle Network News
P.O. Box 219
Mt. Horeb, WI 53572
fax: (608) 924-5961
e-mail: circle@mhtc.net

Request a sample copy of their excellent periodical ($5, paid in U.S. funds) for more information and current subscription rates. Circle sells printed and recorded music written by and for Pagans. Also look online for Circle's web site.

Coming Out Pagan
P.O. Box 12842
Tucson, AZ 85732-2942

Quarterly journal for Gay and Lesbian Pagans. Yearly subscription in U.S. $13, Canada $17.

Fireheart
P.O. Box 462
Maynard, MD 01754

This journal of earth spirituality is professionally produced and comes out at Imbolg and Lughnasadh. Only $7 a year. Sample issue $4.

The Green Egg
P.O. Box 1542
Ukiah, CA 95482

Very professionally produced and often controversial. Sample copy, $4.95. Write for other subscription information.

Hearth Circles
P.O. Box 95
Wauconda, WA 98859
e-mail: ArticDawn@aol.com

A bimonthly, family-oriented Pagan zine. Sample issue, $2. U.S. subscriptions, $18; $22 in Canada.

Hecate's Loom
Box 5206, Station B
Victoria, BC
Canada V8R 6N4

A quality journal of Paganism, professionally formatted. Yearly rates are $18 U.S., $15 in Canada. Write for other information or check out their web site.

History Ireland
P.O. Box 695
Dublin, 8
Eire
From USA: 011 (353) 1-453-5730

Scholarly magazine of Irish history. Write or call for subscription rates.

Hole in the Stone Journal
High Plain Church of Wicca
2125 W. Evans #286
Denver, CO 78023

Professionally produced quarterly focuses on the central Rocky Mountain area. U.S. $12, Canada $17.

Irish American
180 East Central Ave.
P.O. Box 209
Pearl River, NY 10965-0209

A bi-monthly journal for the 44 million Americans of Irish descent. One year subscription: $19.95.

The Irish American News
503 S. Oak Park Ave. Suite 204
Oak Park, IL 60303
phone: (708) 445-0700
fax: (708) 445-0784

Another journal for Irish Americans. Current rates $14 in U.S., $20 in Canada, and $36 elsewhere.

The Irish Echo
309 Fifth Ave.
New York, NY 10016-6548
phone: (212) 686-1266
fax: (212) 686-1756

A journal for Irish Americans. Query for rates.

Keltic Fringe
Box 251 RD #1
Uniondale, PA 18470

A quarterly that approaches Celtic studies—which they spell "Keltic"—from many angles. Focus is not only on mythology and culture, but on present-day issues facing the Celtic nations and their people.

Keltria
P.O. Box 33284-C
Minneapolis, MN 55433

This popular magazine focuses on Druidism and Celtic magick. Write for current subscription information.

New Moon Rising
12345 S.E. Fuller Rd., #119
Milwaukie, OR 97222

Quarterly journal of magick and Paganism. Send SASE for current rates.

Shadow
School of Scottish Studies
27 George Square
Edinburgh, Scotland EH8 9LD

This is the journal of the Traditional Cosmology Society. Write with IRC for information.

Solitary
Box 6091
Madison, WI 53716

A quarterly for solitary Wiccans and Pagans. In U.S., $15 to $36 a year on sliding scale. $3.50 for sample issue.

The World of Hibernia
220 E. 42nd St., Suite 401
New York, NY 10164-2548

A relatively new magazine (1995 premiere) focusing on all things Irish. Write for current subscription rates.

Online Zines

Several of the major Pagan presses, as well as some of the goods and services providers, now have sites on the World Wide Web that carry some of the articles to be found in the most recent issues of their magazines. *Hecate's Loom* and *Connections* are two of the most recent additions as of this writing. Joining the Wiccan/Pagan Press Alliance (membership info can be found in this Appendix), or subscribing to any of the major Pagan journals can keep you apprised of the latest status of Pagans in cyberspace. In the near future it is likely that some new Pagan zines will spring up which will serve only online subscribers.

Music and Video

As of this writing, a new cable television channel is being introduced in the United States called "Celtic Vision: The Irish Channel." Currently a toll-free number has been set up for inquiries. 1-800-4-Celtic. Or call in Ireland, 353-1-662-3434.

Anyone Can Whistle®
P.O. Box 4407
Kingston, NY 12401

This "Catalog of Musical Discovery" carries unique instruments from around the world, many of which include tapes and/or instruction books for learning to play. The most recent catalog featured a Celtic pennywhistle, Gregorian chimes, a German concertina, an Aboriginal digeridoo, and an African rain drum. Also carries novelty items and some recorded music. Write for catalog.

Celtic Video, Inc.
141 E. 33rd Street
New York, NY 10016
(800) 992-3584

Call or write for current catalog.

Circle Sanctuary
See above under "Pagan and Celtic Periodicals."

Green Linnet Records
70 Turner Hill
New Canaan, CT 06840

Sells recorded Celtic music. Request free catalog.

Rego Irish Records and Tapes
64 New Hyde Park Rd.
Garden City, NY 11530

CDs, cassettes, and videos of Irish music and dance. Also some Scottish items. Send $2 for most recent catalog.

Robin Williamson Productions
BCM 4797
London, England
WC1N 3XX

Producer of Celtic books and musical recordings.

Soaring Spirit
Valley of the Sun Publishing
P.O. Box 683
Ashland, OR 97520-0023

Publishers and sellers of New Age music and of mind/body video and audio tapes, including tapes to aid meditation, past-life recall, and astral projection. First copy of their mag-a-log is free upon request, and will continue to be sent free for up to a year if you order from them.

General Pagan Organizations

Covenant of the Goddess
Box 1226
Berkeley, CA 94704

An internationally known Pagan organization. Very active in politics and ecumenical work. Query for membership information. Members receive COG's excellent newsletter.

C.U.U.P.s
(Covenant of Unitarian Universalist Pagans)
P.O. Box 442
Boyes Hot Springs, CA 95416
(707) 939-7559
e-mail: CUUPS@aol.com

National headquarters, which can put you in touch with nearest C.U.U.P.s organization to you.

The Fellowship of Isis
Clonegal Castle
Enniscorthy
County Wexford, Ireland

This is an international organization of Goddess worshipers with a membership of around 10,000. Send one IRC for response to inquiries.

International Wiccan/Pagan Press Alliance
P.O. Box 1392
Mechanicsburg, PA 17055

A membership in the WPPA is open to all, not just to writers and publishers. Current rates are $18 a year U.S., $20 Canada, and $27 elsewhere. The monthly newsletter, *The Midnight Drive*, discusses the trends and news from the Pagan publishing industry, keeps you abreast of the current state of legal problems and other issues facing the Pagan community, and provides ordering information for books from small presses that are hard to find elsewhere.

Pagan Education Network (PEN)
P.O. Box 1364
Bloomington, IN 47402-1364

Organizes Pagans in all communities on the local level to shape politics in favor of religious freedom and to disseminate correct information about our religion. Information and sample newsletter $3.

The Pagan Federation
BM Box 7097
London WC1N 3XX
England

Founded in 1971, this British-based organization seeks to make itself a forum for all European Pagan traditions, and to promote understanding, networking, and exchange of ideas between these diverse groups. Send one SASE or two IRCs for membership information.

Pagan Spirit Alliance
        and
Lady Liberty League
% Circle Sanctuary
Box 219
Mt. Horeb, WI 53572

For membership application to PSA, send SASE to Circle. LLL involves itself in aiding Pagans who face legal difficulties due to their religion.

Witches' Anti-Defamation League
% Celestial Teaching Center
P.O. Box 8706
Kentwood, MI 49518
e-mail: lad@grnet.com

Modeled on the very effective Jewish Anti-Defamation League, this group actively combats discrimination against persons involved in nature religions. Include SASE for response.

Witches' League for Public Awareness
P.O. Box 8736
Salem, MA 01970

Include a business-sized SASE for response. This organization seeks to educate the public about nature religions and tackles discrimination issues.

Witches Today
Box 221
Levittown, PA 19059

An organization whose goal is helping to educate the general public about Witchcraft and Paganism, and in maintaining religious freedom for everyone. If you are interested in aiding their efforts, please write.

World Pagan Network
% Chris West
721 N. Hancock Ave.
Colorado Springs, CO 80903
e-mail: ceile@aol.com

This network is staffed by volunteers (and always looking for others!) from all over the world who attempt to locate local contacts for those who request them. At present there is no charge for this service. Please include a detailed description of the area in which you are searching. If you would like to be listed as a contact person or organization in your area, let them know. If contacting by snail mail, send an SASE or IRC to ensure response.

Odds and Ends

Abyss
RR #1, Box 213 F
Chester, MA 01011
(413) 623-2155

Request this free catalog of magickal supplies. Carries many books and jewelry with a Celtic flavor.

Alternatives
P.O. Box 433
Arlington Heights, IL 60006

Eclectic catalog full of jewelry, oils, incense, cauldrons, medicine bags, books, statuary, and so on. Alternatives provides a toll-free number ONLY to order, do book searches, and to take requests to find special items not in their catalog (800) 357-2719. All others, please write for current catalog price.

Aphrodite's Emporium
628 N. 4th Ave.
Tucson, AZ 85705

Sells books, jewelry, oils, candles, and gifts with a Pagan focus. Catalog, $3.50.

Balefire
6504 Vista Ave.
Wauwatosa, WI 53213

This mail order company carries a large stock of brews, oils, and incenses designed for specific Pagan needs such as scrying, spirit contact, and spellwork. Write for free catalog.

Blarney
373D Route 46 West
Fairfield, NJ 07004-9880
(201) 882-1269

Importers of fine Irish goods including Waterford Crystal, Belleek China, coats of arms, Claddagh jewelry, and woolen clothing. Some items are costly, but worth their price. Catalog $4.

Cash's of Ireland
Mail Order Courier Center
P.O. Box 158
Plainview, NY 11803

Irish imports—clothing, Brighid's Crosses, Claddagh jewelry, and similar items. Request free catalog.

Celtic Heritage Books
P.O. Box 770637
Woodside, NY 11377-0637
(718) 478-8162

Send $2 for current catalog.

Compass Grove
Box 100
Hartland Four Corners, VT 05049

The full-color catalog is worth the $5 asking price. Offers a wide range of Pagan products.

Co-Op Essentials
5364 Ehlich Rd., Suite 402
Tampa, FL 33625

Sells fine essential oils. Prices vary by demand. Send $1 for most current price list.

Dreaming Spirit
P.O. Box 4263
Danbury, CT 06813-4263

Natural, homemade incenses and resins, oils, and tools for using them. Dreaming Spirit welcomes queries about custom blends of incenses or oils. The $2 for their catalog is refundable with your first order.

Dufour Editions, Inc.
P.O. Box 7
Chester Springs, PA 19425

Publishers and sellers of books about and from Ireland. Includes a good selection of hard-to-find mythology, children's books, and poetry from ancient times. Request free catalog.

The Flame
P.O. Box 117
Korbel, CA 95550

The Flame bills its catalog as "complete." They carry all manner of ritual and magickal items. Catalog, $2.00.

Gypsy Heaven
115 S. Main St.
New Hope, PA 18938
(215) 862-5251

Bills itself as "The Witch Shop of New Hope." Request catalog of magickal supplies, oils, jewelry, statues, cards, and similar items.

Halcyon Herb Company
Box 7153 L
Halcyon, CA 93421

Sells not only magickal herbs, but also staffs, brooms, cloaks, drums, and other items of interest to Pagan folk. Current catalog, $5.

Herb Closet
c/o Osaanyin Herbal Cooperative
P.O. Box 964
Montpelier, VT 05602

Incenses, oils, and extracts. Specializes in rare and exotic plants.

Highlander Soaps
P.O. Box 1521
Plainville, MA 02762

Handmade soaps, bath salts, bath oils, dusting powders, and other toiletries that "celebrate the Celtic heritage." Send SASE for brochure and current price list.

Indiana Botanical Gardens
P.O. Box 5
Hammond, IN 46325

Sellers of herbs, teas, charcoal blocks, herbal medicines and some books on alternative health care. Request free catalog.

The Institute of Irish Studies
(Institiuid le Leann na hEireann)
6 Holyrood Park
Dublin 4
Ireland
From Europe: (01) 269-2491
From U.S.A.: (011) 353-1-269-2491

Offers summer courses in Irish heritage and culture through Dublin's prestigious Trinity University. Though the courses are presented at a college level, no prior knowledge of subject matter is presumed. Some classes involve field trips to historic sites as well as classroom work.

Irish Castle Gift and Mail Order
537 Geary
San Francisco, CA 94115
(415) 474-7432

Sells a large variety of items imported from Ireland.

JBL Devotional Statues
P.O. Box 163
Rt. 1, Box 246
Crozet, VA 22932

Includes Irish deities. Request free catalog.

Kenny Bookshop of Galway Book Club
High Street
Galway
Ireland
phone: 011-353-91-62739
fax: 011-353-91-68544
e-mail: queries@kennys.ie

Custom-designed mailing packages sent on approval. Accepts major credit cards. Fire up your search engines and check out Kenny's web site as well.

Leydet Oils
P.O. Box 2354
Fair Oaks, CA 95628

Sellers of fine essential oils. Price list $3.

Light and Shadows
Catalog Consumer Service
2215-R Market St., Box 801
San Francisco, CA 94114-1612

Write for their free metaphysical supply catalog, or fire up your search engines and check out their web site.

Marah
Box 948
Madison, NJ 07940

Sellers of herbs, incenses, oil blends, and other tools. Catalog, $1.

McNamara's Green
P.O. 15822
Seattle, WA 98115

This catalog carries art, jewelry, stickers, sun-catchers, and jewelry with a Celtic flair. Most of it is rather inexpensive. I have ordered from them for years and have always been happy with their products. Catalog and annual supplements, $2.50.

Moon Scents and Magickal Blends, Inc.
P.O. Box 1588-C
Cambridge, MA 02238

Sells all manner of magickal paraphernalia and books. Request free catalog.

Mythic Force
92-734 Nenelea St.
Ewa Beach, HI 96707
(808) 672-3988

Jewelry, art, t-shirts, glassware, and notecards copied from Pagan designs and ancient museum pieces—many of them Celtic in origin. Catalog is $1, and will be credited to your first order.

Nature's Jewelry
27 Industrial Ave.
Chelmsford, MA 01824-3692

Sellers of seasonal and nature-oriented jewelry. Designs include moons, suns, autumn leaves, faeries, snowflakes, cornucopia, jack o' lanterns, dolphins, snakes, and holly. Also an excellent source for gift exchange items for Pagan gatherings and festivals. Write to request a free catalog.

POTO
11002 Massachusetts Ave.
Westwood, CA 90025-3510
(310) 575-3717

POTO is an acronym for "Procurer of the Obscure." Their mail order catalog features services, and rare books and herbs for those in the magickal life. Special orders and requests always welcome. Send $5.00 for current catalog and ordering information.

Really Wild 'n' Mild Celts
P.O. Box 280114
Dallas, TX 75228-1014

Send $1.00 plus an SASE for information on RWMC's God and Goddess art, divinations, and other merchandise.

Sacred Spirit Products
P.O. Box 8163
Salem, MA 01971-8163

Sellers of books, magickal tools, herbs, incense, and other occult items. Catalog, $3.

Shannon
Duty Free Mail Order
c/o Aer Lingus
Building 87, Cargo Plaza
Jamaica, NY 11430-1727

Duty free Irish imports. Request free catalog.

Sidda
1430 Willamette #119
Eugene, OR 97401

Crafters of ritual blades and magick mirrors. Send $1.00 for brochure.

Wildwood Fragrances
717 Spruce St.
Boulder, CO 80306

Creates and sells oils, perfumes, potpourris, incenses, oils, and other items, many constructed to align with the energies of deities or festivals. Also offers a mail-order course in blending ritual oils, incenses, and so on. Catalog is $2, refundable with your first order.

Celtic Folk Tunes

The nine scores in this appendix provide representative traditional or folk tunes from Celtic lands. These may be used during personal or group rituals and/or meditations, either live or prerecorded by you. If you prefer to use recorded music by other artists, please check the Appendix F ("Resources For Women's Spirituality and Celtic Magickal Living") for the addresses of companies that sell recorded Celtic music, both traditional and modern.

The Foggy Foggy Dew (Anglo-Irish)

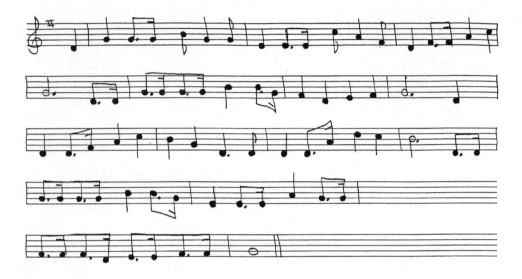

The Kildare Hills Aire (Irish)

The Faery Dance (Scottish)

The Eagle's Whistle (Irish)

King Finnavar (Irish)

Up and In and Out Again (Irish)

Morning Dew (Irish)

Old English Morris Dance (Cornish)

Cookoo's Nest (Irish)

Adbertos. This old Gaulish word literally means "a sacrifice." As a spiritual concept, adbertos was a positive part of the Celtic religious and community world view, in spite of its negative English translation. It referred to giving to others as well as to the deities.

Alignment/Attunement. The art and practice of placing our spiritual and mental selves in sync with the energies of an astronomical event (i.e., a full moon) or another being (i.e., a God or Goddess). This can be done through visualization, evocation, invocation, or ritual.

Anti-Sunwise. A term used in many Celtic traditions to refer to a counterclockwise action.

Archetype. Universally understood symbols defined by Funk and Wagnalls as "standard pattern[s]" or "prototype[s]." They speak to us in the ecumenical language of the subconscious. Sometimes the Pagan deities are referred to as archetypes because they are indwelling, or immanent, as well as possessing separate forms.

Astral Plane. A place generally conceptualized as an invisible parallel world that remains unseen from our own solid world of form.

Athame. A ritual knife and/or magickal tool often associated with air and the east, though sometimes relegated to the realm of the south and fire. It is usually, though not always, double-headed, and set in a handle of natural wood which is sometimes painted black.

Balefire. The traditional communal bonfire of the solar festivals. The name is derived from the Anglo-Saxon word *boon* meaning "a gift" or "something extra." The modern word "bonfire" is virtually synonymous with balefire, but carries no religious connotations.

Bards. The Druids known as bards (*bardoi*) were the poets, singers, and historians who kept alive valuable oral traditions. Their verse, called *cetel* in Ireland and *lay* in Brittany, might also be magickal spells that could curse or bless.

Besom. The traditional Witch's broomstick.

Bless. To bless something or someone is to make it holy or to set it apart as sacred. The word is sometimes used synonymously with "consecrate."

Bodhran. The traditional goatskin drum used in Celtic music.

Book of Shadows. A spellbook, diary, and ritual guide used by an individual witch or coven.

Brehon Laws, The. The law code that governed old Ireland. The Irish name for the laws is *Senchus Mor*, meaning "the great wisdom." The extant version we have dates from around the seventh century C.E., and reflects many centuries of changes from the original. Even with these alterations, which embrace the world view of Christianity, the Brehon Laws were very thorough at addressing and protecting the rights of women. They helped prevent the establishment of the English feudal system after England came to dominate Irish political life.

Brythonic Languages. The Celtic languages of Brittany, Cornwall, England, and Wales. Also known as the "P" Celtic languages due to the softening of the hard "k" sound of the Giodelic Celtic languages to a "p/b" sound.

Burgh. The grassy hillocks or stone cairns of Ireland, Scotland, and the Isle of Man, under which the faeries are said to dwell.

Cairn. The stone burial mounds built by the Celts.

Cath. The word *cath* refers to a type of epic story or myth concerning war which was told as an act of sympathetic magick on the eve of battle. In keeping with the high placement of the art of storytelling in Celtic society, such sessions were referred to until well into the early twentieth century as "the blessing of the story."

Celtic Renaissance, The. In the late nineteenth century, a renewed interest in reviving Celtic culture sparked in Celtic lands, particularly Ireland and Wales. In Ireland, this movement was fueled by the arts, and writers such as William Butler Yeats (who was, by the way, a ceremonial magickian) kept this movement flourishing until well into the twentieth century.

Charge. To empower an object or idea with one's own energy and set it aside for a specific magickal purpose.

Chthonic. Pertaining to the realm of the dead or the underworld.

Circle. The sacred space wherein magick and ritual is enacted. The circle both contains raised energy until it is needed, and provides protection for those inside.

Clan. The extended family system of the Celts. Originally, clans were united by being descended from a single female ancestor, but by the first century C.E. they had become male-oriented. In Welsh, the word for clan is *plant*. Both words mean "offspring of" or "children of."

Coibche. An Irish word for dowry or marriage portion.

Coming of Age. A ritual that recognizes a young person as a spiritual adult. For women, this usually occurs at the onset of menstruation.

Consecrate. To consecrate something is to dedicate it to a higher or sacred purpose. The word is often used synonymously with the term "bless."

Cosmology. A particular (usually culturally based) philosophy about the nature and origin of creation and nature of the universe.

Coven. A group of Pagans/Witches/Wiccans who worship and work together. In Celtic circles a coven may also be known as a grove, a touta, or a sept.

Cup and Ring Markings. Ancient chalk-on-stone or carved-in-stone rendering consisting of meandering lines and circles intersected by lines.

Cyfarwydd. The Welsh word for "storyteller."

Deosil. The act of moving, working, or dancing in a sunwise or clockwise motion. This is the traditional direction one works with for creative magick.

Divination. The act of predicting the future by reading potentials currently in motion.

Dolmen. The standing stones of the Celtic countries, shaped like altars with one large capstone being upheld by two endstones. Another Gaelic word for dolmen is *cromlech*.

Druids. The priestly class of Celtic society; the magicians, singers, poets, judges, priests, and royal advisors. Their power peaked from the second century B.C.E. to the second century C.E. The word *Druid* is sometimes thought to come from the Greek *drus*, which means "oak," but most likely comes from the old Indo-European root word *dru*, which means "steadfast" or "forthright."

Earth Plane. A metaphor for your normal waking consciousness, or for the everyday world in which we live.

Eclectic. In Pagan terms, this is a person or tradition who draws from multi-cultural sources for their practices.

Elements, The. The four alchemical elements once thought to make up the entire universe. These are earth, air, fire and water. The fifth element, pure spirit, is separate from, yet a part of, them all.

Elementals. Archetypal spirit beings associated with one of the four elements.

Eremetic. Pertaining to spiritual traditions or religious sects that emphasize a solitary, hermit-like existence in order to achieve true spiritual enlightenment.

Eric. An honor debt that must be paid to the family of a person who has been wronged or killed.

Evocation. The act of summoning the presence of deities, friendly spirits, or elementals to your circle.

Fith Fath. This type of magick has been widely misunderstood, although the Celtic Druids did purport to have spells called *fith fath* which rendered them invisible. This is probably a metaphor for astral projection.

Folklore. The traditional sayings, cures, fairy tales, and folk wisdom of a particular locale which are separate from their mythology.

Geis. An obligation that bound someone to do or not to do something. The word is often equated with the more familiar Polynesian "taboo," but *geis* also implied a sacred bond with magickal, divine ties. To break it brought horrible misfortunes and even death, usually inflicted by the deity in whose name the vow was made. A *geis* is often the conflict point in Celtic mythic stories.

Giodelic Languages. The Celtic languages of Ireland, Scotland, and the Isle of Mann. The Giodelic languages preceded the Brythonic ones in Celtic lands, with the latter being an offshoot of the former.

The Golden Statute. The first known law declaring universal freedom of religion, enacted in Ireland sometime around 200 B.C.E.

Great Rite, The. The symbolic sexual union, or sacred marriage, of the Goddess and God. It symbolizes the primal act of creation from which all life comes.

Hera. A feminine form of the Greek hero, synonymous with heroine, and preferred by some over the latter word.

Imminent Deity. A God or Goddess who is seen as living within humanity rather than outside of it.

Immrama. The name for epic Otherworld adventures, somewhat akin to the after-death adventures in the mythology of other cultures. Two very good examples of an *immram* (the singular) are the stories of the Otherworld voyages of Maelduin and Bran.

Invocation. The act of drawing the aspect of a particular deity into one's physical self.

Keltoi. The Greek name for the ancient Celts.

Lia Fail. "The Stone of Destiny" used in the crowning of the High Kings of Ireland. Many regard it as the Irish equivalent of Excalibur in the Arthurian myths.

Libation. A portion of food or drink ritually given to a deity, nature spirit, or ghost.

Lorica. A warrior's breastplate, or a blessing or prayer of protection.

Lunar Calendar. A system of keeping time by the phases of the moon.

Lunation. A single cycle of a lunar month, from the new to dark moon.

Matronymic. A designation in a surname that denotes bloodlines through the mother. In Ireland it was once popular for women to preface their last names with the designation *ni*, meaning "daughter of." By the early medieval period, the surname had switched from the mother's name to the father's. Female children adopted the more universally recognized patronymics: Mac, Mc, O', Ab, and Ap, all meaning "son of."

Matriarchy/Matricentric. A matriarchy implies rulership by a woman or a group of women who have hegemony over men and younger women within their tribe. Few, if any, early societies can be proven to have lived under such a system. Matricentric refers to societies in which the central focus of the tribe was a female. These societies usually had a Goddess as a supreme being, and counted as clan members those people linked though blood ties to a female ancestor.

Menhirs. The standing stones from Celtic countries, made of single stones or a circular series of stones. Menhir literally means "long stone." Brittany is famed for its many menhir circles: some of the stones are as much as 64 feet high.

Monadic. That which becomes a single, indivisible unit, and which functions at its peak when in this state. The term can be applied to well-run clans or covens, and the concept was used by the Celts to describe their spiritual unity during battle.

Mysteries. In spiritual terms, this refers to symbols and mythic images whose deeper meanings are not completely comprehensible to the uninitiated, but that are readily apparent to those who have studied and worked within a particular spiritual path. Paganism also recognizes separate male mysteries and women's mysteries, secret teachings that can often only be fully experienced in this incarnation by one gender.

Nementon. A Gaulish word meaning "sacred space."

New Religion, The. A Pagan term used in reference to Christianity; however, it can also be applied to all other non-Pagan religions. These New Religions are sometimes referred to as the "patriarchal religions" because of their exclusive, or nearly exclusive, focus on a male deity.

Niam-Linn. A headband with a jewel or symbol sitting over the center of the forehead, often worn by a priestess.

Ogham. The ancient alphabet of the Celtic people, which consists of series of marks in relationship to a center line. It is used today for both sacred writings and for divination.

Old Religion, The. Another name for European-based Paganism/Wicca, denoting that it was a European faith before the advent of the New Religion, Christianity.

Otherworld. A generic term for the Celtic Land of the Dead, which is also the home of many Celtic deities. Each Celtic culture had its own labels and euphemisms for the various realms of this place which contains an upperworld, middleworld, and underworld. *Tir Na mBan*, or the Land of Women, is one of these labels.

Pagan. Generic term for anyone who practices an earth- or nature-based religion.

Pantheon. The major deities in any religious system that make up the "whole" deity, or the complete power source.

Passing Over. A term used in modern Paganism to refer either to death itself or to Pagan funeral rites.

Patronymic. A designation in a surname that denotes bloodlines through the father. In Celtic countries, Mac, Mc, O', Ab, and Ap serve this function; all mean "son of."

Patriarchy. A term used to designate a society or political unit dominated by males. Also a label for the mindset of the modern world.

Pentagram. The five-pointed star, which has come to symbolize western Paganism. As a symbol it is almost always seen with its apex up, though certain rituals require that it be inverted.

Power Hand. For purposes of magick, this is the hand that is dominant, usually the one with which you write.

Pre-Celtic. Generally regarded, in the Celtic lands, as the time before 800 B.C.E, though some scholars date the first wave of the Celtic "invasion" to as early as 1500 B.C.E.

Rath. A circular earthen fortress sometimes outlined with rocks. These ancient sites, found all over the Celtic lands, are sacred to the faeries and, even today, most natives of the region will not disturb them.

Receptive Hand. For purposes of magick, this is the hand which is non-dominant, usually the one you do not use for writing.

Ritual. A symbolic, systematic, formal or informal, prescribed set of rites whose purpose is to imprint a lasting change on the life and psyche of the participant.

Sabbat. Any of the eight solar festivals or observances of the Wiccan/Pagan year. The word is derived from the Greek word *sabatu*, meaning "to rest."

Seanachai. A Gaelic word meaning "storyteller." The coming of the church to Celtic lands brought a decline of Druidic Bardic influence. These itinerant *seanachai* made storytelling an art form as they took over as the primary keepers of oral lore.

Sept. A term that can loosely describe either one's clan or the clan's holdings.

Shaman. The word comes from an extinct Ural-Altaic language called Tungus, and refers to the priest/esses and medicine people of the world's old tribal societies.

Sidhe. Also *sith*. Literally means "of peace," and refers to the faery folk of Scotland, Ireland, and the Isle of Mann. The sidhe go by many euphemisms, including "the people of peace."

Skyclad. Ritual nudity.

Solar Calendar. A system of keeping time based on the movements of the earth in relation to the sun. Our twelve month common era calendar is a solar calendar.

Torque. A gold or silver neckpiece worn by Celtic warriors and others of high rank.

Touta. A clan that was, in fact, a small chiefdom. This word is sometimes used in Celtic and Druidic circles in place of the term "coven." Technically, a touta differs from a clan because those in it do not have to be related by blood, marriage, or adoption as they would be within a clan.

"So Mote It Be." Traditional words for sealing spells. Mote is an antiquated English word for "must," which affirms our belief that the results of our magick are here and now.

Solitary. A Pagan who works and worships alone without the aid of a larger coven, either by choice or chance. In recent years, the term "solitaire" has also been used. Solitaries can be divided roughly into groups: 1) Solitary by chance, where the practitioner just happens to work alone, either because she has not yet found suitable working partners or because she is in between group situations; and 2) Solitary by choice, where the practitioner chooses to work and worship alone either permanently or temporarily.

Soulfriend. Or *anamchara* in Old Irish. A special friend who shares your spiritual path and is at about the same level of experience and knowledge as you are. Soulfriends function as mutual mentors and students, sharing their wisdom.

Spell. A specific magickal ritual designed for the purpose of obtaining, banishing, or changing one particular thing or condition.

Sunwise. A term used in many Celtic traditions to refer to any clockwise action.

Tara. The County Meath stronghold of Ireland's High Kings from about 300 B.C.E. to 1000 C.E. Only the barest ruins of Tara still remain, and most of what we know of the site today comes from ancient literature.

Theurgy. A word meaning the magickal union of a human being with a divine force.

The Threefold Law. A basic teaching of Paganism, it states that any energy we release, either positive or negative, will return to us three times over.

Transmigration. A belief that the life essence of a living thing would pass immediately from its old vessel into a new lifeform after physical death.

The Celtic Tree Calendar. A system of reckoning the thirteen lunar months of the year by assigning each a sacred tree, which represents the character of the month.

Triple Goddess. The one Goddess in all of her three aspects: virgin, mother, and crone.

Triskele. A symbol that represents the sacred number three. It consists of a circle with three equal-spaced divisions, separated by swirling lines radiating out from the center point.

Tuathail. This Irish word has been adopted in some Celtic circles to replace the more commonly used German word "widdershins" when referring to a counterclockwise motion. However, the root word, *tuath*, means "of the people" or "of the country;" therefore, when used to refer to something that is "backward" it is the equivalent of Americans referring to country people as "bumpkin-like." Also, remember that just because a movement is counterclockwise does not make it negative. Both good and evil magick can be made no matter what direction one moves. The movement is pure power, and only the intent of the spellspinner can determine its character. Author Caitlin Matthews suggests it derives from an old word meaning "to move left."

Wheel of the Year. A conceptualization of the eternal cycle of time.

Wicca. A Pagan tradition based on Anglo-Welsh and other Celtic forms of spirituality. Correctly or incorrectly, it has come to be used as a catch-all term for Pagan traditions from western Europe.

Wiccan/Pagan Rede. "As it harms none, do what you will." A basic tenet of Paganism which prohibits us from harming any other living thing, or from violating anyone's free will. Exactly when this tenet became a conscious part of Pagan spirituality is unknown.

Wiccaning/Paganing. The ritual dedication of a newborn child to the deities.

Widdershins. A German word for counterclockwise or against the sun, popular in many Pagan traditions, Celtic ones included.

Witch. Usually, but not always, a label reserved for Pagans of the Anglo-Celtic, Celtic, and Southern Teutonic traditions.

Works Consulted and Cited

Arnold, Matthew. *On the Study of Celtic Literature*. London: Elder Smith, 1867.

Ashley, Leonard R. N. *The Complete Book of Magic and Witchcraft*. New York: Barricade Books, Inc., 1986.

Berger, Pamela. *The Goddess Obscured: Transformation of the Grain Protectress From Goddess to Saint*. Boston: Beacon Press, 1985.

Bettelheim, Bruno. *The Uses of Enchantment: The Meaning and Importance of Fairy Tales*. New York: Vintage Books, 1977.

Blamires, Steve. *Glamoury: Magic of the Celtic Green World*. St. Paul, Minn.: Llewellyn, 1995.

Brunaux, Jean Louis. *The Celtic Gauls: Gods, Rites and Sanctuaries*. London: Seaby Ltd., 1988.

Budapest, Zsuzsanna E. *The Grandmother of Time*. San Francisco: Harper and Row, 1989.

Byrne, Patrick F., ed. *Tales of the Banshee*. Dublin: Mercier Press, 1987.

Caesar, Julius. *The Battle For Gaul*. Boston: David R. Godine, 1980.

Caldecott, Moyra. *Women in Celtic Myth*. London: Arrow Books, 1988.

Calder, George, ed. *The Book of Leinster* (bilingual edition). Edinburgh: John Grant, 1917.

Campbell, J. F. and George Henderson. *The Celtic Dragon Myth* (bilingual edition, Irish-English). Wales: Llanerch Publishers, 1995 (facsimile of 19th century work, precise date not given).

Campbell, Joseph. *The Mythic Image*. Princeton, N.J.: Princeton University Press, 1974.

_____. *Transformation of Myth Through Time*. New York: Harper and Row, 1990.

Carbery, Mary. *The Farm by Lough Gur*. Dublin: Mercier Press, 1986 (first published 1937).

Carmichael, Alexander. *Carmina Gadelica*. Edinburgh: Floris Books, 1992.

Chernin, Kim. *The Hungry Self*. New York: Perennial Library, 1985.

_____. *Sex and Other Sacred Games*. New York: Times Books, 1989.

Clark, Rosalind. *The Great Queens: Irish Goddesses from the Morrigan to Cathleen ni Houlihan*. Gerrards Cross, Buckinghamshire: Smythe, 1991.

Condren, Mary. *The Serpent and the Goddess: Women, Religion and Power in Celtic Ireland*. San Francisco: Harper & Row, 1989.

Conway, D. J. *By Oak, Ash and Thorn: Modern Celtic Shamanism*. St. Paul, Minn.: Llewellyn, 1995.

_____. *Maiden, Mother, Crone: The Myth and Reality of the Triple Goddess*. St. Paul, Minn.: Llewellyn, 1994.

_____. *Falcon Feather and Valkyrie Sword: Feminine Shamanism, Witchcraft and Magick*. St. Paul, Minn.: Llewellyn, 1995.

Cross, Tom P. and Clark Harris Slover, eds. *Ancient Irish Tales*. New York: Barnes and Noble, 1996 (originally published in 1936).

Crowley, Vivianne. *Wicca: The Old Religion in the New Age*. London: Aquarian, 1989.

Curtain, Jeremiah. *Myths and Folk-lore of Ireland*. New York: Weathervane Books, 1965 (originally published in 1890).

Danaher, Kevin. *In Ireland Long Ago*. Dublin: Mercier Press, 1964.

_____. *The Year in Ireland*. Dublin: Mercier Press, 1972.

Darrah, John. *Paganism in Celtic Romance*. Rochester, N.Y.: Boydell, 1994.

Davidson, H. R. Ellis. *The Lost Beliefs of Northern Europe*. London: Routledge and Kegan Paul, 1993.

_____. *Myths and Symbols in Pagan Europe*. Syracuse, N.Y.: Syracuse University Press, 1988.

Delaney, Frank. *Legends of the Celts*. New York: Sterling Publishing Co., 1991.

Delaney, Mary Murray. *Of Irish Ways*. New York: Harper & Row (Perennial Library Imprint), 1973.

Dillon, Myles. *Cycles of the Irish Kings*. Oxford: Oxford University Press, 1946.

_____. *Early Irish Literature*. Chicago: The University of Chicago Press, 1972.

Dillon, Myles and N. Chadwick. *The Celtic Realms*. New York: Weidenfeld and Nicolson, 1976.

Dudley, Donald R. and Graham Webster. *The Rebellion of Boudicca*. London: Routledge and Kegan Paul, 1962.

Dumezil, Georges. *The Destiny of the Warrior*. Chicago: The University of Chicago Press, 1970.

Eliade, Mircea. *Shamanism: Archaic Techniques of Ecstasy*. Princeton, N.J.: The Princeton University Press, 1964.

Ellis, Peter Berresford. *Celtic Women: Women in Celtic Society and Literature*. Santa Barbara, Calif.: ABC-CLIO, Inc., 1995.

_____. *Dictionary of Celtic Mythology*. Santa Barbara, Calif.: ABC-CLIO, Inc., 1992.

Estes, Clarissa Pinkola, Ph.D. *Women Who Run With the Wolves: Myths and Stories of the Wild Woman Archetype*. New York: Ballantine Books, 1992.

Evans, J. Gwenogryn, ed. *The Black Book of Caermarthen*. Llanbedrog, N. Wales: Pwllheli, 1906.

_____. ed. *The Poetry in the Red Book of Hergest*. Llanbedrog, N. Wales: Pwllheli, 1911.

Evans-Wentz, W. Y. *The Fairy Faith in Celtic Countries*. New York: University Books, 1966 (first published in 1911).

Evola, Julius. *The Metaphysics of Sex*. New York: Inner Traditions International, 1983 (translated from Italian, originally published 1969).

Farrar, Janet and Stewart. *The Witches' Goddess*. Custer, Wash.: Phoenix Publishing, Inc., 1987.

_____. *The Witches' God*. Custer, Wash.: Phoenix Publishing, Inc., 1989.

French, Marilyn. *Beyond Power: On Women, Men and Morals*. New York: Ballantine Books, 1985.

Graves, Robert. *The White Goddess*. New York: Farrar, Straus and Giroux, 1973 (first published 1953).

Green, Miranda J. *Animals In Celtic Life and Myth*. London: Routledge and Kegan Paul, 1992.

_____. *Celtic Goddesses: Warriors, Virgins and Mothers*. London: British Museum Press, 1995.

_____. *The Celtic World*. London: Routledge and Kegan Paul, 1995.

_____. *Symbol and Image in Celtic Religious Art*. London: Routledge and Kegan Paul, 1992.

Harding, M. Esther. *Woman's Mysteries: Ancient and Modern*. New York: Harper & Row, 1971.

Herm, Gerhard. *The Celts: The People Who Came Out of the Darkness*. New York: St. Martin's Press, 1975.

Hoagland, Kathleen. *1000 Years of Irish Verse*. New York: The Devin-Adair Company, 1947.

Hubert, Henri. *The Rise of the Celts*. New York: Bilbo and Tannen, 1966 (originally published in France in 1934).

Hunt, Robert. *Cornish Legends*. Penryn, Cornwall: Tor Mark Press, 1990.

Irish Educational Institute. *Yellow Book of Lecan, Vol.1*. Dublin: Irish Texts Society, 1940.

Jones, Gwyn and Thomas Jones, transl. *The Mabinogion* (revised). London: Everyman, 1993.

Jones, Noragh. *Power of Raven, Wisdom of Serpent: Celtic Women's Spirituality*. Edinburgh: Floris Books, 1994.

Joyce, P. W. *A Social History of Ancient Ireland*. London: Longmans, Green and Co., 1903.

Keane, Patrick J. *Terrible Beauty: Yeats, Joyce, Ireland, and the Myth of the Devouring Female*. Columbia, Mo.: The University of Missouri Press, 1988.

King, John. *The Celtic Druids' Year: Seasonal Cycles of the Ancient Celts*. London: Blandford, 1994.

Kinsella, Thomas. *The Tain*. Oxford: Oxford University Press, 1986.

LaPuma, Karen. *Awakening Female Power: The Way of the Goddess Warrior*. Fairfax, Calif.: SoulSource Publishing, 1991.

Larmine, William. *West Irish Folk-Tales and Romances*. Totowa, N.J.: Rowman and Littlefield, 1973 (originally published in London, 1893).

Larrington, Carolyne, ed. *The Feminist Companion to Mythology*. Hammersmith, London: Pandora Press, 1992.

Lenihan, Edward. *In Search of Biddy Early*. Dublin: Mercier Press, 1987.

_____. *Ferocious Irish Women*. Dublin: Mercier Press, 1993.

Lerner, Gerda. *The Creation of Patriarchy*. New York: Oxford University Press, 1986.

Lincoln, Bruce. *Priests, Warriors, Cattle*. Berkeley, Calif.: The University of California Press, 1981.

Logan, Patrick. *The Holy Wells of Ireland*. Gerrards Cross, Buckinghamshire: Smythe, 1980.

Loomis, Roger Sherman. *The Grail: From Celtic Myth to Christian Symbol*. Princeton, N.J.: Princeton University Press, 1991.

MacAlister, R. A. Stewart, ed. and trans. *Lebor Gabala Erenn, Part 1*. (The Irish Book of Invasions) Dublin: Irish Texts Society, 1938.

_____, ed. and trans. *Lebor Gabala Erenn, Part 2*. (The Irish Book of Invasions) Dublin: Irish Texts Society, 1930.

_____, ed. and trans. *Lebor Gabala Erenn, Part 3*. (The Irish Book of Invasions) Dublin: Irish Texts Society, 1940.

_____, ed. and trans. *Lebor Gabala Erenn, Part 5*. (The Irish Book of Invasions) Dublin: Irish Texts Society, 1948.

MacCrossan, Tadhg. *The Sacred Cauldron*. St. Paul, Minn.: Llewellyn, 1992.

MacManthuna, Seamus. *Immram Bran: Bran's Journey to the Land of Women*. Tubingen, Wales: Neimeyer, 1985.

MacManus, Dermot. *The Middle Kingdom: The Faerie World of Ireland*. Gerrards Cross, Buckinghamshire: Smythe, 1973.

MacManus, Seumas. *The Story of the Irish Race* (44th printing). Old Greenwich, Conn.: The Devin-Adair Company, 1992 (originally published in 1921).

McAnally, D. R., Jr. *Irish Wonders*. New York: Sterling/Main Street, 1993 (facsimile of nineteenth-century work, precise date not given).

McCoy, Edain. *Celtic Myth and Magick*. St. Paul, Minn.: Llewellyn, 1995.

_____. *Inside a Witches' Coven*. St. Paul, Minn.: Llewellyn, 1997.

_____. *Making Magick*. St. Paul, Minn.: Llewellyn, 1997.

_____. *The Sabbats*. St. Paul, Minn.: Llewellyn, 1994.

_____. *A Witch's Guide to Faery Folk*. St. Paul, Minn.: Llewellyn, 1994.

McFarland, Phoenix. *The Complete Book of Magical Names*. St. Paul, Minn.: Llewellyn, 1996.

Mann, Nicholas. *The Isle of Avalon: Sacred Mysteries of Arthur and Glastonbury Tor*. St. Paul, Minn.: Llewellyn, 1996.

Mariechild, Diane. *Mother Wit: A Feminist Guide to Psychic Development*. Freedom, Calif.: The Crossing Press, 1981.

Markale, Jean. *Celtic Civilization* (translation of *Les Celtes et la Civilisation Celtique*). London: Gordon and Cremonesi, 1978.

_____. *Women of the Celts* (translation of *La Femme Celts*). Rochester, Vt.: Inner Traditions International, Ltd., 1972.

Matthews, Caitlin. *The Celtic Book of Days*. Rochester, Vt.: Destiny Books, 1995.

_____. *The Celtic Book of the Dead*. New York: St. Martin's Press, 1992.

_____. *The Elements of the Celtic Tradition*. Longmeade, Shaftsbury, Dorset: Element Books, 1989.

Matthews, John, ed. *The Celtic Reader: Selections From Celtic Myth, Scholarship and Story*. San Francisco: Thorsons, 1991.

_____. *The Celtic Shaman*. Shaftsbury, Dorset: Element Books, 1992.

_____. *The Elements of the Arthurian Tradition*. Longmeade, Shaftsbury, Dorset: Element Books, 1989.

_____. *The Elements of the Grail Tradition*. Longmeade, Shaftsbury, Dorset: Element Books, 1990.

Matthews, John and Caitlin. *The Encyclopaedia of Celtic Wisdom*. Shaftsbury, Dorset: Element Books, 1994.

_____. *Ladies of the Lake*. Hammersmith, London: Aquarian, 1992.

Meyer, Keno, trans. *The Voyage of Bran*. London: David Nutt (facsimile of original bilingual edition of 1895).

Monaghan, Patricia. *The Book of Goddesses and Heroines*. St. Paul, Minn.: Llewellyn, 1990.

Murray, Margaret A. *The God of the Witches*. London: Faber and Faber, Ltd., 1952 (originally published in 1931).

Mynne, Hugh. *The Faerie Way*. St. Paul, Minn.: Llewellyn, 1996.

O'Cathain, Seamas. *The Festival of Brigit: Celtic Goddess and Holy Woman*. Dublin: DBA Publications, 1995.

O'Faolin, Eileen. *Irish Sagas and Folktales*. Dublin: Ward River Press, 1983.

O'Hogain, Dr. Daithi. *Myth, Legend and Romance: An Encyclopedia of the Irish Folk Tradition*. New York: Prentice Hall Press, 1991.

Parry-Jones, D. *Welsh Legends and Fairy Lore*. New York: Barnes and Noble Books, 1992.

Pennick, Nigel. *Celtic Sacred Landscapes*. London: Thames and Hudson, 1996.

_____. *The Pagan Book of Days*. Rochester, Vt.: Destiny, 1992.

Power, Patrick C. *Sex and Marriage in Ancient Ireland*. Dublin: Mercier Press, 1976.

Raftery, Joseph, ed. *The Celts* (transcripts from the Thomas Davis Lecture Series). Dublin: Mercier Press, 1964.

Rees, Alwyn and Brinley Rees. *Celtic Heritage: Ancient Tradition in Ireland and Wales*. New York: Thames and Hudson, 1961.

Rhys, Sir John. *Celtic Folklore: Welsh and Manx (Volume 2)*. Oxford: Clarendon Press, 1901.

Roberts, Jack. *The Sheela-na-Gigs of Britain and Ireland: An Illustrated Guide*. County Cork: Key Books, 1991.

Rodgers, Michael and Marcus Losack. *Glendalough: A Celtic Pilgrimage*. Blackrock, Co. Dublin: The Columba Press, 1996.

Rolleston. T. W. *Celtic Myths and Legends*. New York: Avenel Books, 1986.

Ross, Anne. *Everyday Life of the Pagan Celts*. New York: G. P. Putman's Sons, 1970.

Sanday, Peggy Reeves. *Female Power and Male Dominance: On the Origins of Sexual Inequalities*. Cambridge, England: The Cambridge University Press, 1981.

Seymour, St. John D. *Irish Witchcraft and Demonologie*. New York: Dorset Press, 1992 (reprint of early 20th century work; original publishing date not given).

Sharkey, John. *Celtic Mysteries: The Ancient Religion*. New York: Crossroad Publishing, 1981.

Sheppard-Jones, Elisabeth. *Scottish Legendary Tales*. Edinburgh: Thomas Nelson and Sons, Ltd., 1962.

_____. *Welsh Legendary Tales*. Edinburgh: Thomas Nelson and Sons, Ltd., 1959.

Shuttle, Penelope and Peter Redgrove. *The Wise Wound: Myths, Realities, and Meanings of Menstruation (revised)*. New York: Bantam Books, 1990 (originally published in 1978).

Skene, William F. *The Four Ancient Books of of Wales*. Edinburgh: Edmonston and Douglas, 1868.

Smyth, Ailbhe. *The Irish Women's Studies Reader*. Dublin: Attic Press, 1993.

Squire, Charles. *Celtic Myth and Legend, Poetry and Romance*. New York: Bell Publishing Co., 1979 (originally published in 1905 as *The Mythology of the British Islands*).

Stein, Diane. *Casting the Circle: A Women's Book of Ritual*. Freedom, Calif.: The Crossing Press, 1990.

_____. *Stroking the Python: Women's Psychic Lives*. St. Paul, Minn.: Llewellyn, 1988.

_____. *The Women's Book of Healing*. St. Paul, Minn.: Llewellyn, 1987.

Stewart, R. J. *Celtic Gods, Celtic Goddesses*. London: Blandford, 1990.

_____. *Earth Light: Rediscovery of the Wisdom of Celtic Faery Lore*. Shaftsbury, Dorset: Element Books, 1992.

_____. *The Power Within the Land*. Shaftsbury, Dorset: Element Books, 1991.

_____. *The Underworld Initiation: A Journey Towards Psychic Transformation*. Wellinghorough, England: Aquarian, 1985.

Stone, Merlin. *Ancient Mirrors of Womanhood*. Boston: Beacon Press, 1984.

_____. *When God Was A Woman*. New York: Dorset Press, 1976.

Thomas, N. L. *Irish Symbols of 3500 B.C.* Dublin: Mercier Press, 1988.

VonFranz, Marie-Louise. *Creation Myths*. Boston: Shambhala Publications, Inc., 1995 (originally published 1972).

Walker, Barbara G. *The Crone: Woman of Age, Wisdom, and Power*. San Francisco: HarperCollins, 1985.

_____. *Women's Rituals: A Sourcebook*. San Francisco: HarperCollins, 1990.

Weston, Jessie L. *From Ritual to Romance*. Princeton, N.J.: The Princeton University Press, 1993.

Wilde, Lady. *Ancient Cures, Charms and Usages of Ireland*. Detroit: Singing Tree Press, 1970 (first published in 1890 by Ward and Downey Ltd. of London).

Williams, Selma R. *Riding the Nightmare: Women and Witchcraft From the Old World to Colonial Salem*. San Francisco: Harper Perennial, 1992 (first published in 1978).

Wolfe, Amber. *The Arthurian Quest: Living the Legends of Camelot*. St. Paul, Minn.: Llewellyn, 1996.

INDEX

INDEX

325

INDEX

MAKING MAGICK
What It Is and How It Works

Edain McCoy

How do I raise and send energy? What happens if I make a mistake in casting a spell? What is sex magick all about? What is the Moon's role in magick? Which magickal tools do I need the most?

Making Magick is a complete course in natural magick that answers these and hundreds of other questions. Through exercises designed to develop basic skills, *Making Magick* lays a firm foundation of elemental magickal wisdom. The first chapters begin with an introduction to magick and how it works. You will study Craft tools, learn to connect with the elements—the building blocks of magick—and delve into the intricacies of spell construction and timing. The last half of the book will take you into the advanced magickal arts, which rely on highly honed skills of meditation, astral projection, visualization, and sustaining of creative energy. A special chapter on the tattwas will show you how to use these ancient Hindu symbols as gateways into the astral worlds.

1-56718-670-X, 6 x 9, 304 pp., illus., photos   **$14.95**

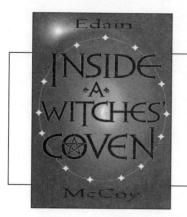

INSIDE A WITCHES' COVEN

Edain McCoy

Inside a Witches' Coven gives you an insider's look at how a real Witches' coven operates, from initiation and secret vows to parting rituals. You'll get step-by-step guidance for joining or forming a coven, plus sage advice and exclusive insights to help you decide which group is the right one for you.

Maybe you're thinking about joining a coven, but don't know what to expect, or how to make contacts. Perhaps you already belong to a coven, but your group needs ideas for organizing a teaching circle or mediating conflicts. Either way, you're sure to find *Inside a Witches' Coven* a practical source of wisdom.

Joining a coven can be an important step in your spiritual life. Before you take that step, let a practicing Witch lead you through the hidden inner workings of a Witches' coven.

1-56718-666-1, 5¼ x 8, 224 pp., softcover   **$9.95**

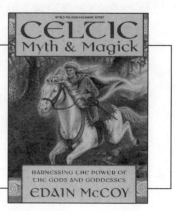

CELTIC MYTH & MAGIC

Harness the Power of the
Gods & Goddesses

Edain McCoy

Tap into the mythic power of the Celtic goddesses, gods, heroes and heroines to aid your spiritual quests and magickal goals. *Celtic Myth & Magic* explains how to use creative ritual and pathworking to align yourself with the energy of these archetypes, whose potent images live deep within your psyche.

Celtic Myth & Magic begins with an overview of 49 different types of Celtic Paganism followed today, then gives specific instructions for evoking and invoking the energy of the Celtic pantheon to channel it toward magickal and spiritual goals and into esbat, sabbat and life transition rituals. Three detailed pathworking texts will take you on an inner journey where you'll join forces with the archetypal images of Cuchulain, Queen Maeve and Merlin the Magician to bring their energies directly into your life. The last half of the book clearly details the energies of over 300 Celtic deities and mythic figures so you can evoke or invoke the appropriate deity to attain a specific goal.

This inspiring, well-researched book will help solitary Pagans who seek to expand the boundaries of their practice to form working partnerships with the divine.

1–56718–661–0, 7 x 10, 464 pp., softcover $19.95